John Shiffman is an investigative reporter for Reuters and a former staff writer at *The Philadelphia Inquirer*. He was a finalist for the Pulitzer Prize in 2009 and 2015. He is the author of *Operation Shakespeare* and, with former FBI agent Robert Wittman, he coauthored *Priceless*, a *New York Times* bestseller published in ten languages. He is a lawyer and lives near Washington, D.C.

OPERATION SHAKESPEARE

*THE TRUE STORY OF AN ELITE
INTERNATIONAL STING*

John Shiffman

Simon & Schuster Paperbacks

NEW YORK   LONDON   TORONTO   SYDNEY   NEW DELHI

Simon & Schuster Paperbacks
An Imprint of Simon & Schuster, Inc.
1230 Avenue of the Americas
New York, NY 10020

First Simon & Schuster trade paperback edition August 2015

SIMON & SCHUSTER PAPERBACKS and colophon are registered trademarks
of Simon & Schuster, Inc.

For information about special discounts for bulk purchases, please contact
Simon & Schuster Special Sales at 1-866-506-1949 or
business@simonandschuster.com.

The Simon & Schuster Speakers Bureau can bring authors to your
live event. For more information or to book an event contact the
Simon & Schuster Speakers Bureau at 1-866-248-3049
or visit our website at www.simonspeakers.com.

Interior design by Paul Dippolito
Map by Paul J. Pugliese

Manufactured in the United States of America

1   3   5   7   9   10   8   6   4   2

The Library of Congress has cataloged the hardcover edition as:
1. Operation Shakespeare, 2004–2009. 2. Technology transfer—Government
policy—United States. 3. Undercover operations—United States. 4. War on
Terrorism, 2001–2009. 5. Terrorism—Prevention—United States. 6. National
security—United States. 7. Intelligence service—United States. 8. United States.
Department of Homeland Security. I. Title.
T174.3.S58 2014
338.973'06—dc23
2013037116

ISBN 978-1-4516-5513-1
ISBN 978-1-4516-5516-2 (pbk)
ISBN 978-1-4516-5519-3(ebook)

This book grew out of a series of articles by the author
that was published in *The Philadelphia Inquirer.*

To Cathy
and
Outkast Platoon

They think the war is coming.

—AMIR ARDEBILI

Our hands are full of business, let's away,
Advantage feeds him fat while men delay.

—HENRY IV, PART I

Contents

Note to the Reader   *xiii*

Map   *xiv–xv*

Prelude—Tbilisi, Georgia, and Iskandariyah, Iraq   *1*

PART ONE: THE LURE (2004–2007)

1   The Storefront—Yardley, Pennsylvania   *15*

2   The Capitalist—Shiraz, Iran   *35*

3   The Captain—Suitland, Maryland   *47*

4   The Producer—Philadelphia, Pennsylvania   *68*

5   The Informant—London, England   *82*

6   The Bazaar—Dubai, United Arab Emirates   *91*

7   Love and Profit—Shiraz, Iran   *103*

8   A Warning—Philadelphia, Pennsylvania   *113*

9   Propositions—Shiraz, Iran   *121*

10   The Magician—Frankfurt, Germany   *126*

11   "A Hero with the Ministry of Defense"—
Wilmington, Delaware   *138*

12   Shakespeare—Wilmington, Delaware   *147*

13   Contagious Enthusiasm—Shiraz, Iran   *159*

PART TWO: THE STING (2007)

14   Mother Georgia—Tbilisi, Georgia   *165*

15   Arrival—Baku, Azerbaijan   *177*

16 The Magic Show—Tbilisi, Georgia   *183*

17 "They Think the War Is Coming"—Tbilisi, Georgia *200*

18 "Very Rich Men"—Tbilisi, Georgia   *213*

19 Takedown—Tbilisi, Georgia   *216*

PART THREE: THE SECRET PRISONER (2007–2012)

20 Coups and Complications—Tbilisi, Georgia   *223*

21 Extraction—Tbilisi, Georgia   *232*

Epilogue—Saipan, Northern Mariana Islands   *251*

Afterward   *255*

Acknowledgments   *257*

Sources   *261*

Note to the Reader

The heart of this book is based on repeated interviews with the participants, as well as hundreds of supporting American, Iranian, and Georgian documents, only a handful of which are available in the public record. The book is also based on two additional key troves of nonpublic information—the contents of Amir Ardebili's laptop, which contained four years of Iranian procurement records, and the full-length undercover videos recorded by U.S. Homeland Security Investigations (HSI) agents. Most participants were interviewed on the record, but a few spoke on a not-for-attribution basis on certain topics, either because they were not authorized to talk publicly or because they feared retribution. The undercover agent who called himself Darius requested anonymity, and the British arms dealer, "Clyde Pensworth," requested a pseudonym. For safety reasons, a handful of facts have been withheld.

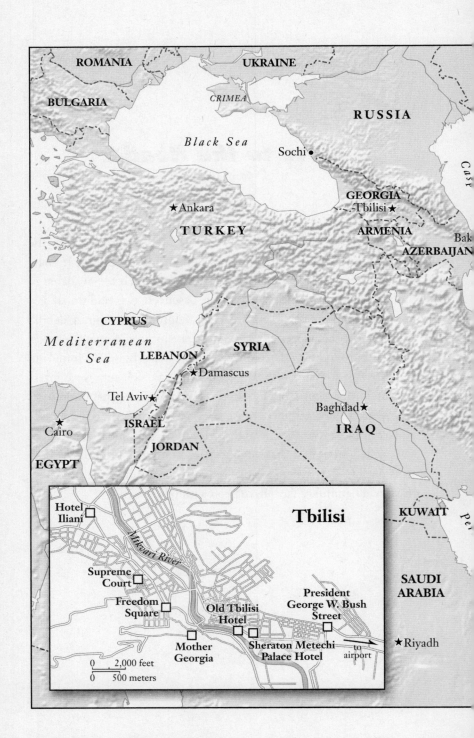

Prelude

Late on a fall afternoon, a small crowd gathered near baggage claim. The modest airport, a two-story burst of sloping steel and glass, otherwise stood largely vacant. The ticket counters were closed, the tourist kiosks bare, all four departure gates empty. Only twenty-four commercial flights landed here daily, and almost all of them arrived and departed in the hazy hours between midnight and dawn.

One man towered above the others in the airport lobby. He stood six-foot-five, with neatly parted brown hair, a square jaw, and stern gray eyes. He was fifty-three years old and looked like any of the Russian and German businessmen who flew here regularly from Moscow and Munich. He spoke Russian and called himself Darius, a name that sounded Persian but could be Baltic.

Sleep-deprived and adrenaline-fueled, Darius fought to remain focused. He had waited on a target in this manner countless times and knew this would be his last major operation. Today's mark was arriving from Tehran. Darius had the man's name, but no picture. He scanned the airport foyer for Iranian counter-surveillance. Nothing stood out, but this was the former Soviet republic of Georgia, birthplace of Stalin, and the legacy of KGB intrigue lingered.

A veteran of the Cold War, Darius carried in his wallet official-looking documents identifying himself as an East European arms broker. Yet he was neither European nor a spy. Darius was a cop, an undercover agent from U.S. Homeland Security. Outside the air-

1

port entrance, an undercover Georgian policeman playing the part of Darius's driver waited beside a black Mercedes SUV with crimson window curtains. Embedded inside the car's rearview mirror were a camera and microphone, ready to record conversations during the ride downtown.

In the terminal, a dour Georgian from the Ministry of Internal Affairs pulled close and discreetly slipped Darius the flight manifest. He skimmed the two-page passenger list until he recognized a name. Darius suppressed a smile, folded the document, and gave a silent signal to his cover team.

. . .

Thirty-five miles south of Baghdad, near a city called Iskandariyah, a cherub-faced second lieutenant from New Jersey set off with his platoon on a routine patrol. Seth Dvorin commanded Outkast Platoon, seventeen men stationed at a major power facility near the banks of the Euphrates River. Lieutenant Dvorin was a Rutgers University graduate and twenty-four years old. This marked his fifth month in combat.

Dvorin's men ventured outside like this virtually every day, beyond the barbed wire and concrete fort, clearing roads in advance of long Army convoys. They lugged M4 carbine rifles, M249 light machine guns, and seventy pounds of gear, sometimes in Humvees, sometimes on foot, always alert for deadly handmade roadside bombs, or IEDs, shorthand for "improvised explosive devices." The enemy hid IEDs everywhere—inside abandoned tires, paint cans, concrete chunks, dead dogs, boxes of candy, mannequins, behind signs and posters. The Army trained soldiers like Lieutenant Dvorin to scan for danger signs—fresh piles of dirt in a roadway, odd objects hanging from trees and electrical poles, or sudden insurgent signals: a flare launch, blinking lights from a nearby home, a single gun shot fired as a convoy entered a village. Lieutenant Dvorin also learned to look for things that weren't there, odd situations, like the absence of children in a place where kids usually played, or a café, busy one day, vacant the next.

The enemy triggered IEDs in three ways: by detonating cord, timer, or remote control. The wired cords were of course easier to spot, and sometimes the remote control triggers could be thwarted by radio wave jammers mounted on the Humvees. But lately, U.S. soldiers in Iraq were discovering more sophisticated remote timers and triggers inside the IEDs, including, incredibly, products manufactured in American factories. Insurgents in both Iraq and Afghanistan were acquiring American-made components to help kill U.S. soldiers—and the growing evidence showed that Iran was smuggling the IED parts from the United States to the battlefield.

Dvorin and his men didn't disarm the roadside bombs; they spotted them and radioed experts from disposal units. They didn't always see them in time. In Iraq and Afghanistan, at least 2,500 U.S. soldiers have died in IED attacks, accounting for nearly half of the total killed by hostile fire. In the coming months, seven of the seventeen men in Lieutenant Dvorin's platoon would be gravely wounded; three would die, killed by remote control IEDs.

"Once you go outside the wire, if you ain't got butterflies, you ain't human," recalled Private First Class Jeffrey Williams, who manned the platoon's .50 caliber gun and lost the use of his legs following an IED attack. Whenever the platoon ventured beyond the wire, Lieutenant Dvorin and his sergeant took turns staying behind at camp. This ensured that if the platoon were attacked, one leader would survive.

.   .   .

At the Tbilisi airport, Darius considered the name on the manifest.

For three years, in countless emails and telephone calls, the Iranian procurement agent had called himself "Alex Dave." Then, three days ago, he had switched to this new name, the one on the manifest. The abrupt change had troubled some of the other Homeland Security agents. Not Darius. He didn't care what the guy called himself, as long as he showed up.

Alex Dave, or whatever his true name, was the prime target of Operation Shakespeare, an audacious U.S. national security sting, one with covert elements in four countries. A symphony of moving parts—false identities, front companies, counterfeit weapons systems, and the lure of a large payday—Operation Shakespeare was designed to catch an agent of the Iranian government as no U.S. law enforcement agency ever had. If the sting succeeded, the agents believed it might mark a turning point in the covert American effort to halt the spread of illicit military sales to Iran. In the long run, Operation Shakespeare could help save American soldiers' lives, as well as protect Israelis and others targeted by the terrorist organizations Tehran supplied, Hezbollah and Hamas.

In Tbilisi, Alex Dave expected to take delivery of three military-grade products he had ordered from Darius: a pair of F-4 fighter jet cockpit computers, major upgrades for Iran's dilapidated air force; a set of precision gyroscopes, the kind required to steer rockets and missiles at targets like Tel Aviv; and a box containing one thousand sophisticated radar microchips, devices quick enough to track and shoot down U.S. fighter jets, including American planes that might be sent someday to destroy Iran's nascent nuclear arsenal. What Darius did not know is that Alex Dave had already successfully smuggled American-made underwater drone components, naval sonar, and the very components showing up in IEDs in Afghanistan and Iraq.

. . .

Lieutenant Seth Dvorin arrived in Iraq as a rookie officer and also as a newlywed. His wife, Kelly, was a graduate psychology student in New Hampshire.

Seth and Kelly had met as students at Rutgers University four years earlier. At the time she was a shy senior, a scholar anticipating a career in counseling. He was a carefree and brash sophomore, a C-plus student. She wore little makeup and kept her brown hair flat and straight to her elbows, like Cher. He used so much mousse and experimented with so many different hairstyles that his frat brothers nicknamed him Vidal. Seth sometimes augmented his look with a small hoop in each ear. He spoke with a low, guttural voice, not unlike Springsteen. Though his ruddy cheeks made him appear younger than his twenty years, Seth exuded a confidence and kindness that Kelly hadn't found in other Rutgers men. He carried a genuine interest in other people's problems, and not in a gossipy way. She believed there was something sort of wise about him.

Seth's unusual maturity and empathy could be traced to childhood trauma. Growing up, his parents fought bitterly, and to escape Seth spent a lot of time hanging out at the homes of friends and relatives. His mother, a teacher, and father, a policeman, divorced when Seth was eight. The boy remained close to both parents and became the de facto mediator and family peacemaker. He was happiest when he found ways to make everyone else happy. Seth learned to hide disappointments and resentments, but his parents' divorce shook him deeply and he witnessed acts of selfishness and unfairness that transformed him. What emerged was a nice guy, a person with an unusually strong sense of justice and duty to community. In high school, Seth wrote a paper advocating that colleges ought to pay student-athletes because universities reaped millions from their talents. When he adopted a cat at a shelter, he picked the scrawniest one, reasoning that the better-looking cats were more likely to find homes. When Seth was seventeen, he brought a U.S. Army recruiter home to dinner, eager for the sergeant to repeat for his mother the importance of national service. This was long before 9/11, and within his circle of suburban high school friends, Seth was the only one even considering enlisting.

On their first date, Seth took Kelly to a Mexican restaurant near campus, followed by ice cream at Thomas Sweet's and a visit to a local arcade. That summer, they handwrote a list of forty-one date ideas, and in the year that followed crossed off almost all of them: dance at a Dave Matthews Band concert, stroll the Wildwood Boardwalk, visit New Hope on a Sunday afternoon, picnic in Central Park, spend a lazy day watching Stanley Kubrick movies, go to a Yankees-Phillies game in the Bronx. As they fell in love, they talked about a future together. After graduation, she intended to become a psychologist. He planned to serve a few years in the Army and then become a federal agent, maybe for the FBI or Secret Service. That fall, Seth accompanied Kelly on several doctoral program interviews and grew serious about his own schoolwork. In the summer between his junior and senior years, he spent a month backpacking across Europe with a frat brother. While abroad, he mailed Kelly a box of Swiss chocolates. The note said, "Look at this and think of me whenever you are lonely."

During Seth's final semester, he applied for the Army's college-graduate officer program. He did not enlist to avenge 9/11 or because he fantasized about becoming some sort of Special Forces soldier working secret ops in the Middle East. Seth stood just five-foot-seven and weighed a somewhat doughy 170 pounds. Mostly, he enlisted because he believed he ought to. "From the time that I first met him," Kelly recalled, "Seth talked about a greater sense of duty to his fellow man and country. It sounds cheesy, but that's really how he talked, and what he wanted to do." On his Army application, the college senior wrote, "In regard to the reasons that I desire to join the United States Army as an officer . . . perhaps the most important is my lifelong desire to serve my country."

.   .   .

While Darius staked out the Tbilisi airport, fellow undercover agents prepared a downtown hotel suite for the anticipated meeting with the Iranian arms broker. They installed a dime-sized camera inside a wicker trash basket and checked the feed on a second camera hidden inside a painting hanging on a wall. Working beside the Homeland Security agents at the hotel was a technical ace from an obscure Pentagon agency, the Defense Criminal Investigative Service.

The Pentagon special agent's presence underscored the nature of the work. Darius and his colleagues were part of a small, elite band of Homeland Security agents, mostly former Customs men, who worked in the shadows, usually undercover, to prevent enemies from acquiring American-made weapons. These weren't theoretical threats in some future war; the Homeland Security agents were chasing current dangers playing out on today's battlefields, trying to prevent enemies from acquiring American-made night vision equipment, radar microchips, infrared targeting scopes, drone technology, and triggers for IEDs—weapons that might be used against U.S. soldiers like Seth Dvorin. The Pentagon coined a clumsy slogan for the program, "Protecting the Warfighter," and though largely unknown to the public, the task was as critical to individual U.S. troops as it was to national security.

With Operation Shakespeare, Darius and his colleagues hoped to strike back against Iran's murky and elusive black market arms network. They hoped to prove wrong a widely held assumption that U.S. law enforcement wouldn't or couldn't operate overseas, that the degree of difficulty—overcoming legal, bureaucratic, budgetary, diplomatic, and logistical hurdles—was too high. Darius marveled that even the Central Intelligence Agency, unfettered by the kind of legal restrictions that constrained U.S. law enforcement, had struggled to stop the Iranians and Chinese from acquiring American-made weapons and military technology. Following 9/11, the CIA created eleven overseas counter-proliferation sting operations similar to Operation Shakespeare. Only one succeeded.

. . .

It takes the Army about a year to forge an officer.

One clear West Texas evening during his final month of training, Seth Dvorin, still earnest and inquisitive, found himself sitting atop a picnic table on an Army base near El Paso, cradling a forty-ounce bottle of King Cobra malt liquor wrapped in a brown paper bag.

He wore a gray Rutgers T-shirt, cargo pants, and a great big black cowboy hat, a symbol of his new adventure. The year had been harder than he had expected, mentally and physically, and offered rare chances to see Kelly. Seth sat beside classmate James McCormick, a combat vet eight years older. McCormick wore a white wife-beater and camouflage pants. A unit barbecue had just concluded, and the two men remained, wordlessly studying the final embers on the grill. In a month, they expected to receive their first command assignments. Like any soldier, Seth considered that he might be sent into combat and killed. But what he feared more than death, he told McCormick, was failing as a leader. He thought about it constantly.

"Okay, man, tell me again," he said to McCormick. "What it's like to lead under fire? What's it like to tell someone to do something that might cost him his life?"

At thirty-four, McCormick was perhaps the oldest and most experienced soldier in the officer-candidate class. A compact West Virginian with a bushy blond mustache, McCormick had adopted Seth, treated him like a little brother, impressed that a smart, slight Rutgers grad with soft hands would sign up, knowing he'd be sent to Iraq or Afghanistan. Seth drove a Mustang and drank and cussed as well as anyone in the Army, but he also wore Coke-bottle glasses, sang karaoke, told corny jokes, kept a plaid baby blanket in his locker, and bragged about his college sweetheart, Kelly. His roughest feature was his New Jersey accent.

At the picnic table, Seth asked again about combat. His friend told him to expect guerrilla and asymmetrical attacks. The enemy won't wear uniforms. There won't be traditional front lines of battle. It will be what the Army calls 360-degree warfare.

Seth asked about leadership again.

"Never show fear, never hesitate," his mentor said. "Make a decision, even when you're not sure. A leader doesn't order his men to do anything he wouldn't do. A leader doesn't push his men forward. He leads from the front."

Seth's combat assignment came quicker than expected. Just days after he arrived at his first post, Fort Drum, New York, the Army ordered him to Iraq. Seth and Kelly had just moved into a new off-post apartment; now he would deploy in two weeks. Seth took Kelly on a long stroll by a lake and proposed. He didn't have money for a ring or time to arrange for a large wedding, but she didn't care. A week later, they married on the steps of the Watertown library before a small gathering of family members. She wore a white sleeveless gown she found on summer-end clearance at JCPenney for $20. He wore his Army dress uniform. They wrote their own vows. "In you, I have found a best friend and a life love," Kelly told Seth during the ceremony. "I love your zest for life, willingness to help those in need and your unique sense of humor. I promise you my loyalty, support, understanding and friendship. Life is full of many surprises and twists and turns. I will be by your side through them all. You are the man I want to walk through life with, the man I want to grow old with."

. . .

In the Tbilisi airport terminal, a stabbing pain in Darius's left foot spiked, and he leaned to his right. His gout flared whenever he became tense, and was made more irritable by lack of sleep.

The secret Georgia operation was unfolding during an unusually tense fall between Tehran and Washington. President Bush, frustrated by Iranian support for insurgent attacks against U.S. troops in Iraq, had recently made his most public threat to date: "I have authorized our military commanders in Iraq to confront Tehran's murderous activities." And just days ago, Iranian president Mahmoud Ahmadinejad had visited New York, where he'd offered bellicose remarks at the United Nations and at Columbia University. Even as the U.S. agents waited for the target at the airport, *The New Yorker* magazine was reporting that the Pentagon and CIA were rushing plans for a military strike against Iran. The agents followed it all on CNN and the BBC, aware that a successful mission, however small, might aid a U.S. attack, and that a screwup would hand the enemy an untimely propaganda coup.

Darius swiveled to his right flank and stole a glimpse of the two men leading Operation Shakespeare, Homeland Security supervisor John Malandra and U.S. Justice Department prosecutor Dave Hall. Despite inevitable tensions, Darius liked Hall and Malandra. They shared his aggressiveness and his assessment that The G—the U.S. government—was too mired in bureaucracy and petty politics to effectively stop the Chinese and Iranians from stealing American military technology. "The G is like one giant Dilbert cartoon," Darius liked to say. Darius felt the closest kinship with the prosecutor, a karate black belt who liked to accompany undercover agents into the field, an unusual trait that made his bosses nervous. The prosecutor stood beside Malandra, a former Philly street cop who carried the looks and swagger of a middle-aged Kirk Douglas. Normally a man in constant motion, Malandra was calmly leaning against a currency exchange kiosk, casually licking a vanilla ice cream cone. Darius recognized the undercover trick. What looked less like a cop than a guy enjoying an ice cream cone?

. . .

On that morning five months into combat, Lieutenant Dvorin's platoon approached a narrow stretch of bullet-riddled homes about ten miles from base. He ordered two thirds of the soldiers to dismount from the Humvees, spread out, and scan for IEDs on foot. Dvorin joined them, leading from the front, patrolling about seven yards ahead of the next man, a protocol designed to reduce injuries in case a bomb exploded. Shortly after ten o'clock, he saw a suspicious object in the roadway. It looked like scrap metal, perhaps part of a wheel rim. Dvorin turned and ordered his men back, a warning that probably saved lives. As the lieutenant yelled, an insurgent triggered the IED by remote control, launching shrapnel in all directions.

Many hours later, in the small southern New Hampshire town

of Jaffrey, the first flakes of a heavy snowstorm began to fall. Kelly Dvorin slept in a friend's apartment there on nights when she attended graduate classes. She pulled into the parking lot after a long day cradling a box of chocolates, by now the ritual comfort food of choice for nights when she especially missed her husband. Kelly put a can of minestrone soup on the stove and sat down to watch television while the soup simmered.

There was a knock at the door and she stood to answer it. A tall, middle-aged man in an olive uniform with wire-rim glasses removed his hat and asked if he could step inside. Kelly assumed he was soliciting donations for some sort of military charity. It was frigid outside and her first instinct was politeness. She invited him to sit at the kitchen table. She didn't sense danger until he began speaking.

"Ma'am, I'm with the Army . . ." Kelly didn't hear the precise words that followed. Her heart thumped over the officer's voice. His mouth moved in slow motion. But she understood. Seth was dead. Killed in combat.

Her defenses kicked in, a classic stress response, one she'd studied in her psychology coursework. "Are you sure?" she said. Kelly did not cry or yell. "Are you sure?" she repeated. "You're probably in the wrong house. It's easy to make a mistake."

He shook his head. No mistake. Her husband had been killed during a patrol that morning. The Army officer apologized again. There were things Kelly needed to begin thinking about. Did she want her husband's body embalmed? Did she have religious instructions for handling Seth's body? Where would she like the body delivered? Did she know where she wanted Seth buried?

Each query hit Kelly like an assault, a brutal confirmation. Embalmed? *He's dead.* Religious instructions? *He's dead.* Which cemetery? *He's dead.*

She fell silent.

"Um, ma'am," the officer said, breaking her trance. "I think something's burning."

It was the soup.

Kelly's mother and stepfather raced up Interstate 95 through the snowstorm. When they arrived long after midnight, they found Kelly lying on a mattress someone had pulled into the center of the living room. She was curled up, between two friends from school, locked in the fetal position.

. . .

Darius scanned the Tbilisi airport once more for counter-surveillance. The plane was due in minutes. His mind swirled. Would the Iranian arms broker show? Would he fall for the sting? If so, what intelligence might he reveal about Iranian procurement networks? Might he point the agents to American war profiteers betraying the troops? And once in handcuffs, would the Georgians let the Americans haul the Iranian back to the United States to face justice?

Or were the Iranians already wise? Had they figured it all out? Had the U.S. agents unwittingly become targets of a reverse Iranian intelligence op?

The Americans understood that the Iranian flying to meet them could be anyone. They knew him only as a guy on the other end of countless emails and phone calls. The men leading the U.S. team—Darius, his undercover partner, the supervisor, and the prosecutor—were staking their reputations on capturing a man who remained an enigma.

An arrival announcement came over the airport loudspeaker, first in Georgian, then in English. The crowd inched forward. The double doors hissed open and the first passengers with rolling suitcases filed out.

In twenty-four hours, the Americans would know whether their effort would pay off, or if they would go home fools.

PART ONE

The Lure

2004–2007

CHAPTER 1
The Storefront

On a mild spring morning in April 2004, a black Mercedes S430 sedan pulled into a low-rise office park. The robin's-egg blue building stood on a narrow suburban road near the New Jersey state line, thirty minutes from Seth Dvorin's boyhood home. The driver who stepped out of the Mercedes had a shaved head and an affable face. He wore a white dress shirt tucked into tan slacks that bulged a bit at the waist. In his wallet, the man carried a driver's license and business cards that identified him as Patrick J. Lynch. He carried a briefcase and walked purposefully inside, past the offices of a dentist and a chiropractor, and unlocked Suite 106. A small sign beside the door declared this the offices of Cross International.

Cross rarely received visitors, but anyone who wandered in the front door would have likely found Lynch seated at one of two desks, busy on the telephone or on a desktop computer. At his elbows were strategically strewn invoices, each topped with the company's globe-like logo and motto, "Cross International—Your Dependable Partner, Serving Your Acquisition, Logistics and Transportation Needs." The walls were lined with posters of jet fighters and aircraft carriers, and a coffee table by the front door held neatly stacked copies of *Jane's Fighting Ships* and other encyclopedias of modern warfare.

A quick check of public records or the Internet would reveal just enough about Cross International to assuage any suspicions—Cross had been in business since the mid-1990s and its state, county, and federal tax and incorporation records were in good order. Although Cross was a fairly generic name, a Google search of "Cross International" usually returned reaffirming hits, links to well-established import-export trade directories. Almost all of these links cited Suite 106 in Yardley and the Cross phone number, 215-496-1372.

The Cross website was understated and featured a standard, American-style business mission statement: "Cross International is a worldwide procurer of military and defense-related items and technology facilitating the needs of various customers throughout the world. Cross seeks to solve the difficulties associated with procurement through their many years of experience in the international logistics and acquisition business. Through a network of relationships, Cross has access to various international inventories that can facilitate many of your defense needs. Cross is an authorized broker for many U.S. and Canadian manufacturers. Cross also provides freight forwarding, brokerage and transportation assistance and guidance relative to the movement of sensitive commodities throughout the world."

The customers Patrick Lynch hoped to attract would instantly understand what Cross really offered. Cross helped foreign corporations—often no more than state-run front companies—buy sophisticated, American-made military-grade equipment and technology. Cross not only promised to help foreigners find the highest-quality items for the best price, it facilitated the hardest part of any global arms deal: navigating, and, if necessary, circumventing the byzantine U.S. regulations that limit export of military products to certain nations. "Freight forwarding . . . sensitive commodities throughout the world" meant that Cross could smuggle contraband military equipment to banned nations by routing it through ports like Vancouver, Dubai, Amsterdam, or Singapore. The practice, known as "transshipping," was the primary method of sending contraband to China, Iran, Pakistan, and war-torn countries in Africa.

To attract the right kind of customer, Lynch had embedded certain terms and phrases in the company website's metadata, the invisible keywords that search engines like Google use to link search terms to websites. In the webpage's metadata header, he had typed: "Laser, tanks, infrared, night vision, night targeting system, tandem warhead, reactive armor, grenade launcher, forward looking infrared, F-14, assault rifle, M4 carbine, M24 sniper rifle, M240 machine gun, unmanned aerial vehicle, sonar, radar, electronic combat systems, military cryptology, kinetic energy weapon systems."

On an average day, Patrick Lynch received a handful of fresh foreign queries for American-made military equipment and sophisticated electronics. Each query usually contained dozens of RFQs, or requests for price quotes. The RFQs often arrived in the form of an Excel spreadsheet with product or part numbers. Like any arms broker, Lynch would turn to the Internet, Google each product, figure out what it was and who made it, how much it cost, how long it took to manufacture, how it might be shipped, what export regulations applied, and what the profit margin might be. Discreet research could be intense and time-consuming.

With so many sales variables, it was not uncommon for negotiations to stretch across months. One recent successful transaction had lingered for nearly a year. It involved a Japanese client who sought something called an AN/PEQ-2. Lynch looked it up and found that an AN/PEQ-2 is an Infrared Target Pointer/Illuminator/Aiming Laser, and is deployed by U.S. troops in Iraq and Afghanistan. The device, made in New Hampshire, is a waterproof, rifle-mounted spotting laser that can project a red dot on a target miles away. The man who emailed Cross sought five of them, priced at $1,200 each. He asked if the aiming laser could be exported to Japan, and a Cross employee told him that it could not, as this would violate U.S. export law. So the man supplied Cross with an address in California for delivery. Lynch and his Cross colleagues replied that the law still requires them to certify the name of the end user, or final recipient. No problem, the Japanese buyer assured them. He promised to come up with a company name, and made a date to meet Lynch and other Cross executives in Los Angeles.

Only when he was arrested did the Japanese man learn Lynch's true identity—an undercover agent for Homeland Security Investigations (HSI), a division of U.S. Immigration and Customs Enforcement (ICE). Cross International was an undercover HSI company.

.   .   .

With its technical superiority, the U.S. military has created an unrivaled and formidable military machine, a superpower. With superior night vision and targeting software, the U.S. Army owns the night. With undetectable submarines and massive aircraft carriers, the U.S. Navy dominates every ocean, above and below the surface. With stealth fighters and bombers, the U.S. Air Force rules the skies.

The American advantage is so pronounced that on many battlefields the greatest threat to U.S. soldiers, sailors, and pilots is an enemy firing back with American-made weapons and technology. These tiny weapons of modern war—precision microchips, missile-guiding gyroscopes, night vision scopes, radar-cloaking material—can alter the balance of power. The most valuable military components are often the smallest state-of-the-art devices, most no larger than a stick of chewing gum, but nonetheless lethal, capable of guiding missiles, jamming radar, pinpointing submarines, and triggering countless weapons, from wireless IEDs to nuclear explosions.

To maintain its strategic and tactical advantages, the U.S. government long ago adopted a matrix of laws and regulations restricting the sale of sensitive technology and munitions overseas. But in a global economy fed by the speed and anonymity of Internet communication and cheap international shipping, it is growing increasingly difficult to enforce smuggling laws. Worse, an outdated and needlessly bureaucratic regulatory scheme—one filled with inherent conflicts of interest—has hamstrung law enforcement. As a result, America's technical advantage is evaporating.

Throughout history, the practice of war has evolved at the pace of technology, from ancient metal body armor to medieval armadas to atomic weapons. The nations with the most advanced technology usually win the wars and enjoy the spoils, political and economic dominance. "Tools, or weapons, if only the right ones can be discovered, form 99 percent of victory," the British general and military historian J. F. C. Fuller said in 1919. "Strategy, command, leadership, courage, discipline, supply, organization and all the moral and physical paraphernalia of war are nothing to a high superiority of weapons."

In the fifth century BC, Athens became a superpower in part by developing a fleet of sophisticated and expensive warships, triremes powered by oars. The nimble galley ships, built with pegs and rods, rather than nails and screws, dominated the Mediterranean Sea— so much so that following a victory against the Persians in 480 BC, Themistocles urged his fellow Athenians to preserve this advantage by preemptively burning the enemy's dockyards. His idea was rejected as immoral, and, sure enough, decades later, the Persians struck back by secretly bankrolling a proxy navy led by the Athenians' archrivals, the Spartans. "While it lasted, the age of the trireme anticipated issues facing today's nuclear world," Bard College classics professor James Romm has written. "Then as now, a single advanced weapon loomed so large that nations tried to strip it away with surgical strikes."

In the late fifteenth century, the advent of the mobile cannon triggered the rise of a European military machine that would grow to dominate global affairs for nearly five hundred years. Consider that at the outset of the artillery age, Europe controlled just 15 percent of the world's landmass. "But by the early sixteenth century, Europe would emerge as the richest, most dynamic and most powerful region on the planet," military historian Max Boot writes in *War Made New*. "In the years ahead, its explorers, merchants, preachers, settlers, sailors and soldiers would subdue much of the rest of mankind, controlling 35 percent of the earth's landmass by 1800 and a staggering 84 percent by 1914."

This technology revolution began in 1494, at the height of the Renaissance, when the French invaded the Italian city-states of Naples, Venice, and Florence. France sent 27,000 traditional soldiers to Italy, primarily a mix of archers and cavalrymen in armor, carrying lances and swords. But France also deployed dozens of newfangled mobile cannons. Though gunpowder had arrived in Europe a few hundred years earlier and some had developed rudimentary cannons, the French improved the technology dramatically. They developed a cannon with significantly more explosive force and crafted iron ordnance that could travel farther and faster than standard stone cannonballs. As important, the French cast the cannon from bronze, a lighter metal, which allowed the artillery to be mounted on raised wooden carriages and, thus, for the first time, be wheeled by horses rather than dragged by oxen. When the French forces invaded, the Italian armies took traditional positions in castles built of stone. The new cannons obliterated the castles. Many years later, a Florentine politician, Francesco Guicciardini, reflected on the profound changes wrought by the new weapon. "[Previously] when war broke out, the sides were so evenly balanced, the military methods so slow and the artillery so primitive, that the capture of a castle took up almost a whole campaign." The introduction of modern, mobile, powerful artillery turned "everything upside down," he wrote. "Wars became sudden and violent . . . cities were reduced with great speed, in a matter of days and hours rather than months."

England soon surpassed France in cannon technology, and beginning with the 1588 battle against the Spanish Armada, grew to dominate the seas, and therefore much of the world. As England built its empire, Britain sought to protect its technological advantage. In 1610, the British made it illegal to export ordnance, gunmetal, and iron ore without a government license. Other European nations adopted similar, rudimentary export controls. Milan forbade the emigration of skilled arms workers. Tuscany banned the export of munitions, powder, and metal to the Barbary Muslims.

In early U.S. history, trade and tariff policy rarely addressed counter-proliferation. Presidents imposed exceptions during war—Lincoln's blockade of the Confederate states—but until World War I the United States, largely neutral in foreign affairs, promoted free trade. Indeed, for three years preceding America's entry into the war in 1917, U.S. nonmilitary exports continued to flow to Germany. The Trading with the Enemy Act of 1917 formed the basis for an export-control framework that survives to this day, and the government published a list of thousands of embargoed foreign companies and individuals, a forerunner to the current prohibited entities lists. Under the regime, American shippers were required to obtain a government license before exporting products to a person or business on the list.

Following World War I, a series of Senate hearings fanned suspicions that U.S. munitions manufacturers had helped push the nation into war. The backlash spurred postwar export controls on munitions to certain countries, and by 1935, reflecting the American return toward isolationism, Congress adopted the Neutrality Act, which forbade the United States from trading with any nation at war with another. One provision created a National Munitions Control Board to license exports. United States policy shifted abruptly again at the outbreak of World War II, from neutrality to support for the Allies. In 1940, the United States banned aviation fuel and machine tools to the Japanese, and even before Pearl Harbor, Roosevelt imposed a complete ban on military items to Japan. By 1941, the ban extended to trade with Germany and Italy. This did not, however, prevent several major American corporations from continuing to do business with the Nazis or their proxies, according to documents unearthed decades later by journalist Charles Higham. In his book *Trading with the Enemy*, he writes that at the height of the war Standard Oil smuggled fuel to the enemy through Switzerland, and, with authorization from Detroit, a Ford factory in France built trucks for the Nazis. But these acts were overshadowed by the tremendous technological advances during the war, from the development of the atomic bomb to radar. The United States won the decisive battle of Midway in part because American ships carried rudimentary radar that could detect incoming enemy planes from miles away, while the Japanese largely relied on scout planes and spotters.

After the war, U.S. policymakers struggled to contain communism, in part by limiting technology exports to the Soviet Union, while at the same time working to rebuild the European economy, for which free trade was critical. Some Americans viewed the Soviet Union as an untapped market; others took a more cautious view. In a 1946 report to President Truman, White House counselor Clark Clifford advised that the surest way to influence the Soviets was to engage them in trade, though he warned, presciently, that "the United States should avoid premature disclosure of scientific and technological information relating to war matériel." Truman's inclination after the war was to embrace free trade. His administration shrank the wartime list of controlled goods and abolished the Trading with the Enemy list. Reflecting the prevailing free trade vision, the Commerce Department assigned just one person to enforce export controls.

The era of free trade did not last long. After the communists seized power in Czechoslovakia in 1948 and the Soviets detonated their own atomic bomb the following year, Truman was compelled to tighten export controls. New lists were drafted restricting many shipments to the Soviet Union and its satellites. The Commerce Department enforcement staff morphed to fifty. The anticommunist philosophy solidified by 1950, and would shape U.S. export policy for the duration of the Cold War and beyond. President Eisenhower found many Soviet trade restrictions "damned silly"—the data showed that the embargoes carried little practical effect. But anticommunist political currents were too swift to navigate a change in direction.

From this Cold War structure emerged a rubric in which export licensing decisions were made either by the State Department, sensitive first to foreign policy concerns, or by the Commerce Department, a government agency created to promote American business, not restrict it. The Pentagon and other agencies held only advisory roles. Toward the end of the Cold War, the military began to push back. The Pentagon interceded, for example, in 1988 to dissuade State and Commerce from approving a Maryland company's request to export 500,000 injectors of a nerve gas antidote to the Iraqi army. A short while later, the Pentagon got the White House to block Commerce Department approval of a New Jersey company's request to supply Iraq with furnaces that could be used to produce missiles and nuclear weapons. Although the United States won a quick victory over Saddam Hussein in 1991, coalition forces were surprised to discover a significant amount of American-made munitions and technology in Iraqi military stocks.

After the war, President George H. W. Bush declared nonproliferation of sensitive and military technology to terrorists and rogue states a priority. But the policy shift—attempting to regulate trade with specific end users instead of whole countries—did not fit well with an export enforcement system designed to fight the Cold War. What's more, as technology evolved rapidly in the 1990s and 2000s, weapons systems, like everything else, became miniaturized and therefore easier to smuggle—a military computer that once filled a room could now fit on a thumb drive. President Bill Clinton struggled, too, to balance the emerging security threats with the burgeoning global economy. Stymied by a split Congress, Clinton adopted a series of administrative reforms—he granted the Pentagon the power to review dual-use license applications, but he also relaxed restrictions governing satellites and computers. Clinton's successors each touted "reform," yet as late as 2013, the government was still struggling to cull the lists of restricted items and focus on the most dangerous.

Robert Gates, who first confronted the issue as a deputy CIA director for Ronald Reagan and again as defense secretary for

George W. Bush and Barack Obama, believes that U.S. export policy is so broad—"a byzantine amalgam of authorities, roles and missions scattered around different parts of the federal government"—that it neither promotes commerce nor protects national security. After becoming deputy CIA director, Gates recalled, "it soon became apparent that the length of the list of controlled technologies outstripped our finite intelligence monitoring capabilities." In many cases, Cold War–era regulations restricted basic, off-the-shelf items—latches, wires, and lug nuts if they could be used in an airplane, for example—from export. "We were wasting our time and resources tracking technologies you could buy at RadioShack," Gates told a group of business executives in 2010. "Frederick the Great's famous maxim that 'he who defends everything defends nothing' certainly applies to export control."

Although the Obama administration embarked on an ambitious series of reforms, U.S. export control remains fractured. The State and Commerce departments, now assisted by the Pentagon, still decide which products can be exported where. The Treasury Department maintains its own list of sanctioned countries and individuals—nations, terrorists, and suspected criminals, such as Syria or al Qaeda, to whom nothing can be exported. A separate and equally strained triumvirate shares responsibility for enforcement: Commerce, FBI, and Homeland Security. Commerce's three-part role—promoting trade, licensing exports, and enforcing the law—creates inherent conflicts of interest. Not surprisingly, the Commerce marketing and licensing divisions dwarf the law enforcement section. Commerce employs perhaps one hundred federal agents nationwide and a token handful overseas. The FBI plays a larger role than Commerce, but Homeland Security deploys the most resources.

Federal law enforcement turf battles are legion, but are exacerbated in the counter-proliferation arena by the clash of cultures between FBI, Commerce, and Homeland Security. The FBI approaches the problem from a counterespionage point of view. Commerce focuses on licensing enforcement. Many Homeland Security agents are former Customs officers with smuggling expertise. Each agency enjoys unique powers. Only FBI agents can deploy Foreign Intelligence Surveillance Act wiretaps. Only Commerce agents can issue administrative sanctions. Only Homeland Security agents can search packages at the border without a warrant. The three agencies can't even agree on military smuggling nomenclature. The FBI calls it "technology transfer." Commerce calls it "export enforcement." Homeland Security calls it "counter-proliferation." A string of twenty-two government audits dating to 2001 have documented poor export coordination, administration, and enforcement. In 2007, the Government Accountability Office placed export controls on its "High Risk List," a dubious honor reserved for the nation's most troubled government programs. A 2010 government briefing paper described the current mix of export enforcement agencies as "confusing . . . disjointed and inefficient." Change is proving difficult. As part of its reform initiative, the Obama administration created a unified export enforcement center, a clearinghouse in which the law enforcement agencies will share information about cases. Even creation of the center became a bureaucratic chore. The grand opening of the coordination center was delayed for nine months as Commerce, FBI, and Homeland Security officials bickered over how they would cooperate.

Every year, American businesses report to the authorities more than nineteen thousand suspicious contacts from foreign buyers, and U.S. agents open approximately 1,800 new counter-proliferation investigations. And every year, U.S. authorities announce about thirty or forty arrests for military technology smuggling, mostly inside the United States. Most of the smugglers are middlemen caught buying or selling American-made military gear for the Chinese, the Pakistanis, the Iranians, or the Russians. Most arrested know little more than the details of their own schemes. Mostly, they are expats out to exploit one or two contacts from the homeland. They cannot provide large-scale portraits of the vast shadow networks of procurement agents deployed by the Iranian, Russian, Chinese, and Pakistani governments. The best U.S. law enforcement targets—foreign procurement agents—are virtually untouchable inside their own countries, and employ the Internet, freight forwarding companies, and express mail services to keep the illicit purchases at arm's length. As late as 2004, U.S. law enforcement agents had never nabbed an insider—someone living in Iran or China with intimate knowledge of their nation's military supply network—seized his files, and brought him to justice in the United States. The U.S. agents were constantly on the hunt for such an elusive, high-value target.

. . .

Patrick J. Lynch, the undercover agent posing as a Cross International arms broker, was really Patrick J. Lechleitner. Everyone called him P.J.

Lechleitner worked for Immigration and Customs Enforcement, or ICE, which was part of the sprawling Department of Homeland Security. ICE agents were split between an immigration division and an investigations division. The immigration side employed Enforcement and Removal Operations agents, or ERO agents, and the customs side employed Homeland Security Investigations agents, HSI agents. Lechleitner was an HSI agent, one of approximately seven thousand. HSI agents investigated transnational border crimes, primarily serious immigration violations, human trafficking, drug smuggling, and child pornography. A small percentage, perhaps a few hundred, worked arms and technology smuggling cases. Lechleitner was a rookie agent, but HSI had assigned him to counter-proliferation because he held unusual qualifications.

Born in 1972, Lechleitner grew up two hours west of Yardley, in a rural eastern Pennsylvania county called Schuylkill, at the edge of Appalachia. Once a prosperous coal and railroad hub, Schuylkill was already declining by the time Lechleitner entered elementary school. His parents were natives; they shared working-class Irish Catholic roots and had met during high school. Lechleitner was the sixth of seven children. Five of his siblings still live in Schuylkill County.

In high school, Lechleitner held one ambition, joining the Navy. He sought travel and adventure, the kind his father, his uncle, a brother, and a sister had found in the service. His dad had been a rescue and deep-sea diver—trained, as it happened, by Master Sergeant Carl Brashear, the civil rights icon portrayed by Cuba Gooding Jr. in the movie *Men of Honor.* A month after graduating from high school, Lechleitner reported for basic training in Florida.

P.J. Lechleitner's interests lay in science and history, technology and strategy, and so he sought an assignment in cryptology, the signals intelligence track that includes codes, eavesdropping, and communications, working amidst the military's deepest secrets. Lechleitner scored well on aptitude tests and got a lucky assignment. The Navy posted him aboard the USS *Belknap*, the guided missile cruiser in the Mediterranean that hosted the Sixth Fleet's commander, a three-star admiral.

As a crypto technician, Lechleitner processed the admiral's communications, which meant he was exposed to almost everything the commander of the Sixth Fleet read—the threat reports, the diplomatic cables, and the political intelligence, things that revealed the true capabilities and limits of American military might. He arrived aboard the ship in 1991, just as groundbreaking advances in computer technology and cell phones were creating unexpected opportunities to collect oceans of intelligence data. In his new job, Lechleitner was stationed at a central collection point and became privy to much of what America's secret listening devices were picking up in the Mediterranean theater. He received a crash course in geopolitics—how the world really works, why some things happen and some things don't, why some events are more trivial than they appear to be and others more ominous. There were moments of boredom, to be sure, but few of his six hundred shipmates enjoyed such an interesting job. The vast majority performed rote chores; they might as well as have been working in a factory back in Schuylkill County. Cables to the admiral could arrive at any hour. Given the time difference with Washington, it was not unusual for Lechleitner to conduct an urgent brief at 2 a.m., the admiral standing in his pajamas, the subject matter a Flash message from the White House Situation Room. At age eighteen, Lechleitner was seeing and hearing things classified at the highest levels.

He served five years, mostly in Europe, then returned to central Pennsylvania and enrolled in a local college, planning to become a cop, just like his uncle and other friends. "I liked the rule of law; it fit my personality," Lechleitner recalled. After a year in college, he ran out of money and dropped out. He moved to northern Virginia, near Pentagon friends with connections. There, he won a job as a police officer in affluent Fairfax County. He patrolled a sector near Dulles International Airport for five years, combining it with classes at George Mason University. By his senior year, Lechleitner grew restless with suburban police work and applied for a slew of federal agent jobs, from U.S. Customs to the FBI. He hoped to find something as interesting as cryptology, something that might require overseas travel.

It turned out he got his pick of agencies. Several moved swiftly to hire him. Here was a seasoned cop with a military background who already held top secret clearances. The National Security Agency struck first and hired him as an internal affairs officer. Lechleitner soon left NSA for a better offer, but the months he spent at the agency's headquarters in Fort Meade, Maryland, proved invaluable. It exposed Lechleitner to the other side of the secret signals network, the civilian intelligence community. He would become the rare federal agent who could navigate the distinct and often insular worlds of street cops, soldiers, and spies.

The better offer came from Customs—higher salary, more interesting work, sweeter pension. His dad, the Navy vet, didn't like it, and told him so. His father couldn't understand why he would give up a presumably cool job at NSA in favor of busting dirtbag drug smugglers at airports. "Why do you want to spend your life searching people's underwear?" his father asked. Lechleitner shrugged and talked about the differences in benefits. For security reasons, including his own safety, he was not allowed to tell his dad what Customs had in mind.

By the time Lechleitner arrived in Yardley in mid-2003, the undercover storefront was considered a bit of a backwater. Originally created as a vehicle to enforce the Iraqi oil embargo in the mid-1990s, the undercover agents who worked at Cross International had made several contacts, started a few investigations, but had little to show for their efforts. The operation was inconveniently situated in the northern Philadelphia suburbs, and when Lechleitner showed up, only one other agent, a supervisor, was still working there.

At the time, the undercover operation boasted only a handful of active, promising international arms proliferation cases. In addition to the AN/PEQ-2 laser-spotter case, they were targeting a New York aerospace company suspected of shipping military aircraft parts overseas. The agents were also pursuing a relatively minor, five-year-old investigation of an Iranian agricultural commodities broker. The target was assumed to be still living out of reach in Dubai, but a quick records check by the agents would have shown that the woman had recently moved to Southern California. When Lechleitner's supervisor retired, the pace began to quicken.

Customs merged with the Immigration and Naturalization Service to become Immigrations and Customs Enforcement in 2003, but Lechleitner's assignment did not change. In addition to working as an undercover HSI agent four or five days a week in Yardley, Lechleitner also spent two or three days a month on an effort called Project Shield America. This was a Homeland Security outreach campaign in which agents visited U.S. defense contractors and high-tech manufacturers to discuss export security. It was impossible to visit every exporter in the region—annually, an estimated 2,600 companies shipped about 400,000 tons of cargo and mail from Philadelphia International Airport, and millions of tons more on an estimated 2,700 cargo ships. To winnow the numbers and identify the American businesses worth approaching for Shield America, Homeland Security agents data-mined government and shipping records, no small matter—in fiscal 2004, local companies filed more than 354,000 Shippers Export Declarations. The agents began by comparing the Pentagon's list of approved contractors with applications to Commerce and State for export licenses. They paid particular attention to those companies whose export license applications had been denied. The agents also scoured financial intelligence reports supplied by a special HSI unit in New York and foreign-based analyses from the CIA.

Once Lechleitner identified a vulnerable or suspect U.S. company, he made his Shield America visit overtly—as an HSI agent, carrying a badge and gun. He brought with him a twenty-five-page PowerPoint presentation designed to simplify the confusing and complex export rules, win the trust and cooperation of manufacturers, sellers, and exporters, and provide them with a formal method of reporting suspicious foreign contacts. Whenever he visited a business, Lechleitner tried to meet with as many potential sources as possible—corporate executives, export managers, technicians, scientists, engineers, salesmen, brokers, freight forwarders, anyone in the supply chain who might come in contact with foreign customers. If these folks couldn't understand the rules, how could they be expected to follow them? As important, how could they be expected to help enforce them?

Lechleitner usually began his PowerPoint presentation with a patriotic pitch, laying out the consequences of munitions smuggling. Export enforcement, his opening PowerPoint slide explained, is designed to prevent America's enemies, including terrorists, from "obtaining arms, weapons systems and controlled technology used to develop weapons of mass destruction." There are four primary export laws, he explained. The first law, the Arms Export Control Act, and the companion International Traffic in Arms Regulations Act, regulate the export of military weapons, from small arms to missiles, on an ever-changing list maintained by the State Department. The second law, the Export Administration Act, regulates the export of certain "dual-use" commodities, items that have both a civilian and military application. This list is maintained by the Commerce Department, and includes, for example, night vision technology, flame retardant chemicals, and certain types of radar. The third and fourth laws, the Trading with the Enemy and International Emergency Economic Powers acts, prohibit virtually *any* export, military or commercial, to certain countries, including Iran, Cuba, and Syria. The rules also require an American manufacturer-shipper to create formal internal management protocols, including making a serious effort to determine the end user, or true final recipient of an exported product.

What made a foreign query suspicious? Lechleitner offered four common warning signs: *1. Cash sales.* Legitimate dealers will insist on pro forma invoices or letters of credit. *2. Buyers reluctant to name an end user.* Legitimate buyers expect to be required to provide end user certificates. *3. Buyers who refuse warranty or installation assistance for complex goods.* Legitimate buyers expect the seller to warranty the product and to service it if necessary. *4. Illogical requests.* Legitimate buyers tend to make sensible purchases. Undersea companies shouldn't make inquires about desert gear; clothing companies shouldn't order microchips.

Near the close of his presentation, Lechleitner explained how American exporters could help him try to catch black market brokers. If you receive a suspicious overseas query, Lechleitner told manufacturers, don't ignore it or reject it out of hand. Call HSI and let us help you respond, he told them. He always kept that last part tantalizingly vague.

To remind his audience of the stakes—in the wrong hands, their equipment might be used against U.S. troops—Lechleitner ended every presentation with the same image, a photograph of rows of tombstones at Arlington National Cemetery.

.   .   .

His Shield America efforts paid off quickly.

In April 2004, a Philadelphia ship manufacturer called Lechleitner with a tip about a query from Pakistan. The foreign broker's name set off alarm bells.

Yasmin Ahmed was well known to American law enforcement. For more than a decade, Ahmed and her husband had been smuggling munitions to embargoed countries in the Middle East, including Pakistan and Iran. Their company, Neaz Trading, kept offices in Dubai and Karachi. In 2001 and 2002, they smuggled $200,000 worth of military radar from Connecticut. They skirted U.S. regulations by falsifying export documents, claiming the radar was destined for the Bangladesh air force. When U.S. undercover agents in Connecticut got wind of the scheme, they planted transmitters inside one of the shipping containers, and traced the radar to Pakistan, not Bangladesh. Posing as American brokers, the undercover agents then lured Ahmed to New York City with the promise of future deals. She was arrested moments after stepping into a limousine the agents had waiting for her at the airport. Nearly simultaneously, the agents discovered that Ahmed and her husband were also conspiring with an American broker in Florida to smuggle parts for the M109 self-propelled howitzer cannon and the M113 armored personnel carrier to Dubai. Although the shipment had already departed the Port of Charleston, South Carolina, and was moving across the Atlantic, the HSI agents were able to intervene before the ship reached the Middle East. Ahmed pleaded guilty to smuggling charges, served nine months, paid a $50,000 fine, and was deported to Karachi. Now, less than a year later, she was back in business, shopping for more contraband American-made military equipment.

The balls on this woman, Lechleitner thought. *Finally, a righteous case.*

Lechleitner paid a visit to the Pennsylvania shipping company manager who'd received the new query from Ahmed. While there was always a risk that the company manager was working with the bad guys and could blow Cross's cover, Lechleitner decided the man seemed trustworthy enough to take into his confidence. He thanked him and handed up a HSI-written script to email to Ahmed in Pakistan:

"Thank you again for your request for parts. I must apologize for the delay in responding but due to an unexpected increase in business I am unable to fulfill your request for parts at this time. However, we have worked with a company in the past on similar matters and they would be able to assist you in obtaining the requested parts. The company is Cross International, located at 1790 Yardley-Langhorne Road, Suite 106, Yardley, PA 19067. I have already advised my contact at Cross, Patrick Lynch, of your request and they are currently working on pricing and availability. Feel free to contact Patrick at crossintl@aol.com. Thank you again for your business and I look forward to working with you in the future."

The ruse worked. Ahmed replied to Cross within twenty-four hours. In short order, she and Lechleitner were negotiating for all manner of electronics and munitions.

During this week in April 2004, Lechleitner and his colleagues received another equally intriguing Shield America tip. This one came from an aircraft manufacturer south of Philadelphia. A first-generation American, he told Lechleitner that he was offended by the clumsy nature of the inquiry. This email had arrived from someone calling himself Alex Dave. The man claimed to be based in Dubai. But a quick Google search revealed that Alex Dave's email address was linked to phone number 98-711-2351809. "98" was the country code for Iran.

Lechleitner gave the aircraft factory owner the same script, referring Alex Dave's business to Cross International. Within days, the American undercover agent and the Iranian broker were emailing directly, and Alex Dave was sending Cross International a flurry of requests. To begin, the Iranian sought prices for American jet parts and radioisotopes.

CHAPTER 2
The Capitalist

SHIRAZ, IRAN

The man looking to buy radiological isotopes and U.S. fighter jet parts—"Alex Dave"—lived in the Iranian city of wine, flowers, and poets.

On a warm June morning in 2004, Amir Hossein Ardebili, a trim, ambitious man with olive skin, aquiline nose, and receding crown of black hair, woke to the comforting aroma of chai, his mother's tea. Her brew included a strong mix of loose dark leaves and pinches of rose petals. She spent more care preparing the tea, pouring it from the kettle to a glass cup and back again to check color and consistency, than she did laying out the assortment of breakfast cheeses, warm breads, honey, basil, and chives. She could not be rushed. "Patience, patience," she often admonished her boys. By the time Ardebili arrived downstairs, the tea had been brewing for a proper fifteen minutes. At the table, he instinctively plucked a sugar cube from a bowl, stuck it on his tongue, and swirled it into his gums. Ardebili gripped the cup of chai before him and took the first invigorating sip of the day. The tea rushed caffeine to his brain; sugar residue lodged to his teeth.

The morning sun cast soft light across Iran's sixth largest city and into the modest Ardebili home, a two-story stucco building tucked into a semi-affluent northwestern neighborhood. Six hundred miles south of Tehran, Shiraz is the leafy capital of the Fars province, a culturally significant region of mountains and valleys. In ancient times, foreigners called the Fars region Persis, a term that evolved into the word that defines Iranian culture, Persian. The word for the official language of Iran, Farsi, is derived from Fars.

Beyond the 1,500-year-old center city and exurban sugar and cement factories grow lush fields of figs, artichokes, pistachios, apricots, mulberries, and yellow plums, but since the Islamic Revolution, no vineyards for Shiraz wine. Iran's greatest poets, Hafez and Sa'di, lived and died in Shiraz, and the legendary ruins of Persepolis, the fulcrum of Persia's first dynasty, are located an hour's drive to the east. Darius the Great, considered the Thomas Jefferson of ancient Iran, ruled at Persepolis from 522 to 486 BC. His empire stretched from India to Eastern Europe, and Darius was said to have introduced the rest of civilization to the paved road and the postal service. Modern Shiraz is also known for its eponymous university, where Ardebili had studied electrical engineering, history, and poetry. The sprawling campus is a short stroll from Ardebili's house, on the opposite side of the city's dry riverbed.

Although twenty-nine years old, Amir Ardebili still lived in his boyhood home with his parents, Zahra and Nasrollah, and younger brother, Afshin. The arrangement was not unusual—many Iranians remained in their parents' homes for economic or familial reasons. Amir planned to move out once he found a wife; living with single male friends would have proved a distraction from his new all-consuming and lucrative business. Besides, he was the only breadwinner in the family. His father had recently retired, and his brother was unemployed.

The Ardebili family was entrenched in Iran's middle class. Amir's sixty-year-old father was a retired senior official for the municipal tax administration. Although an uncle was becoming a nationally known jewelry designer, he had yet to earn his fortune. Amir's grandfathers had been local leaders but were not wealthy. His mother's father had been a respected local religious cleric, and his father's father was once an important government executive for the city of Shiraz, the equivalent of a chief of staff—famous enough, the family liked to brag, that a mailed envelope bearing only the name "Ardebili" and the city "Shiraz" would find its way to his home. Amir held

great respect for his grandfathers, but he saw a different path to
success.

The young Ardebili did not aspire to be a public servant or religious cleric. He was a capitalist. A businessman. And his new enterprise was just beginning to grow.

Until recently, Ardebili had worked for a large, state-controlled
company called Shiraz Electronics Industries. It was a steady job
that paid a respectable $650 a week. SEI was one of a half dozen
government-run outfits supplying foreign electronic and military
equipment to the Iranian army, navy, and air force. SEI also maintained a lab dedicated to reengineering samples of the most modern and sensitive foreign military equipment. Such labs had created
knockoff Iranian versions of American weapons systems, including
surface-to-air missiles. What SEI could not adequately replicate—
night vision goggles and military-grade radar, for example—it
bought in bulk. To circumvent the international embargo crippling
the Iranian economic and military infrastructure, and to shield
any hint of government involvement, SEI hired freelance brokers
to operate as secret middlemen. At SEI, Ardebili's job was to serve
as the primary contact for these freelance brokers, mostly Iranians
working inside Iran. He forwarded orders from SEI to the brokers,
and the brokers pivoted to the Internet to find Western companies
willing to fulfill the requests, ordering anything from refrigerator
pumps to radioisotopes to stealth technology. SEI often demanded
American-made products, especially electronics, because the Americans usually made the most advanced technical components. The
American parts were also the most difficult to acquire because they
could not be shipped directly, requiring a dose of extra guile on the
part of the Iranian brokers. A successful broker needed to work discreetly, employing transshipment points—places like Dubai, Singapore, or former Soviet republics, countries where the items could be
legally shipped from the United States, and then quickly reloaded
for final transit to Iran. The brokers also had to devise ways to

pay their American suppliers. Because they could not legally wire funds directly from an Iranian bank to a U.S. one, they set up special accounts with banks in Zurich, Dubai, and Frankfurt to launder money to America.

. . .

Several international banks did their utmost to help Iranians like Ardebili skirt U.S. restrictions. From the mid-1990s until approximately 2008, six of them systematically falsified or concealed wire transactions—to slip the payments past computerized U.S. money laundering filters, the banks routinely stripped any information linking wire transfers to Iran. This included deleting any Iranian-sounding surname, address, bank code, phone number, and email domain. When U.S. investigators discovered widespread deception by the six banks, they levied huge penalties. Lloyds TSB bank was hit for $350 million, Barclays Bank PLC for $298 million, and Standard Chartered Bank for $227 million. ING Bank NV forfeited $619 million, and ABN Amro Bank NV (now the Royal Bank of Scotland) forfeited $500 million. Credit Suisse, the bank Ardebili used at least a dozen times to funnel payments to American manufacturers, was later forced to forfeit $536 million.

Credit Suisse's circumvention of U.S. banking restrictions can be traced to at least 1986, when President Reagan first imposed restrictions on financial transactions with Libya. That year, Credit Suisse issued a directive to employees to conceal references to Libya in certain wire transfers: "Payment orders of Libyan banks or government organizations to third party accounts in the United State or with U.S. banks abroad are to be executed without stating the name of the ordering party." Over the years, the bank honed its evasion methods, motivated in part by the need for speed—delayed, rejected, or seized payments ate into profits. In 1994, Credit Suisse instructed employees to begin substituting the term "By order of A client" for actual Iranian client names. In 1995, Credit Suisse employees were told to omit bank identification codes from future Iranian transactions, and to use something called "cover payment messages" to mask the true originator.

Credit Suisse distributed a pamphlet to Iranian clients entitled "How to Transfer USD Payments," which explained how best to avoid the automated U.S. banking filters. As part of another marketing endeavor to Middle East clients, Credit Suisse pledged to manually inspect every wire transfer to or from Iran, and to wipe away any incriminating data. "It is absolutely impossible," the bank promised potential customers, "that one of your payment instructions will be effected without having it checked in advance by our specially designated payment team at Credit Suisse in Zurich and all team members are most professional and aware of the special attention such payments of yours do require." The promises paid off. In 2003, when the British bank Lloyds decided to terminate all U.S. dollar transactions with Iranian customers, almost every Iranian customer at Lloyds moved to the more accommodating Credit Suisse. From 2002 to 2005, the number of Iranians banking with Credit Suisse jumped from 49,000 to nearly 200,000. Amir Ardebili was one of these new customers.

．　．　．

During the five years he had worked as an acquisition agent for the state-operated SEI, Ardebili learned a great deal about the military, environmental engineering, and the way various radar systems operate. He even spent a few exciting months at an Iranian nuclear facility. Yet Ardebili came to realize that he could make a great deal more than $650 a week if he became a freelance broker himself. A swift middleman could make tens of thousands in a good month. "And," Ardebili recalled years later, "it is better to be your own boss." In early 2004, he quit SEI and opened a small office with a partner and a secretary.

His mother did not approve.

Five months into the new venture, she was still giving him dirty looks at breakfast, daggers that suggested he was acting self-ishly, recklessly putting his career, even his family's well-being, at risk. Why had he quit a perfectly good, stable job? His father was retired! His brother was unemployed! How would they live if the new business failed? And when did he plan to find a wife? He was twenty-eight! Soon, the neighbors would begin to wonder what was wrong with him.

Ardebili did not argue with his mother. His timing, he knew, was poor. His slightly younger brother, Afshin, held no immediate job prospects, though this was neither unusual nor his fault. At least one third of the young adults in Shiraz were unemployed, and most of those who were employed held jobs that made a tiny fraction of what Amir had earned at SEI. Amir understood the career risks better than his mother, but he was also deeply mindful of what surely exac-erbated his mother's worry—the recent death of his other brother. The brother had died mysteriously, after falling from a third-floor window. His absence hung over every conversation.

To Amir, his brother's unexpected death simply reaffirmed his decision to depart SEI. For as long as he could remember, the future had always seemed unsettled. Like a lot of Iranians his age, Arde-bili had lost boyhood friends during the eight-year Iran-Iraq War in the 1980s, likely killed by American armaments sold to Iraq. He was too young to remember the 1979 Islamic Revolution and U.S. embassy takeover, but the events that followed, especially the eco-nomic embargoes that stunted the Iranian economy, shaped his worldview. Culturally, America fascinated him, from its Hollywood movies to its free enterprise ethos; politically, however, he remained suspicious, sincerely frightened of current leaders like George W. Bush and Dick Cheney, and their true intentions toward Iran. Arde-bili wasn't sure what to make of the 9/11 attacks. Many of his con-temporaries argued that Israel or Bush had staged them, a possibility he did not entirely dismiss. And yet, although he believed in God and loosely followed the news from Tehran, Ardebili carried only two true passions—business and mountain climbing.

Ardebili briefly considered engaging his mother, to try to explain that his new business required a different pace. He would not earn a weekly paycheck; there might be weeks where he might not be paid at all. The new work was trial and error, delays and frustrations, but soon, with his SEI connections, hard work, and a bit of good luck, he envisioned a comfortable future. By his mid-thirties, he expected to be able to buy a home of his own, perhaps take his parents on a first-ever trip overseas, to Turkey, possibly even to America or Canada. So far, business had been good; he'd moved on from small-time initial sales in the Asian computer chip market to the European and American military black market. Already, he was working on a $1 million deal to buy North American–made sonar on behalf of SEI and the Iranian navy. If Ardebili succeeded, the commission on this single deal would almost match his annual salary at SEI. How to make his mother understand?

Ardebili stared at his tea, and did not speak for a few moments. Finally, he held the glass aloft and softly threw his mother's own words into the air. "Patience, patience."

■ ■ ■

The nascent arms dealer stepped out into the Shiraz morning, a new Gigabyte-brand laptop in a black bag flung over his shoulder. He strolled halfway down an alley to tree-lined Bargh Street, and up one block to Karim Khan-e Zand Boulevard, the frantic main highway that ran parallel to the river. At the corner of Bargh and Zand, he nodded, as he did every day, to a fruit vendor, the same middle-aged man stationed there since Ardebili had been in high school.

"*Salaam,*" Ardebili said. *Peace be with you.*

"*Salaam, mohandes,*" the old man replied, invoking the honorific that came with Ardebili's college degree in engineering.

Ardebili walked about two blocks, past his neighborhood drug-store and market, beyond a subway stop under endless construc-tion, until he reached a shoeshine stand. He liked to stop here most mornings, whether his shoes needed buffing or not. He viewed it as a silent act of charity. The leathered old man clearly needed the money, and though he and Ardebili rarely spoke, he seemed to appreciate the gesture. The fledgling broker liked to use this time to gather his thoughts. He relaxed, contemplating the busy pan-orama and, ultimately, his place in it. Schoolchildren scurried past on the sidewalk. Cars and scooters crept up the jammed boulevard. Exhaust fumes choked the city air. Two months ago, he'd been far from here, in his favorite place, up in the Zagros Mountains with friends, on a four-day hike among fig and pomegranate trees, to a summit nearly eleven thousand feet above sea level. He could close his eyes and still smell that pristine air, relish that majestic view. Ardebili imagined that his new work would be a lot like mountain climbing—incredibly challenging, but once he reached the summit, unbelievably rewarding.

The shoeshine usually ended with the same ritual: the old man refused to take any payment, Ardebili insisted, they haggled for a bit, then settled on a fair price. Ardebili enjoyed the game. It was a tune-up, his first negotiation of the day.

In ten minutes' time he had reached his modest office, a win-dowless single room with three desks and three chairs. He arrived before his partner, Sina Tavokoli, and their secretary. He opened his laptop, turned it on, and stepped over to the fax machine. For secu-rity reasons, SEI and other government-run companies liked to fax their requests, rather than email them. This eliminated the risk that independent brokers like Ardebili might simply forward the requests to the Western suppliers, leaving telltale SEI or Iranian government fingerprints on the emails. Ardebili didn't like it—it created extra work in English, a language he was still struggling to learn—but he understood the rationale.

Ardebili called his company SBC Technology Group. The letters *S* and *B* stood for Sayeh Bahar, a nod to Shiraz's lush heritage. *Sayeh* means "shade" and *bahar* means "spring," though in this context it was a reference to a blossom on a regional fruit tree. The romantic yet misleading name fit Ardebili's business plan. The *C* in SBC didn't stand for anything. It was just part of the facade. Virtually everything about his company was fake, designed to create a patina of legitimacy.

He cast the company website on a navy blue background and topped it with the SBC logo—red block letters embedded inside an infinity symbol. "Our mission is to provide our customers with high-quality, cost-effective solutions for spare and communications parts and equipment that keep aircraft operating safely, on time and on budget. Customer satisfaction is our highest priority." The website offered a Dubai address—no more than a mail drop—and claimed an association with a well-established American company. "SBC Inc. is a subsidiary of The Churchill Companies, Minneapolis, Minnesota, a multi-billion dollar financial services company." Ardebili had stumbled upon Churchill during a random Google search, and conveniently appropriated its apparent assets and respectability, without contacting anyone in Minnesota. SBC also purported to be an authorized Middle East and Russian distributor for five American electronics companies, three of which primarily produced equipment for the U.S. military. While it was true that SBC conducted business with some of these U.S. firms, buying equipment from them for the Iranian government, the American companies hadn't authorized the resale of anything. Nonetheless, Ardebili had begun downloading product spec sheets and instruction manuals from the Internet, relabeling the cover sheets with his SBC logo, and sending the newly forged documents to prospective clients.

On this morning, Ardebili logged on to his Hotmail account and scrolled through his messages. He used the online name "Alex Dave" because it sounded American. He found it relatively easy to engage U.S. salesmen, as long as he remembered to pretend that he was in Dubai, not Iran. He'd slipped up a few times early on, ruining deals, but he exercised more caution now, and by mid-2004 found himself involved in serious negotiations with so many companies he had trouble keeping them all straight: an aerospace metals company in North Carolina; a military-grade microprocessor factory in Colorado; a military cargo-jet spare-parts supplier in the Midwest; a Vermont company producing high-performance inertial sensors and transducers used by NASA; a billion-dollar California company selling chemical and electronic analyzers; a Washington company making sonar capable of detecting commando divers swimming in busy harbors. On each deal, he hoped to earn a 10 to 15 percent commission.

On this Monday in April 2004, Ardebili and his partner were finalizing a deal with LinkQuest, a San Diego company that manufactured precision underwater acoustic instruments—remote modems and Doppler radar devices used for deep-sea targeting and mapping. These were deployed primarily by oil companies in the North Sea, Alaska, and East Asia, but also by the U.S. Navy. Ardebili shielded his identity from LinkQuest by using the address and name of his freight forwarding company in Dubai, Jabal Al Dhanna General Trading. To skirt the financial embargo and obscure from LinkQuest the fact that he was operating inside Iran, he routed the payments through friendly third-country banks. For this deal, he wired $12,200 through Credit Suisse Zurich, which was instructed to forward the money to a Bank of America account in California. Within days, a FedEx driver in San Diego would pick up the LinkQuest package addressed to the Dubai front company. The FedEx box would make a brief stop in Dubai, and within a week arrive inside Iran. This shipment, one of four Ardebili ordered from LinkQuest to Iran in 2004, contained a UWM3000, a deep-sea data transmitter. The U.S. Navy deploys the UWM3000 aboard its Unmanned Undersea Vehicle, which is the equivalent of an underwater Predator drone. It is used primarily to conduct recon and to clear mines.

Although Ardebili typically queried American manufacturers directly, he sometimes engaged U.S. and European middlemen. These were Western brokers who facilitated deals between sellers and buyers; they were handy because they were located inside America and, theoretically, could place orders without raising suspicions. These brokers also offered one-stop shopping for virtually any military or electronic item; Ardebili knew that if he found a reliable, connected U.S. broker, it would be like striking gold. Not long ago, while on the hunt for jet aircraft parts, an American manufacturer had referred him to one such potential broker, a company called Cross International in Pennsylvania. Ardebili had begun exchanging email with a Cross salesman named Patrick Lynch about a wide variety of requests. Lately, they'd been discussing the logistics of obtaining radioisotopes.

In the afternoon, the most important email of the day arrived, a response from a Canadian manufacturer to Ardebili's query for military sonar. This was the Big One, the deal he'd been tempted to tell his mother about. His deals rarely topped $20,000 or $30,000. This one would be for $990,000.

SEI, working on behalf of the Iranian navy, had asked Ardebili to lay hands on a state-of-the-art sonar device called a CTS-24 from the Canadian manufacturer. The CTS-24 mounts to the hull of a warship and uses medium-frequency sonar to detect enemy mines, submarines, and commando divers. The sonar works in shallow or deep water and automatically detects up to three targets at once. It includes an instant video playback system, an invaluable tool for training sailors engaged in war games.

It was no secret that Iran's navy was the weakest link in its armed forces. Though Iran could not hope to match U.S. forces in the Persian Gulf, it could certainly cause a lot of trouble, especially if it tried to block the Gulf entrance at the Strait of Hormuz, through which

40 percent of the world's seaborne oil passed. Since the revolution, the Iranian and American navies had played a game of cat and mouse in the Persian Gulf, quietly testing, probing each other. Everyone understood things could escalate quickly. In 1988, the American and Iranian navies had engaged in a brief shooting war over U.S. escorts of Kuwaiti oil tankers; and months later, the USS *Vincennes* had shot down an Iranian commercial airliner, killing 290 people. The Iranian navy had expanded marginally since then, but the Americans still held an enormous advantage beneath the surface, where their submarines moved largely undetected. Sophisticated sonar like the CTS-24 could help Iran locate those U.S. subs.

Ardebili forwarded the $990,000 offer to his SEI contact, and then began typing up a response for the Canadians. He wrote that the naval sonar could be shipped from Ontario to Dubai and then to Kiev, its purported final destination. The end user, Ardebili wrote, would be the Institute of Merchant Marine of Ukraine, a legitimate organization that knew nothing of the deal. Using a knockoff Photoshop program, Ardebili had created a phony end user certificate, complete with a bogus logo, Cyrillic lettering, and the forged signature of the institute's general director. "The application of the CTS-24," Ardebili typed on the fake Ukrainian certificate, "is to provide underwater acoustic detection of objects for ship safety."

Ardebili told the Canadians to expect the $990,000 payment to be wired from his Dubai bank to the Royal Bank of Canada, routing and account numbers to follow shortly. He closed his letter with an American-style colloquialism. "We trust that this is the beginning of a long and mutually beneficial relationship."

CHAPTER 3

The Captain

The top secret briefing at the Office of Naval Intelligence took place inside a secure, windowless room known as a SCIF—a Sensitive Compartmented Information Facility, which meant the walls, ceilings, and floors were sealed and specially wired with electronics designed to thwart enemy listening devices. All electronics, from smartphones to thumb drives, were barred from the SCIF. Naval Intelligence kept offices at the Pentagon of course, but it conducted the heart of its 24/7 intelligence work inside a battleship-gray headquarters on a suburban federal campus just southeast of Washington. On this late fall morning in 2004, the briefing had an audience of one, a Navy reservist assuming command of a one-hundred-man intelligence unit assigned to help protect the eastern seaboard.

Captain David L. Hall, forty-nine years old, with a stubble of white hair, had spent the last twenty years splitting time between the Departments of Justice and Defense. He was a full-time federal prosecutor and a part-time officer in the Navy Reserve. Hall held three Ivy League degrees, and was qualified as a rifle sharpshooter and karate black belt. In the courtroom, he prosecuted drug dealers, mobsters, con artists, gang-bangers, and bank robbers. On occasion, and to his delight, he took up more exotic, complicated investigations, like art theft and arms smuggling. In the Navy, his deployments varied, though they always revolved around intelligence. Shortly after 9/11, the Navy recalled Hall to full-time duty and had assigned him to the Pentagon as a warning officer, essentially a senior analyst on foreign terror threats. In this role, he briefed the deputy defense secretary and vice chairman of the Joint Chiefs of Staff on a daily basis. He also spent time in Guantánamo on work that remains classified.

This morning's thirty-minute intel briefing did not strike Hall as particularly unusual or alarming. The brief contained a standard domestic threat assessment. A junior officer neatly summarized potential domestic terror targets, from Navy warships to commercial vessels to U.S. ports, and potential consequences. Since 2001, Hall had given dozens of similar briefings himself. Yet as he exited into the crisp Washington morning, khaki garrison cap atop his nearly bald head, something nagged at him. He couldn't place it; something was off.

Hall walked to his car, retrieved his DOD and DOJ cell phones from the glove box, and began the slog north to Wilmington, Delaware, and his full-time prosecutor job. As he navigated the Suitland Parkway to the Capital Beltway to Interstate 95, his mind slowly shifted gears, from the Navy briefing to pending criminal cases in Delaware. Nearing Baltimore, his unease grew until it hit him: in the Navy, he was tackling serious national security issues—potential terrorist attacks against the United States or U.S. Navy ships. The job, in part, required him to think like a terrorist: how to use existing, available, cheap technology to create massive damage, the way the 9/11 hijackers had used box cutters to transform jetliners into missiles. By contrast, in his day job as a federal prosecutor in Wilmington, despite ten years' experience, Hall was handling small-scale credit card fraud and petty public corruption. His part-time Navy job had become far more relevant and rewarding than his full-time job.

.   .   .

Born in San Francisco in 1955, Dave Hall grew up across the bay in Marin County. The Marin he experienced growing up was not yet the liberal, suburban enclave it is today; the region was still *Leave It to Beaver* territory. As a teenager, Hall's only brush with the counter-culture and the Summer of Love came through the car window, as his parents drove curious out-of-town guests through Haight-Ashbury. But it was still California, where people tended to think in terms of possibilities, not limitations. Hall's parents certainly stressed this. Follow the rules, they told him; but when you run into obstacles, don't retreat, find another path. Keep trying, even if you find your-self banging your head against the wall.

In his late high school years, Hall's father landed an executive position with a shoe polish company near Philadelphia and the family followed him there. Hall was accepted at Dartmouth, and after graduation entered Yale's MBA program largely because his new bride was enrolled as a PhD candidate there. After earning the graduate degree, Hall entered a special Navy officer commis-sion program, joining a line of soldiers and sailors in his family that stretched back to the Revolutionary War. His great-great-grandfather had served as a Confederate officer and was executed by Union troops in 1863. During World War I, his grandfather was executive officer of the USS *Louisville*. In World War II, his father served as a combat Marine, and survived landings at Guadalcanal, Tarawa, Saipan, Tinian, and Okinawa. "I always assumed I would join the military; it just seemed natural," Hall recalled. "I think it's probably hard for someone whose family isn't a military fam-ily to understand. Military families beget military families. I think if I came from a line of firefighters, I probably would have been a firefighter."

In the Navy, Hall chose the intelligence path because he believed his critical thinking skills would add the greatest value, and because he was already twenty-six, four or five years older than most officer candidates. He quickly embraced the Navy's clearly stated core creeds—leadership, courage, honor, commitment. To Hall, these precepts were more than words on a mission state-ment, and he liked that they were an important part of the evaluation process. Navy work wasn't easy or glamorous. Living quarters were cheap, the separation from his wife and children harsh. Hall didn't make the money most Dartmouth/Yale men might, but he felt fulfilled.

After two years, he entered Penn Law School in Philadelphia. He found he loved the rule of law and everything it stood for. Rules and justice kept the universe from disorder. The best way to enforce the rules, he decided, was to prosecute criminals. In 1990, he became an assistant U.S. attorney in Philadelphia, and in his first year drew two significant cases. In one, he helped convict a crew of old-school wiseguys on methamphetamine charges. In the other, he prosecuted a pair of notorious crack-dealing brothers responsible for shooting a Philadelphia officer. In the mid-1990s Hall partnered with prosecutor Robert Goldman on several unorthodox art crime and national security cases—investigations that would make international headlines, alter his career trajectory, and later, during Operation Shakespeare, invoke visions of déjà vu.

Throughout this time, Hall continued to serve in the Navy Reserve. His younger brother, Steven Richard Hall, was a full-time Navy copilot stationed aboard the *Roosevelt*, a nuclear carrier. Steven Hall flew an EA-6B Prowler, a long-range jet packed with electronic countermeasure devices designed to eavesdrop, jam enemy radar, and, if necessary, launch HARM missiles. "Steve was the picture of fitness," Hall recalled. "Zero body fat, full head of hair. In college he was a national champion oarsman, and he still looked ten years younger than he was." In late 2001, Steven Hall developed a rare, aggressive cancer. He died about eight months later at age forty-two. Steven Hall's death hit Dave Hall like a sucker punch. It didn't change his outlook on his work. But, in the back of his mind, he could not help but think about his brother whenever he came across someone trying to sell or buy weapons systems that could be used to shoot down a U.S. military aircraft.

Once or twice a year, just to get away, Hall liked to drive up to an obscure New Hampshire river, not far from Dartmouth, climb into waders, and plant his legs deep in rushing water. Most people fish with live bait or artificial lures made of plastic and metal, using a spinning rod and reel loaded with a wispy fishing line. Spin fishing is certainly a fine way to catch a lot of fish, run up your stats, put a few trophy trout on the wall. Hall prefers fly-fishing. It offers a more sophisticated and ultimately rewarding challenge. Fly-fishing is a dance of timing and finesse, science and artistry. To cast a fly rod properly is an act of sport as sublime as pitching a curveball or draining a twenty-foot putt. A typical trout fly is nearly weightless, so getting it in front of the fish means learning how to cast and control yards of heavy line, in the air and in the water. It's a pursuit that requires a refined knowledge of entomology and physics within a particular river, an ability to match the correct fly with the season and topography, and to know where and when to cast the lure. To target a fish he can't see, a fly fisherman must consider a moving three-dimensional zone several feet wide and cast just ahead of this window, softly enough so that everything lands naturally, without a splash—first the fly, then the transparent leader and regular fishing line. A savvy fish will be wise to the slightest abnormality, and a fly fisherman will cast over and over, until he senses a hit, a ripple on the line. When that happens, he must play it cool, neither too quick nor too slow on the hook, knowing that if he spooks the target, it'll be gone in a flash. A fish can spook for any number of reasons. It might be because of something the fly fisherman does, or something he doesn't do, or something he can't control, like a cloud floating over the sun, casting a new shadow. Fly-fishing takes patience. But when the fisherman hooks one, man, is it sweet.

. . .

In Hall's view, you didn't need access to top secret intelligence to grasp the serious nature of the threat.

Arms and military technology proliferation poses the most destabilizing factor in geopolitics, a greater danger to U.S. national security than terrorism. *Who do you think arms the terrorists?* Hall would argue. *Rogue nations and arms dealers.* In almost every region of the world, illicit arms and technology shipments tip the balance of power. In the Middle East, the Iranian effort to acquire sophisticated weapons, nuclear or not, terrifies not only Israel but also pro-American and neutral Persian Gulf states, which fear the expansion of Islamic fascism. In the Pacific theater, China is building a modern navy and launching satellites capable of challenging a quarter century of U.S. dominance on the oceans and in space. Nuclear aspirations aside, North Korea has emerged as one of the world's largest arms dealers, supplying despots and terrorists on virtually every continent. The proliferation threat, Hall believed, represents a fundamental menace, one the United States can't necessarily see clearly over the horizon. He often cited as an example his first arms proliferation case: A few years before the first Gulf War, a Pennsylvania manufacturer had smuggled arms to South Africa. The South African firm, in turn, had sold the arms to Saddam Hussein in Iraq. When Allied troops invaded Kuwait and Iraq, those American-made weapons were turned against U.S. troops.

The South African case, prosecuted when Hall still worked in Philadelphia, had introduced him to the diplomatic sensitivities that permeate arms smuggling cases. The protracted case also burnished Hall's reputation for tenacity and occasional insubordination. The South African firm was called Armscor and its offenses could be traced back to the 1980s, when the apartheid government ran South Africa. Armscor was the acquisition arm of the South African government, and notorious in the 1980s for selling weapons to rogue nations. Long before Hall inherited the case in the mid-1990s, a grand jury in Philadelphia had indicted ten Americans, eight South Africans, and Armscor itself for smuggling arms from Pennsylvania. Most defendants pleaded guilty and two South Africans were convicted at trial. Armscor, however, argued that it could not be charged—as an arm of the South African government it was entitled to sovereign immunity.

Hall and his prosecutor colleague Robert Goldman pushed to take Armscor to trial, but by the mid-1990s the geopolitical environment had changed. The new post-apartheid president, Nelson Mandela, was promoting reconciliation, which called for degrees of forgiveness for past sins. The South African ambassador in Washington was pressuring senior U.S. officials to drop the case against Armscor, and Mandela raised the issue during meetings with Clinton and his vice president, Al Gore. Hall and Goldman found themselves on the opposite side of an argument with one of the most significant and popular political figures of the twentieth century. They couldn't fathom why Mandela wouldn't want to prosecute a company once run by white supremacists—men who had enforced apartheid and distributed arms to the enemies of his political party, the African National Congress. To Hall and Goldman, the rule of law demanded that they be prosecuted. U.S. political and diplomatic officials had other ideas. They informed Hall and Goldman that maintaining good relations with South Africa was more important than a single case. The affair was becoming a sore point between Clinton and Mandela, they said. It needed to go away, quickly and quietly.

It didn't go away. The Philadelphia prosecutors pushed, meeting repeatedly with senior Justice Department officials and the South African ambassador. When Hall and Goldman briefed Attorney General Janet Reno, they argued that it would look terrible if the United States dropped the case for political reasons. They also told their boss, the U.S. attorney in Philadelphia, that if the charges against Armscor were dropped, they would resign and go public in protest. The threat carried great career risk for Hall, who had a young wife and three small children at the time. To Hall's great relief, Reno agreed to stand by her prosecutors and told the White House so. The case against Armscor went forward and the South Africans agreed to a plea deal. The South African episode fit Hall's personal mantra: *Don't expect life to be linear. Do expect unpredictable obstacles. If you have a righteous goal, press on.*

Lately, Hall saw proliferation mistakes of the past repeating themselves. Having joined the Navy during the Cold War in 1984, he well remembered widespread debate concerning whether Pakistan and India were capable of obtaining a nuclear weapon. The U.S. government had pledged to try to stop this from happening; yet within a decade, Pakistan and India were exploding nuclear warheads, and atomic weapons were now in the hands of a Pakistani government riddled with al Qaeda sympathizers. Elsewhere, enemies on multiple continents were smuggling U.S. military technology out of the United States and reverse engineering it. There was a reason why the Russian space shuttle looked a lot like the American one, why the Iranian Toofan surface-to-air missile was a clone of the American version, why the Chinese rockets used the same telemetry as the American ones. Wittingly or not, American companies had sold them the parts, piece by piece.*

And while it was certainly critical to focus on the most dangerous weapons—items like nuclear components, tanks, and Stinger missiles—that didn't mean the United States could afford to ignore the smuggling of smaller arms and electrical components. State-of-the-art night vision goggles and advanced sonar obtained by an enemy could strip the U.S. military's ability to dominate in darkness and under the sea. As accurately portrayed in the Tom Hanks movie *Charlie Wilson's War*, one weapon in the hands of insurgents

---

* There are exceptions. For example, the Russian K-13 missile, also known as the Atoll, is a clone of the U.S. Sidewinder. But the technology was not stolen. In 1958, a Taiwanese fighter fired a Sidewinder into a Chinese plane, and though the missile lodged inside the aircraft, it did not explode. The Chinese gave the missile to the Soviets, who reverse engineered it.

can change the outcome of a war. In Afghanistan in the 1990s, the Soviet Union's domination of the skies provided a lethal advantage for years, until the CIA smuggled rocket-propelled grenades and Stinger missiles to the mujahedeen and insurgents began downing Red Army helicopters.

As a Navy officer, Hall understood how tiny, seemingly innocuous items like airplane gears, radar chips, and modems—things other than weapons that fire bullets, mortars, and missiles—can pose a threat to U.S. forces. Armies, air forces, and navies are mobile beasts with thousands of moving parts. In war, repair, resupply, and replacement are crucial. Poor supply and logistics crippled Napoleon in Russia, Rommel in North Africa, and Cornwallis at Yorktown. Modern technology only exacerbates this dynamic. Fighter jets and tanks are precision machines that require constant maintenance. Parts and components fail. Without the proper spare part, a tank can be immobilized and a fighter grounded. Mechanics joke that the most important part is the one you don't have. Every military in the world, including the U.S. Navy, faces this problem, especially when deployed in battle. This is why, scattered across bases and aircraft carriers, wily U.S. logistics officers and mechanics employ "hangar queens," planes that will never fly, but are instead permanently grounded so their parts can be cannibalized for other aircraft. It's why the Iranians appear to have an insatiable, almost infinite, appetite for aircraft parts; nearly half their air force is grounded for lack of proper parts. A lack of these basics is why Iran Air's fleet of Boeing 727s averages one major accident a year, and why, for safety reasons, the European Union has banned many Iran Air aircraft from its airports.

Iran surely represented an immediate threat. But Hall believed the long-term menace from Beijing posed a potentially greater harm to U.S. national security, in part because the Chinese effort to acquire restricted American military technology is so well coordinated. According to a Council on Foreign Relations analysis, China is engaged in a "methodical, deliberate and focused course of modernization of its military, developing power-projection and advanced early warning intelligence, reconnaissance and surveillance capabilities to address a range of possible contingencies with emphasis on the domains of maritime, air, space and cyber and information war." Because Beijing's ability to "develop, produce and, most important, integrate indigenously sophisticated military systems [is] limited," China steals whatever it can from the United States.

The Chinese target nearly everything from night vision to space flight. They deploy sleeper agents to burrow into the American defense industry, engineers and scientists who earn advanced U.S. degrees, become citizens, and develop sufficient trust to earn top security clearances. Dongfan "Greg" Chung, an engineer who arrived from China in the 1970s and worked for Rockwell and Boeing for decades, stole 250,000 pages' worth of aerospace and military trade secrets, including Space Shuttle and Delta IV rocket data. The Chinese sleeper agent Chi Mak, an engineer, spent twenty years climbing the ranks of a major U.S. defense contractor, all the while secretly sending plans for submarine noise suppression systems back to Beijing.

The Chinese also deploy teams of agents to the United States with instructions to create American businesses. These "American" companies openly purchase U.S. technology, knowing they can avoid the embargo as long as they falsely claim that the equipment will remain inside the United States. One such Chinese agent in Virginia, Shu Quan-Sheng, provided Beijing with the design and development of a cryogenic fueling system for space vehicles. In Massachusetts, a company created by a Chinese couple, Chitron Electronics, smuggled tens of thousands of military-grade electronic components to a China-based defense manufacturer over a decade. Among the components the Chinese company smuggled were tens of thousands of devices called MAPCGM0003 phase shifters, microchips long sought by the Chinese, Pakistanis, and Iranians because they can be deployed in a radar scheme that can pinpoint some U.S. fighter jets.

. . .

There's an old saw in law enforcement: Small cases, small headaches. Big cases, big headaches.

Counter-proliferation cases—good ones—can create big headaches. The typical arms smuggling investigation is unconventional, complicated, time-consuming, and risky. It requires months, even years of investigation, and can involve undercover work overseas, which is expensive and requires the cooperation of U.S. diplomats and foreign police. For many U.S. attorneys—the political appointees who run the Justice Department's ninety-three branch offices around the country—it makes more sense to focus instead on traditional cases, things like drugs, bank robberies, illegal immigration, and white-collar fraud. It's also easier; half of those kinds of cases just walk in the door, the product of a street arrest or tip from a disgruntled spouse or employee. The easy cases buoy the statistics that make everyone in a bureaucracy look good, including the U.S. attorneys' regional counterparts at the FBI, Drug Enforcement Administration (DEA), IRS, and Homeland Security. The typical career-minded prosecutor is even less likely to seek an arms-smuggling case—why give up sure-fire short-term convictions to pursue a single complex case that may come up empty?

These are just the political considerations. The legal hurdles in arms smuggling cases are so specialized, so complicated, they present a steep learning curve for anyone new to the work. The contraband involved is unlike anything else in criminal law. Consider the difference between cocaine and a gyroscope: cocaine is illegal in virtually any form, and any amount. It comes in white powder or crystalized rock, which almost any adult can recognize. The drug has but one purpose. A gyroscope, on the other hand, might be legal or not, depending upon its specifications and final foreign destination. To the layman's eye, a poker-chip-sized gyroscope isn't easily recognizable; it looks a lot like scores of similar electronic gizmos. A gyroscope has a myriad of uses—it can orient a compass, help play an iPhone game, or steer an intercontinental ballistic missile. A federal agent or prosecutor working counter-proliferation has to take the time to properly identify a particular gyroscope, learn how it can be used, know where it can be exported and where it can't, and why. To determine its legality, the agent and prosecutor must consult a ridiculously complex set of Treasury, State, and Commerce regulations, lists, licenses, exceptions, and miscellaneous orders. Some items are explicitly banned from export to certain countries but not others; lists can change as fast as foreign governments rise and fall, or as quickly as technology evolves.

Perhaps the most challenging obstacle for agents and prosecutors is the legal standard of proof. In a counter-proliferation case, unlike many other crimes, prosecutors have to demonstrate that a smuggler is aware of the law, understands exactly what he is doing, and that he is *purposefully and willfully* violating the law by exporting an American-made product banned to a certain nation. Sometimes, prosecutors and investigators get lucky. Sometimes smugglers boldly—and stupidly—make it easy by laying out their state of mind in email messages. "We can't say we're shipping to Iran because that violates U.S. law," or "Don't say the end user is in Iran or the American company won't ship it!" But the feds don't get that lucky very often. On occasion, agents manage to catch one or two smugglers within an organization and, by promising a lighter sentence in return for cooperation, get them to email co-conspirators and trick them into making incriminating statements. This, too, is fairly rare. Often the only way to prove willfulness is the most complicated—set up a sting, go undercover, get the smuggler to unwittingly admit everything on hidden videotape. Stings aren't easy. They require subtlety, research, creativity, money, patience, and risk—things The G doesn't often do very well.

Senior U.S. government officials insist that counter-proliferation is critical to national security and that they have poured resources into the effort. Every few months, the Justice Department releases an informal list that summarizes "major export enforcement criminal cases." The document exceeds fifty pages, and though it has a disclaimer that it doesn't include every case, the case summaries are widely touted within the government as a successful scorecard on export enforcement. But this document amounts to little more than a compilation of greatest hits; it reflects neither the true threat posed by counter-proliferation nor the government's response. The government does not release precise and comprehensive statistics on export control.* A nationwide review of court records for this book reveals a pattern from 2003 to 2013 in which approximately forty people were prosecuted each year under the primary arms and military technology smuggling statutes. In the cases against individuals, only a third of them were significant enough to warrant a sentence of more than a year or two in prison.

A handful of cases are brought each year against corporations, and some of the most egregious involve some of America's best-known defense contractors—Northrop Grumman, Raytheon, Hughes, UTC, and ITT. In other words, companies that reap billions each year from U.S. taxpayers, and market themselves as defenders of freedom and champions of U.S. troops, have also been severely fined for exporting sensitive military technology to China, Iran, Russia, and elsewhere.

Hughes, for example, shared critical rocket guidance and satellite technology with the Chinese, helping Beijing end a streak of failures and launch twenty-seven consecutive missiles and satellites, significantly improving the accuracy of China's intercontinental

---

* The Commerce Department releases annual statistics of convictions in which agents from its law enforcement agency, the Bureau of Industry and Security, participated. But the review of court records for this book reveals that the Commerce statistics are inflated—and in several cases inaccurate—and include minor export violations for which no jail time was served.

ballistic force, placing western U.S. states at risk. A Northrop subsidiary sold the inertial navigation source code for Air Force One to a Russian company, revealing classified capabilities, limitations, and vulnerabilities of the president's plane. Raytheon got caught sending sophisticated military communications equipment to Pakistan; to skirt rules, the company slightly tweaked its equipment and employed semantics to alter the equipment's official use from "military" to "commercial." A subsidiary of United Technologies Corporation—UTC—helped China develop its first modern military attack helicopter. U.S. prosecutors said the Connecticut-based company "purposely turned a blind eye to the helicopter's military application" because UTC believed the project would help secure a civilian helicopter deal worth as much as $2 billion. The civilian copter deal never materialized, and the Chinese instead used the UTC technology to develop its first attack helicopter—the Z-10, outfitted with 30-millimeter cannons, antitank guided missiles, and air-to-air missiles.

The giant Pentagon contractors all paid large fines. Northrop incurred $15 million, Raytheon $25 million, Hughes $32 million, and UTC $75 million.* Despite the damage to national security, no one went to prison following any of the investigations, and each company resumed billion-dollar Pentagon contacts.

Perhaps the worst transgression was committed by ITT, one of the best-known names in corporate America. Founded as International Telephone & Telegraph in 1920, ITT grew into a massive conglomerate in the 1960s and 1970s, acquiring some 350 companies, including Avis rent-a-car, Hartford Insurance, Sheraton hotels, and Wonder Bread. During this period, ITT also bought and grew

---

* The Air Force One issues occurred in 1998, before Northrop acquired the subsidiary responsible, Litton Industries. The satellite case involved both Raytheon in Massachusetts and Raytheon in Canada. The UTC subsidiary is Pratt & Whitney Canada Corp.

defense businesses that performed lucrative contracts for the U.S. government. In the late 1970s, one such subsidiary, ITT Night Vision, began supplying night vision to the U.S. military from its factory in Roanoke, Virginia. Over the next thirty years, ITT NV became the primary night vision supplier to the U.S. armed forces, completing Pentagon contracts worth more than $500 million. ITT NV engineers and scientists worked alongside U.S. government counterparts developing restricted and classified technology, creating the game-changing device that allowed U.S. forces to fight in the dark. "This technology gives our U.S. allied forces a decisive combat advantage, enhances the principles of surprise, maneuver and security, as well as our ability to apply discriminate firepower against identifiable belligerent enemy forces while avoiding unnecessary collateral damage to innocent civilians," a U.S. Air Force colonel explained during a federal case involving smuggled night vision. "In enemy hands, these devices can enable hostile forces to track and fire on our aircraft at night, direct fire against our ground forces with deadlier accuracy at much greater distances and effectively target our key equipment. The direct result is the loss of American lives."

And yet during the same thirty-year period in which ITT NV designed and manufactured this key advantage for the U.S. military, the company also repeatedly and systematically violated U.S. export laws by sending sensitive and sometimes classified material about night vision overseas. Court records show that ITT NV managers did so to boost corporate profits. ITT NV discouraged complaints from employee whistle-blowers and repeatedly misled U.S. government officials for years, even after it became clear they were under investigation. "There was a culture at this company where they viewed export laws as an obstacle to making money, and they actively and willfully worked to circumvent the U.S. laws to increase profits," said Dean Boyd, the Justice Department's national security spokesman. One export compliance specialist quit after just seven weeks on the job at ITT NV. "The problems are much greater than anyone could imagine," he wrote in his resignation letter.

The illegal and secret cost cutting began almost from the outset. In the early 1980s, ITT NV outsourced the manufacture of night vision optical assemblies to a Singapore company called Electro Optics without a required license from the U.S. State Department. ITT NV sent the data to Singapore for at least a decade, until 1994, when the company finally applied for a license. The State Department granted ITT NV a license, but with limitations, restrictions the company simply ignored. The pattern repeated itself again six years later when ITT NV won a new license, then promptly began violating virtually every significant proviso, including overseas manufacture. U.S. government investigators did not learn of ITT NV's duplicity until 2004, but by then the United States was engaged in two wars, and production in Singapore could not be suspended without affecting the supply of night vision equipment to troops on the battlefields of Afghanistan and Iraq. ITT NV was too tied to the war effort to face immediate sanctions. Like giant banks and investment houses at the core of the Wall Street collapse, the government deemed ITT too big to fail.

During the same period, ITT NV also skirted security rules covering two of the most important and cutting-edge aspects of night vision—countermeasures and thermal imaging. Government investigators say both episodes may have cost U.S. troops major critical advantages on the battlefield, now and in decades to come.

The countermeasures were designed in the 1990s to prevent enemy troops from using lasers and related weapons to blind U.S. soldiers and pilots wearing night vision goggles. The specs of one countermeasure, a filter that could block lasers, were classified "SECRET/NOFORN," which meant that the designs were too sensitive to share with any foreign government, no matter how friendly. In 1999, an ITT NV manager informed its countermeasure filter subcontractor in California that it needed to cut production costs.

To save money, the California company asked the State Department for permission to build a key component in China. The State Department said no, citing national security concerns. The ITT NV manager, now desperate to find savings, engaged his Singapore manufacturer, Electro Optics, to produce the lens. The ITT NV manager did not ask the State Department for permission; he just did it. To save even more money, Electro Optics forwarded these sensitive designs to a factory inside China, which set to work producing thousands of the lenses.

Once the special lenses were produced, they needed to be coated. This, too, was a sensitive and complex process. As one ITT NV manager wrote to another: "Specification is very demanding and worse, it is a classified specification which prevents us from going to off-shore coating suppliers." The manager plunged ahead anyway, and contacted a British company with ties to ITT NV's Singapore supplier. Without obtaining permission from the U.S. government or confirming that the British company had the appropriate security clearances, the ITT NV manager mailed a copy of the classified specs to England. When the package had not arrived a week later, a British manager expressed concern that the drawings had been lost in the mail. The specs arrived eventually, but to the great surprise of the British manager, they were marked classified. The Brit did not have a U.S. security clearance. The American told him to just go ahead and open the package and start calculating a price quote. Only then did the ITT NV manager submit a State Department application to send the classified specs to the British. On the paperwork, the ITT NV manager lied and declared that the British company held the proper security clearances. The State Department flatly rejected the application. "The specifications are classified secret/no foreign," a State Department official wrote. "Light interference filters are the critical technology for electro-optical countermeasures for U.S. military/national security night vision systems." The ITT NV manager told the British firm to begin work anyway, and issued a purchase order for twenty thousand units.

ITT NV also illegally outsourced production of "next-gen" technology, a revolutionary system that combined the strengths of night vision with thermal imaging. By blending the two systems, soldiers could see in the dark *and* through smoke and clouds, a great tactical advantage, U.S. officials said, "that could mean the difference between life and death." Without bothering to ask for State Department permission, ITT NV shared these highly sensitive thermal optical designs with the Singapore company, Electro Optics, which employed two Chinese engineers. To further circumvent security rules, ITT NV set up the equivalent of a front operation inside the United States to serve as a conduit for sending sensitive next-gen night vision to Electro Optics. The ITT NV deception appeared to touch nearly every aspect of the next-gen project: the American company also sent a critical switching device to a Japanese company for manufacture, without bothering to seek a State Department license, and did not object when some switches were assembled in China.

Following a lengthy criminal investigation, one that ITT NV fought for years, U.S. authorities announced criminal charges against the company in 2007, along with a settlement. For repeatedly ignoring export rules, for sending classified information overseas, for exporting sensitive optical, laser, and enhanced night vision technology, and for making false statements to regulators, the company was fined $100 million, a record for an arms technology case. At a press conference announcing the case, the U.S. attorney in Roanoke, John Brownlee, said, "Simply put, the criminal actions of this corporation have threatened to turn on the lights on the modern battlefield for our enemies and expose American soldiers to great harm." Under the terms of the settlement, ITT NV agreed to dedicate half of the $100 million toward developing new night vision technology for the U.S. military to make up for the losses created by the company's disclosures to foreign armed forces. Despite the repeated and well-documented misdeeds of ITT NV managers, not one was charged with a crime, and therefore, not one was sent to prison.

.　.　.

By any measure, the United States Attorney's Office in Delaware is tiny, nearly a backwater. With only a dozen full-time prosecutors, it is less than a tenth of the size of the prestigious U.S. Attorney's Office in Philadelphia, where Hall had worked from 1990 to 2001. He hadn't planned to transfer to Wilmington, but while temporarily deployed to the Pentagon following 9/11, he'd received an unexpected and intriguing recruiting pitch.

The offer had come from Colm Connolly, the well-regarded and ambitious new U.S. attorney in Delaware. Connolly was best known as lead prosecutor during a scandalous case in which a prominent attorney had killed the governor's secretary, stuffed her body inside a cooler, and dumped it into the Atlantic. The case had inspired three books and a made-for-TV movie, and catapulted Connolly's career. Connolly viewed the U.S. attorney's job as a stepping-stone to the next political appointment, perhaps a federal judgeship. As part of his pitch, Connolly told Hall he wanted to make big cases, but had inherited a crop of largely inexperienced prosecutors. Connolly deftly promised Hall that he could become his ace, handling anything in Delaware with an international, national security nexus. Hall liked Connolly and the concept, but held reservations. He credited much of his success in Philadelphia to the stable of federal agents he'd worked with repeatedly—solid investigators from the FBI, HSI, and the Navy Criminal Investigative Service (NCIS). For jurisdictional reasons, Hall figured he'd probably lose contact with most of those agents if he moved to the Delaware office. What's more, Wilmington, despite its reputation as a national banking hub, acted a lot like a small town. The official slogan, proudly displayed on signs at the city limits, didn't help: "Wilmington: A Place to Be

Somebody." But Connolly charmed Hall. He pitched the offer as if the U.S. Attorney's Office in Delaware were a law firm seeking to expand its practice. This enticed Hall, as did the prospect of a much shorter commute. In the spring of 2003, when his Pentagon tour ended, Hall accepted the offer to transfer from Philadelphia to Wilmington.

For eighteen months, Hall paid his dues, taking his share of low-grade drug and fraud cases. He also worked directly with Connolly on the U.S. attorney's big crusade, a political corruption investigation of two prominent Delaware county officials. The corruption case focused on a local police chief and county administrator. The investigation had uncovered what appeared to prosecutors to be police resources deployed for political purposes and also a sweetheart $2 million loan to the county administrator by an heir to the DuPonts, Delaware's royal family. The government's evidence included FBI wiretaps, a lie detector test, a secret romance, a hot tub, and enough gossipy details to guarantee headlines. But as an outsider, Hall didn't share the enthusiasm of his colleagues. Shortly after the indictments came down, the case hit a snag. The judge, nearing retirement and boasting a reputation for irascibility, expressed doubts about the charges, encouraging the defense to file a bevy of motions. Hall could tell the case was going to eat up a good chunk of his efforts, time he'd planned to spend on national security cases.

Now, as Hall sped up I-95 on that April afternoon in 2004, he recalled Connolly's law firm analogy, and smiled to himself. *Yep*, he thought. *How apt.* He knew friends who'd been lured to white-shoe law firms with the same kind of pitch—"We want you to expand the practice!"—only to find themselves handling DUI cases for the spoiled sons of major corporate clients.

We're at war, Hall thought, *and I'm stuck prosecuting small-town corruption, minor-league fraud, and nuisance gun cases.* Hall dreaded the week that lay ahead. He expected to spend most of it drafting pre-trial motions for the corruption case.

And yet a short while after returning from Washington, Hall caught a break. He received a call out of the blue from the new HSI group supervisor for counter-proliferation in Philadelphia. The group handled export enforcement cases in Pennsylvania, Delaware, and West Virginia. Hall didn't know the man. Their conversation was brief, but it struck Hall that the HSI agent hadn't called about any particular case, which was unusual. Instead, the supervisor said he had a couple of ideas best discussed in person. Could Hall drive up to Philadelphia to meet with a few of his guys at the old Customs House?

CHAPTER 4

The Producer

ICE is the creature of a shotgun marriage. When the Department of Homeland Security was created in 2003, two existing agencies—the U.S. Customs Service, a division of the Treasury Department, and the Immigration and Naturalization Service, a division of the Justice Department—were merged into one. The new hybrid agency was named Immigrations and Customs Enforcement, or ICE. At the time, the merger made sense to anyone outside Customs and INS. Both agencies worked the borders: Customs policed goods, INS policed people. Under the post-9/11 law enforcement scheme, they would work together. But policymakers in Washington failed to understand the vast cultural difference between Customs and INS.

INS, created in 1933, was an agency with a single focus—detaining and expelling illegal aliens. INS agents were usually more interested in a suspect's immigration status than any crimes committed. INS operated largely within its own bureaucratic constructs. It even used a language all its own. In most cases, agents who picked up illegal aliens didn't make *arrests*; they made *administrative detentions*. Suspected illegal aliens who were handcuffed and carted away were called *detainees*, never *inmates* or *prisoners*. These detainees were housed in special INS *facilities*, never prisons. The accused faced a judiciary system outside the normal American criminal court framework, with cases presided over by special *administrative immigration judges*. This sprawling INS system remained under constant stress—roughly 33,000 aliens in custody, scattered in more than 250 facilities across the country, an underfunded and poorly managed program, struggling to perform a thankless and perpetually politically charged task.

Customs, by contrast, traced its formation to 1789, when agents were sent to the frontier border with little more than a weapon and badge. Two centuries later, Customs still trained agents to think creatively and embrace that frontier mentality. Empowered to investigate any cross-border crime, Customs agents dabbled in a little bit of everything. They made criminal cases as simple as nabbing drug smugglers at the border, and as complicated as money laundering, child pornography, and arms smuggling. Many agents enjoyed the low-key, lean, agile nature of the U.S. Customs Service; they didn't get the headlines the FBI got, but most didn't care. They seemed to embrace their relative anonymity. Older agents would tell younger ones, "You want credit, go to a bank."

When the INS-Customs merger was announced, nobody groused publicly. But resentments simmered. Some Customs agents bristled when tasked to help round up aliens, and some Immigration agents struggled when assigned to work nonalien criminal cases. In whispers, agents on the street continued to identify each other by the label "legacy Customs" or "legacy Immigration." Even the name of the new agency rankled many Customs agents, who believed it stripped them of their heritage and identity. Because the word "Immigration" came first—on everything from the new letterhead to badges to IDs—it naturally followed that people began calling everyone who worked at ICE "immigration agents." It was at once embarrassing and confusing. Everyone knew what a customs or an immigration agent was. But what the hell was an ICE agent? And what kind of acronym was ICE anyway? It sounded ridiculous. Former Customs agents soon came up with a creative solution. Instead of identifying themselves as ICE agents, they started calling themselves Homeland Security agents—which was the truth, and, they found, made it a lot easier to get their calls returned. Eventually, the informal name was formalized and the customs-oriented agents became Homeland Security Investigations agents, or HSI agents.

Perhaps the starkest metaphor for the split that divided the two legacy agencies was the offices they kept in Philadelphia. The Customs legacy squads remained in the old Customs House, a magnificent Art Deco building that towered seventeen stories above the historic Old City skyline, the upper floors narrowing into an octagonal lantern of white high-relief terra-cotta. The Customs House lobby featured an elaborately decorated three-story rotunda, anchored by eight serpentine marble columns and murals of ships, planes, seahorses, and several images of a reclining Neptune. Two grand circular staircases curled up from the lobby to the second floor, where HSI kept its regional headquarters. The legacy Immigration agents remained twenty blocks away, cramped inside a drab former INS building with a lobby that carried all the ambiance of the local Department of Motor Vehicles.

⋅ ⋅ ⋅

On a brisk winter morning in November 2004, Dave Hall flashed his prosecutor's credential in the Customs House lobby, bypassed security, and climbed the spiral staircase to the second floor, bound for the office of the new HSI counter-proliferation supervisor.

On paper, ICE is led by an assistant secretary of homeland security—a political appointee who also holds the title of Director—and assorted deputies in Washington. The twenty-six field offices are supervised by powerful regional managers known as special agents in charge, or SACs. But the most important people inside ICE and its subdivision HSI are the group supervisors—*group supes*—the men and women who direct squads of six to ten agents. Each squad is assigned a specific duty, from airports to seaports to immigration to sex trafficking to counter-proliferation. The group supes drive cases and an HSI squad's productivity. A good group supe is a strong player-coach, a creative leader who motivates, inspires, and gets his people what they need. The job is critical because ICE, like any government agency, is burdened with its share of mediocre agents and middle managers who are more focused on their paychecks, pensions, and job security than fighting crime. There is even a term for these agents—they are "retired on the job." HSI squads tend to mimic the metabolism of their managers. "Group supes run HSI," says Andrew McLees, a senior official in Philadelphia at the time. "Finding good ones might be my most important job."

Hall knew the new counter-proliferation group supervisor, John Malandra, only by résumé: Age fifty-three. Thirty years in law enforcement. Former Philly vice cop. Surveillance and wiretapping expert. Post-9/11 hitch overseas. Past chief of ICE's global counter-proliferation section in Washington. Recently returned to Philadelphia to finish out his career. Reputation for moving quickly and getting things done.

Malandra met Hall at an unmarked, locked side door on the second floor. He led him to a cozy office overlooking coffee shops on Chestnut Street. Two counter-proliferation agents, P.J. Lechleitner and Michael Ronayne, joined them. Malandra carried a full white mane and wore it longer than most cops and federal agents. He spoke in rapid, clipped bursts of information, like a street cop talking into a police radio.

Malandra began with an update on the Yasmin Ahmed case: *Okay, the Pakistani lady, Yasmin. She's back in contact with P.J. Looks like she wants FLIR. Says she gonna sell it to the Pakistani navy. Puts her at the top of our list . . .*

Hall, the Navy man, knew that FLIR stood for forward looking infrared radar, a laser-guided targeting system that can peer over the horizon. While primarily deployed for directing surface-to-ground missiles such as the Hellfire, a FLIR system's laser, thermal imager, and daylight camera could be used for surveillance, assault, and armed reconnaissance missions. The FLIR BRITE Star II, produced by a company in Oregon, had no legitimate civilian use and was restricted for sale only to U.S. allies—and even then, each sale had to be individually approved by the U.S. State Department. Deployed extensively in battle by U.S. forces in Iraq and Afghanistan, the BRITE Star was versatile and small, about the size of an NFL football, and very expensive. Mounted on a helicopter, aircraft, boat, or tank, the device could help hit a moving target at several miles. A single unit sold for $1.5 million.

The FLIR Ahmed sought included a night targeting system compatible with weapons systems deployed in antiship warfare. Lechleitner, still based at the undercover Cross storefront, reported that negotiations had progressed to the point where he believed he had a deal, at least in principle. Given Ahmed's prior record of smuggling military gear to Dubai and Pakistan, the agents were taking her inquiries seriously. But Ahmed, now safely back in Pakistan, was too savvy to risk a return to the United States to consummate the transaction. After all, she was still on probation in Connecticut for the 2003 arms smuggling conviction.

Malandra proposed a sting. They would lure Ahmed to a third country, perhaps a city in Eastern Europe, a place where she would feel comfortable traveling and where the United States could expect the local government to cooperate. Hall jumped in, pressing Malandra to be sure to pick a country that would allow extradition to the United States; otherwise the exercise would be futile. Together, Hall and Malandra fleshed out the rest, forming a quick bond: they'd set up the sting in an East European warehouse, show Ahmed the FLIR system, tease out details of her contact with the Pakistani military, arrest her, and haul her back for prosecution. If Ahmed wired the $1.5 million or carried cash to the Baltics, they'd confiscate the money. The case would more than pay for itself.

There was one big hitch, however. HSI was having trouble coming up with the *flash*—an actual FLIR to dangle in front of Ahmed during the sting. It was one thing to ask the Navy to borrow a FLIR for a domestic sting, it was another to take the sensitive and very valuable weapon overseas. "We had a chicken and egg problem," one of the participants recalled. "We didn't want to ask a foreign government for help until we knew we would have a FLIR to use as flash, and we didn't want to ask the Navy for help until we knew exactly where we would be taking it and when."

To Hall, this seemed like a good problem to have. He was impressed by Malandra's approach: *Okay, there's a problem, a roadblock. Let's see how we can solve it.* Too many supervisors tended to throw up their hands at this point and say the opposite: *Well, it's great that we've come this far. But there's not much we can do if she won't enter the United States.* Hall believed too many counter-proliferation cases ended unsatisfactorily. The goal simply seemed to be to get the bad guys to wire a deposit and confiscate the money. *That'll show 'em!* Malandra aspired higher, and this was harder. It required a totally different approach.

To catch serious arms dealers working for the Iranians, Chinese, or North Koreans, Hall believed, a prosecutor and HSI agents couldn't target them the way they'd target a drug dealer or a gangster. They couldn't go after them one by one, and they would need more than an undercover website and fake office in the United States. They would need to create undercover platforms in multiple dimensions. They would need to open foreign bank accounts. They would need to create foreign-based undercover companies and win permission from foreign governments to conduct stings overseas. All of this would require strong cop-to-cop relationships.

Malandra seemed to get that. In the office that day, Malandra, Hall, and the agents dreamed large. They began talking about much more than Ahmed and Pakistan. They discussed leveraging Cross International's existing infrastructure, maybe even move it offshore, to create an undercover framework that might enable them to successfully target multiple arms dealers for years to come.

. . .

John Malandra kept his office at Customs House clinically neat and sparsely decorated. But three things stood out, even to a casual visitor: a Girard College calendar on the wall, a poster of Girard College pinned above his computer monitor, and, on the bookshelf, a small bust of Stephen Girard.

Malandra was born in South Philadelphia in 1955. His father died when he was eight months old. His mother raised him with his brother in a two-story brick row house, not far from the church where they filmed portions of *Rocky*. His friends, mostly Northern Italians, stuck together, rarely straying more than four blocks in either direction. They played ball in the street and swam under the fire hydrant.

At age seven, his mother reluctantly sent young John and his brother to a local boarding school for fatherless boys. The experience changed their lives. The unusual school was more than a century old, the legacy of Stephen Girard, a French immigrant often credited as the father of American philanthropy. A successful nineteenth-century banker and merchant, Girard supplied the cash that helped Philadelphia survive a yellow fever epidemic and later helped finance the U.S. Army during the War of 1812. When Girard died in 1831, he may have been the richest man in America. His will provided that his fortune be used to create a nonsectarian school for poor, fatherless boys. The will's trustees built a forty-three-acre campus a mile north of the city's museums and named the elementary and secondary school Girard College. With its Greek Revival dorms, classrooms, libraries, and gargantuan gym, Girard was built in the style and grandeur of the U.S. Naval Academy campus in Annapolis. The school opened in 1848, and its alumni have included generals, admirals, architects, doctors, and professional ballplayers.

Girard was not a military school, but the regimen was strict and spartan. Boys left personal possessions at home; toys were banned— most families couldn't afford them anyway. The boys slept together in dorm rooms large enough to accommodate thirty beds; they used toilets without partitions; they studied, played, and fought together nine months out of every year. The academic day began at 7:30 a.m. with classes until the lunch hour. The boys spent afternoons in mechanical school learning a trade—print shop, auto shop, metal shop, electric shop, wood shop. They ate dinner family style, canned fruit for dessert four days a week; every Friday, each boy received a large ginger cookie called a Hum Mud. In eighth grade, students were assigned to cadet corps and practiced military drills. Before, during and after lunch, boys worked menial tasks—they waited tables, loaded dishes, swept hallways, or shoveled snow. The cadet corps and menial jobs ceased in the early 1970s, just after Malandra graduated, when busybodies complained that the marching glorified war and the jobs violated child labor laws. "But it was absolutely the best thing," Malandra recalled. Girard taught him discipline, organization, loyalty, humility, charity, teamwork, and the value of hard work.

Of the 160 boys who began with Malandra in elementary school, only thirty-nine made it to high school graduation. Cosseted inside the walls of Girard, Malandra missed the turbulent 1960s, and when he entered college in 1974, he confronted the disorder, sloth, and selfishness that existed in the real world. He saw friends from the neighborhood flailing aimlessly and fellow students taking college for granted. He felt lucky. "I don't think there's a boy who graduated who doesn't believe his life would be very different, if it wasn't for Girard College. It's a school that gave guys who'd had a bad break a good break. . . . We're the kind of guys who work hard, keep our mouths shut, do our jobs."

As a supervisor for Customs and then HSI, Malandra became a father figure to many agents: He worked them hard but inspired loyalty. He invited agents to his family beach house and arranged for their nieces and nephews to ride the Zamboni at Flyers games. Throughout HSI, Malandra was regarded as a closer, someone who received an assignment and found a way to get it done. "A lot of people in government spend a lot of time trying to avoid trouble," a younger colleague recalled. "Malandra spent that energy on accomplishing the task at hand. He taught me how to be creative: You take things right up to the edge of what's okay and what's not. You never cross the line, but sometimes you push things." Inside HSI, Malandra was universally respected, but not always loved. He had a quick temper and became exasperated with agents he believed lazy or stupid. If Malandra liked you, he'd do almost anything to help you. If he didn't, he might pass you in a hallway without so much as a hello.

.   .   .

At about the same time as Malandra began meeting with Hall to try to put together an overseas operation, a first-of-its-kind export case was materializing in eastern Tennessee. The investigation involved an obscure and controversial portion of the law, the deemed export section, which makes it a crime to release sensitive information to foreigners visiting the United States. The law serves several purposes. It is designed to prevent foreign companies from establishing U.S.-based subsidiaries for the primary purpose of skirting the export laws by creating a legitimate American mailing address. The law is also designed to prevent other nations from sending their smartest citizens to work for U.S. companies as part of an effort to steal sensitive American technology and intellectual property. China, for one, finds it more efficient to deploy large numbers of scientists and students to the United States, instead of professional spies. The deemed export law applies at almost all levels, including to foreign graduate students conducting research at American universities. Foreign students cannot work on sensitive projects without a license from the State Department.

This does not sit well with some university researchers, who find the export law at odds with the spirit of race and equality laws. At U.S. universities and technical conferences, most research is conducted openly, and the reflex is to share, rather than to withhold, findings. But sensitive scientific knowledge can be as valuable on the black market as software and hardware, planes and tanks, or guns and ammunition. The disclosure of secret-sauce ideas behind certain weapons technology—rocket propulsion or wing design—can help a nation leapfrog past years of expensive and difficult research, and catch up to U.S. forces on the battlefield. In a free society in which information moves at the speed of the Internet, it is difficult to prevent some of the smartest Americans from disclosing, whether by sloppiness, naïveté, or outright espionage, what they know to foreign governments.

Most major U.S. corporations and research universities have hired compliance officers to try to enforce the deemed export law, but some scientists chafe at attempts to limit academic freedom. They don't like being told which students they can hire as assistants and which they can't. John Reece Roth was one such academic. A graduate of the Massachusetts Institute of Technology and Cornell University, Roth had joined the faculty of the University of Tennessee as an assistant professor of electrical engineering in 1978. Over the next quarter century, Roth became a preeminent researcher on plasma, a state of matter between liquid and gas. Plasma actuators are formed when electrodes are set on a dielectric material and voltage is applied, causing the air to ionize, creating the potential for an alternative to traditional flight controls such as flaps and ailerons. Roth had published hundreds of scientific papers on plasma and a two-volume treatise, *Industrial Plasma Engineering*, which was also translated into Chinese. Plasma was Roth's life. He put vanity Tennessee license plates, "Plasma," on his Buick and named his cat Plasma. Roth enjoyed working closely with graduate students on his research, some of which was funded by the U.S. military.

In 2003, the Air Force solicited proposals from academia to study the use of plasma actuators to steer drones. If drones could be outfitted with plasma actuators, the Air Force believed it could shrink the size and weight of the pilotless aircraft. Miniature drones would be harder to spot in the sky, stay aloft longer, and maneuver with greater ease and accuracy, particularly in urban settings. The plasma drone research was one of hundreds of next-generation projects funded by the Air Force each year. Atmospheric Glow Technologies, a Knoxville-area company run by one of Roth's former students, Daniel Sherman, submitted the winning bid for the plasma drone project. Atmospheric subsequently hired Roth as a consultant. The work on the design phase was successful enough that Atmospheric won a second contract to conduct technical experiments. Again, the company retained Roth as a consultant.

The plasma drone project was not classified, but Roth's sub-contract contained a standard proviso that it was subject to deemed export controls. This meant foreigners could not participate in the project without State Department authorization.

For the Air Force plasma project—titled Plasma Aerodynamics for Munitions—Roth proposed to use two graduate assistants, Truman Bonds, an American, and Xin Dai, a Chinese national. When Sherman, Roth's partner, cited the deemed export rules and objected to using a foreign student, Roth divided the work. The American student was tasked to handle the export-controlled data and the Chinese student was assigned to nonsensitive aspects of the project. Roth soon found this impractical and began sharing weekly progress reports with Xin, the Chinese student. In 2006, as Xin neared graduation, Roth informed Sherman that he planned to replace the Chinese student with an Iranian graduate assistant. When Sherman again objected, Roth appealed to university officials. The officials were aghast. They not only rejected the use of an Iranian student but expressed surprise that a Chinese student had been permitted to work on a military project for so long. And when a university official learned that Roth was about to depart for a lecture tour in China, she reminded him not to take sensitive plasma drone data with him. Roth apparently ignored her. On his flight to China, the professor carried with him a printout of the latest update on the drone project, a thumb drive with earlier project updates, and a laptop that contained a paper related to another potential Pentagon weapons project.

Whether by arrogance or sloppiness, or both, Roth's disdain for security continued once he arrived in China. He asked a graduate student back in Knoxville to email him a draft paper containing data about a drone project. The student did so, but when Roth couldn't get his university laptop to connect to the Internet, he turned his computer over to a Chinese technician for assistance. When the technician couldn't resolve the issue, Roth directed his Tennessee graduate student to forward the drone document to the email account of one of the professors hosting him in China. When Roth returned to the United States, his luggage was searched and the sensitive documents discovered, triggering the first-of-its-kind criminal export case against an American professor.

Roth was indicted for taking sensitive data to China and for providing drone project access to his Iranian and Chinese students. At trial, he claimed he did not willfully violate the law, that much of the information was already in the public domain, and that the export law should not apply to preliminary research. On the witness stand, however, he displayed flashes of arrogance that probably served him poorly before the jury. "I do think that academic freedom and research is going to be severely impacted by some of the things that have cropped up in this investigation. . . . This apparent contention that any export controlled information must not go out of the country . . . is going to make it virtually impossible for scholars to take their laptops out of the United States."

Roth was convicted and the judge gave him four years. At age seventy-four, the professor reported to prison, still maintaining his innocence. In his university office, he left behind a collection that included laboratory notes, patents, and three hundred scientific articles drafted over a quarter century. Shortly after Roth departed, the university, acting on advice of its attorneys, shredded the contents of his office.

. . .

Hall and Malandra spent much of the next year pursing the Ahmed deal for a FLIR system, but they also took care to grow the legend of Cross International and target other suspected smugglers. A Pennsylvania company helped them try to stop the flow of U.S. goods to a Canadian company making weapons for the Iranians, and a Kentucky company helped the HSI agents investigate a Chinese American suspected of smuggling chemical warfare detection kits to China. Malandra and his agents traveled to Canada and the Caribbean to set up bank accounts and enlist the help of legitimate companies. They also began talking to an aggressive HSI agent based in Germany, who was setting up an undercover arms company based in the Baltics. The agents scurried to get everything in place. If an arms broker agreed to meet them overseas, whether Ahmed or someone else, they wanted to be ready.

Meanwhile, to keep the bosses happy, the agents pursued a few smaller, simpler cases. They discovered, for example, a low-level Iranian smuggler with outstanding charges living in California, and this made for an easy arrest. They also pursued leads for the Bureau of Alcohol, Tobacco, Firearms and Explosives and other HSI regional offices, mostly minor gun smuggling cases down at the docks. Not every "easy" case went smoothly. In late spring 2005, the agents received a tip about a British man selling military-grade thermal imaging cameras on eBay. They engaged the suspect by email, and wired a $1,000 deposit to him in London. They never heard from the man again, or recovered the money, and the rip-off triggered a mound of embarrassing paperwork.

By summer 2005, Hall believed they were nearly ready to take their operation overseas, and have their undercover agents, including Lechleitner, try to meet with targets outside the United States. An international arms conference would be best, they concluded, because it would provide excellent cover and allow the undercover agents to meet multiple brokers in the same week. They chose the biennial Dubai Airshow, the world's third largest, which loomed in November. Dubai was a short flight from Iran, and close enough to Pakistan that it might lure the likes of Yasmin Ahmed. Lechleitner began making arrangements to attend.

Still, Hall believed their team lacked one critical element—an insider, someone who could teach undercover agents like Lechleitner how to act and what to say, someone with established black market credentials willing to vouch for the agents, even travel with them to Dubai. It would help if this insider were a foreigner, as arms dealers were always suspicious of Americans. Hall asked Malandra if he knew anyone like that. Yeah, Malandra replied, as a matter of fact, he did.

CHAPTER 5

The Informant

Clyde Pensworth, salesman to despots and dictators since 1962, boarded the express train from Paddington Station to Heathrow. He carried a suitcase, a British passport, and, compliments of the U.S. government, an airplane ticket to Dubai and instructions to meet P.J. Lechleitner.

A wisp of a man approaching seventy, Pensworth looked more like a bookkeeper than a merchant of death. His two front lower teeth were cross-eyed, and his sunken face accentuated by unruly salt-and-pepper eyebrows. On his right hand he wore his only false hint of wealth—a gold ring encrusted with three large diamonds, a gift ages ago from a grateful Middle Eastern client. From a distance, particularly on the streets of London or any other Western capital, Pensworth looked like an anonymous pensioner. But up close his wizened gray eyes—cold, calculating, with more than a hint of malice—betrayed the soul of a ruthless dealmaker who embraced each of the world's violent conflicts as the next business opportunity. In certain Third World corners, Pensworth was still known by the code name he'd given himself, The White Man.

The White Man kept a low profile. As testimony to his stealthy existence over decades, only a handful of his deals had ever surfaced publicly, finding their way into unlinked news accounts and court files. These included Pensworth's association with the East German Stasi in the 1980s and the North Koreans in the 1990s. More recently, he'd been tied to deals to sell attack helicopters to Robert Mugabe's murderous regime in Zimbabwe and to subvert the

Darfur embargo by offering tanks and planes to Sudan. Pensworth was despicable and he knew it. As he once remarked to an American acquaintance, "People like me shouldn't exist."

Pensworth claimed to be chummy with several notorious arms dealers. Perhaps most notable was Monzer al-Kassar, a Syrian linked to black market deals in the Balkans, Somalia, and Palestine. Like Pensworth, Kassar played all sides: he was charged but acquitted in the *Achille Lauro* terror attack; he was Oliver North's conduit for arming the contras in Nicaragua; and he resupplied Saddam Hussein before the two U.S. invasions. The DEA ultimately caught Kassar in a sting involving Colombian narco-rebels, eight thousand assault rifles, tons of C-4 explosive, and a dozen surface-to-air missiles. At Kassar's trial, Pensworth offered to testify on his behalf as a character witness.

Pensworth lived modestly southwest of London, and liked to meet clients and associates in the Lobby Lounge of the Grosvenor, a four-star hotel adjacent to Victoria Station. Strolling distance from Parliament and Buckingham Palace, the Lobby Lounge projected the air of an old-school British club—vaulted ceilings, high-backed maroon chairs, hushed conversations, the kind of place where afternoon tea was considered high art and longtime patrons like Pensworth still ordered the fruitcake. He affectionately called it "The Office."

As the airport express train rushed from central London, Pensworth wondered if his Dubai hotel would be Western enough to stock a decent chardonnay. He imagined that it would be. Despite the seven-hour flight that lay ahead, Pensworth felt invigorated. Dubai was one of his favorite places to do business, a modern-day Casablanca, infested with spies, hustlers, bankers, and strongmen of every nationality. The city-state's free port offered the kind of efficiency and discretion Pensworth valued. A package from America could arrive in Dubai by plane in the morning and be aboard a boat to Iran by late afternoon.

Dubai also hosted one of the world's largest aviation conferences, the Dubai Airshow, which usually drew 35,000 attendees, among them royalty, defense ministers, corporate chief executives, and arms brokers. The 2005 show would begin in two days, and Pensworth planned to make the most of it. In the coming week, a staggering $35 billion worth of legitimate contracts would be consummated; tens of millions more would secretly change hands on the black market.

The black market. The term rankled Pensworth. So often the only determining factor between what constituted a black market deal and a so-called legitimate one were matters of geography and politics. Still, weapons and high-tech electronics were often as easy to wash as dirty money. Once you smuggled them to a free port like Dubai, you could forward them pretty much anywhere.

Pensworth's great skill was finance. The consummate middleman and dealmaker, he created and shepherded the dull but obligatory international paperwork, from banking letters of credit to export documentation, that playboy arms merchants like his friend Kassar needed to conduct business. In five decades, Pensworth had developed an extensive network of global banking and military contacts—though the British Empire had retreated, two thirds of its financial network remained in its former colonies. So long as he remained once removed from the arms deals, and the shipments never touched British shores, Pensworth committed no English crimes. He drew constant scrutiny and surveillance from the spies at MI5 and detectives at Scotland Yard, as well as various journalists and human rights groups. But nobody ever pinned anything on him.

They'd come close, though. A year earlier, a report had exposed and nearly spoiled a major deal to sell Antonov 26 cargo aircraft, T-72 tanks, and pistols to the Sudanese government. The deal had touched four continents: to sell arms to Africa, Pensworth and his partner had used an Iranian banker, a British Virgin Islands shell company, and factories in China and Ukraine. The way Pensworth and his partner had crafted the shipments, wire transfers, and end user certificates, the deal neatly skirted European Union and United Nations embargoes on arms to Darfur. Although the publicity scuttled the tanks and pistols portion of the deal, the aircraft project still succeeded.

And yet, for all his wheeling and dealing and 007-style tales—like the night a Warsaw arms dealer tipped him for his services with three prostitutes—Pensworth never made his fortune. He was a hopeless gambler and, he readily admitted, a terrible one, consistently burning through proceeds from arms deals, usually on ponies. Pensworth lived a hustler's life. He started a detective agency. He tried his hand at interior design. He bought three racehorses and seven greyhounds, losers all. He opened a lesbian bar. Everything tanked. When friends would ask how he was doing, Pensworth would say, "Nickels and dimes. Nickels and dimes."

Which was one of the reasons he was headed to Dubai, on secret assignment for his new friends from Philadelphia. He needed the money.

. . .

You hire a snitch, you dance with the devil.

It's a law enforcement axiom. But who better to help bust a crack dealer than another crack dealer? Who better to bring down a mob boss than another mobster? As long as there have been cops, they've been making deals with informants, deploying one criminal to catch another, a process fraught with ethical and practical issues: Is it moral to use one criminal to help catch another? Can agents control their snitch? Can they trust him? Who controls the line between sting and entrapment?

More so than most snitches, Pensworth's unsavory pedigree rankled a lot of people in American and British law enforcement. Here was a man with access, inside knowledge, and a proven track record, but the people with whom he did business were among the most evil in the world. More than a few were linked to genocide. Pensworth made it clear that neither morals nor politics played a role in his business. He held no allegiances, except to money. He insisted on running cases his way—in part because he believed most cops didn't know what they were doing, and in part because he wanted to make sure he made a little something on the side.

Pensworth didn't consider himself a snitch, per se. Though he'd been helping the Americans, quietly, since the latter days of the Reagan administration, he'd also been working with America's adversaries. The way he viewed it, he helped everyone. He was nobody's man. Pensworth was so dirty that Western governments kept him on the edges of projects, using him carefully. He was a setup guy. Law enforcement and intelligence agencies rarely included him in actual stings. That way, his name was less likely to surface if a clandestine operation turned sour and drifted toward public scandal, or if a case reached the trial stage, where the routine exchange of evidence risked putting all his unsavory exploits on display.

Perhaps the government with which he had the worst relations was his own. The British refused to deal with Pensworth, and resented his relationship with the Americans and Iranians. Truth be told, the British were still trying to put Pensworth in prison, failing in part because English conspiracy laws were rather toothless. Several times MI5 had asked the Americans to break off contact with the White Man. "He brought a lot of controversies," recalled a U.S. federal agent stationed in London. "I'd get calls from our headquarters in Washington, saying 'The word's come down: You can never meet with that guy again.' And then two months later, a CIA case officer would call and say, 'Hey, that buddy of yours, can you call him?' They didn't have a choice. They had to deal with him. He was dealing with all these people who were hitting law enforcement and intelligence agencies' radar screens." Eventually, the Americans and the English struck an uneasy gentleman's agreement: the United States could continue to use Pensworth as an informant, but they could never meet with him on British soil. Pensworth soon became a frequent visitor to Philadelphia.

At pubs just blocks from Independence Hall, over glasses of dry white wine and pints of local brew, Pensworth set about schooling the Americans on the gray and black market arms trade. He enjoyed working with the agents and found them quick learners. The White Man taught the Americans how to better portray themselves as businessmen, not cops. He taught them nuances that helped them hone the perspective of someone trying to skirt rules, not enforce them. He taught them the cadence of the trade, how to respond to unsolicited queries, how to craft vague but legal end user certificates, how to demand a realistic deposit, where to bank, how to negotiate, when to close a deal, and when to walk away. He taught them the lingo and abbreviations that black market dealers would expect them to know—beyond RFQ (request for quote), FOB (freight on board), PO (purchase order), LC (letter of credit), EUC (end user certificate), and CIF (cost, insurance, and freight). He emphasized that every inquiry should be taken seriously, even the seemingly inconsequential. Too many law enforcement agents, he said, foolishly ignored low-dollar, low-quantity requests for arms and sensitive technology, assuming they came from small-time operators. Not necessarily so, Pensworth would lecture. These were probably probes, tests to measure the worthiness and safety of a company. Many of his best relationships and biggest deals, he told the agents, had begun with a simple order, a so-called one-off. You never know where things might lead. He'd met his friend Kassar on a one-off.

Pensworth described the tricks black market arms dealers used to mask deals with cutouts, shell companies, and middlemen, placing at least one layer between the true buyer and true seller. Every extra layer cut into profits, but also created a buffer in case something went wrong. The Iranians, Chinese, and North Koreans almost always took such precautions, and they would immediately become suspicious of any American buyer or seller who insisted on working without a middleman.

Most important, Pensworth taught patience, something he believed the Americans sorely lacked. Black market deals usually took months, even years, to develop, he explained. Arms brokers surfaced and disappeared as randomly as feeding fish. It was not uncommon for a buyer to vanish inexplicably on the eve of a deal—break off contact for weeks—only to surface again, just as suddenly, eager to complete the transaction. There were just too many variables to know for sure why one deal worked and another got scuttled. Sometimes, it was financing; sometimes, it was a Customs issue. Or a buyer found a better deal elsewhere. Or a buyer's client changed his mind. Or his government was overthrown. One just had to play it cool. Remain patient. Keep at it. Because even if an arms broker gave you a reason why he'd backed out of a deal or had disappeared for a few months, he was probably lying—playing you. It didn't mean he wouldn't ring again months later and propose a different deal. He might. Pensworth's point was that it was pointless to try to follow the logic. Cops who tried were wasting their time.

Pensworth relished his role as teacher. He regaled captive audiences of U.S. agents with stories of strongmen, generals, and Western diplomats, self-aggrandizing yarns stretching back half a century. At one point, the Americans brought him to Washington, where he spoke to more than a hundred agents, answering question after question for nearly two hours. Pensworth considered the session an honor, a highlight of his sub rosa career. Now his stock was rising further—the United States was sending him to Dubai on a secret mission.

The Americans were paying his expenses, plus a modest consulting fee, dangling the vague prospect of a handsome cut for his participation in undercover deals to come. But Pensworth wasn't helping the Americans for the money, at least not entirely. He was doing it for the thrill. He got off on playing detective/spy, working all sides. As he explained one afternoon to the Philadelphia HSI agents, he'd caught the undercover bug as a young man, while serving as a military policeman in a former British colony in the Middle East in the 1950s. The story, captured on audiotape, is vintage Pensworth. He is the central character, the cops are bungling and impatient, the buyers treacherous, the spies cagey.

"Some local blokes in a restaurant became my friends, and one night they told me they wanted to buy a few pistols. I reported this back to my officer in charge, and he spoke with the funny people— you know, MI5, MI6 and all that. After a lot of this and that, they got back to me said, 'We'd like you to follow up and meet these guys.' I agreed that I should do it. I picked up the chap I was supposed to meet, who wanted to buy just one pistol and some bullets. The police followed me in military vehicles, and they were supposed to wait, but the asshole chief copper rushed the other guy as soon as I greeted him. I thought, 'Shit, he hasn't even taken the pistol from me yet.' So I slipped the ammunition in his bloody pocket! As they took him away, the guy gave me a look and slashed fingers across his throat."

Pensworth had played this game for fifty years now, surviving as friends and clients had been jailed, murdered, or simply disappeared. Lately, though, things were changing. Back in the glory days, before 9/11 and the Internet, when the rules of the game were clearer, people spoke in person, meetings mattered, and Pensworth was treated like a big shot, the White Man. Now, things were less predictable and more dangerous. The Internet had created a double-edged sword. The web offered anonymity but also presented governments with an incredible surveillance tool. Pensworth used the telephone and email carefully. He wasn't paranoid, just cautious. Ironically, what worried him most was the evaporating rule of law that followed 9/11. American definitions of conspiracy and legal rendition now seemed to be whatever the Americans said they were, depending on the circumstances. And plenty of countries, it seemed, felt obliged to do whatever the Americans asked. In some ways, his trips to Philadelphia were becoming as dicey as his journeys to Tehran.

The White Man had made six trips to Iran since 1980, and he carried a strong affinity for the Iranians. They were smarter than the Americans realized, and quite skilled at reverse engineering military hardware and technology. They were gracious hosts, too, treating him like a brother, especially the senior officials at the Ministry of Defense. Although Pensworth never felt completely trusted, and always experienced a small sense of relief whenever he departed Imam Khomeini International Airport in Tehran, his relationships grew quickly and profitably. He even claimed—in a story that strains credulity—that the Iranians once asked him to ferry a sealed message to a senior Israeli official, a task that gave him an enormous mental high. Pensworth tried to avoid politics, but he shared the Iranians' frustration with the United States, and their fear that a misguided American president might order an attack. Some twenty-five years on, and most Americans remained hung up over the 1979 hostage crisis. They couldn't look past it. And the way Pensworth saw it, the U.S. 2003 invasion of Iraq had been bloody stupid. Saddam Hussein had been keeping the Iranians at bay. The war had created more problems than it had solved. If the Americans were smart, they would try harder to court the Iranians as allies. The Iranians were insecure, but they were more pragmatic than the West believed. With threats on every border, they were willing to overlook the past to secure the future.

But Pensworth's secret mission for the Americans in November 2005 was not a diplomatic one. His job was not to broker peace between Iran and the West, or to deliver some sort of secret message. The White Man was flying from London to Dubai to meet Lechleitner and introduce him to two prolific Iranian arms brokers, men the United States hoped to put in prison.

CHAPTER 6

The Bazaar

DUBAI, UNITED ARAB EMIRATES

P.J. Lechleitner's thirteen-hour flight from Dulles descended as the morning's first light reached the Arabian Peninsula. An endless desert stretched below, flat brown sand divided by impossibly straight roads, grids pierced only by the occasional milk-white walls of an encampment. In minutes, a gleaming city-state appeared on the horizon, silver and sun-bleached, construction cranes and half-finished towers dotting the skyline. The plane put down at Dubai International Airport and rolled to the gate. From a cramped middle seat in coach, Lechleitner unpacked his burly frame and grabbed his carry-on gear. Stepping into the air-cooled terminal, he fished out his sunglasses and a wallet with cards identifying him as Patrick J. Lynch, arms broker for Cross International of Pennsylvania.

Lechleitner and his traveling partner, fellow undercover HSI agent Mitch Worley, found the taxi queue and told the Pakistani driver to take them to the Metropolitan Hotel. The exhausted Americans, squinting into the morning sun, helped hoist the luggage into the trunk, and climbed into the backseat.

The Dubai trip marked Lechleitner's first truly undercover mission. His work in Yardley had been almost exclusively by phone and email, and he was eager to meet a target in person. Over the next four days, as the Dubai Airshow played out, the Philadelphia agents expected to meet four arms dealers—two get-togethers arranged by Lechleitner and two by Clyde Pensworth, who was due from Heathrow in a few hours. The British informant would also serve as their sensei, make introductions and accompany them to meetings.

The four appointments were: Yasmin Ahmed, the Pakistani broker looking for a FLIR system and who-knew-what-else; Esmaeil Azizi, a heavy-hitter Iranian suspected of smuggling arms, technology, and aircraft to Iran from the United States, Russia, Britain, and Africa; an as yet unidentified Tunisian, a Pensworth contact said to be diverting U.S. arms to war-torn African nations; and Alex Dave, the mysterious and prolific Iranian broker interested in a little bit of everything.

Lately, Alex Dave seemed to be in the market for large quantities of radioactive material—tritium, promethium-147, strontium-90, and nickel-63. The Iranian had not explained why he wanted the material. Tritium, for example, has a range of uses: it is a component deployed in the triggering mechanism of thermonuclear weapons but also a key ingredient for innocuous self-luminescent devices, such as exit signs, aircraft dials, and wristwatches. Lechleitner's most recent exchange with Alex Dave had included a formal proposal for the radioactive material, which came to $224,000, shipping included.

The taxi carrying Lechleitner and Worley sprinted from the airport to Casablanca Road and across Dubai Creek, the wide river splitting the city. It was nearly rush hour, and the driver chose the southern approach to the primary expressway, Sheikh Zayed Road, bypassing the ancient Deira and Bur Dubai neighborhoods and their warrens of alleys and souks. The modern Dubai that the jet-lagged Americans glimpsed from the taxi window at eighty-five kilometers an hour looked a lot like Vegas, a gaudy canyon of office towers in the shape of sails and sailboats, the city's architectural theme. The expressway raced through the financial district toward the sprawling construction site of the Dubai Mall, soon to boast an astounding four million square feet of shops and restaurants, a monstrosity anchored by a four-story aquarium, indoor ice rink, and Bellagio-style lake with dancing fountains. Nearby, South Asian laborers were erecting Dubai's crown jewel, the Burj Khalifa, destined to become the world's tallest building, rising half a mile above the desert.

The taxi whipped south beyond the new construction. The driver swerved onto a raised exit ramp that crossed back over the highway, and he deposited the Americans in front of an unimpressive five-story cream and burgundy structure. The building looked like a large Red Roof Inn, circa 1979, and it faced the expressway. This was the Metropolitan Hotel.

In a city filled with five-star accommodations attached to world-class attractions, the HSI agents found themselves marooned at the Metropolitan. Natty marble floors and wood paneling in the lobby belied moldy rooms, rumbling, dripping pipes, and a location far from anything interesting in Dubai. The agents hadn't had much choice. All the best hotels had long ago been booked by airshow attendees. The Metropolitan did offer one saving grace for the agents' cover, an underground reputation for sin. The hotel's largest bar, the Rattlesnake, hosted Dubai's most notorious upscale den of prostitution. Each night, shortly after ten, a creepy mix of Western businessmen and expensive East European women began circling one another at the bar as a Japanese cover band crooned Motown hits in the background. Further adding to the Metropolitan's unabashed ethos, the hotel's Italian restaurant was named Don Corleone.

Lechleitner and Worley checked in, dropped their bags in their rooms, and met their Dubai-based colleagues in the lobby. The local HSI agents arrived with bad news: U.S. diplomats had taken a second look at the undercover plan and reconsidered. Embassy officials no longer wanted Lechleitner and Worley to meet with one of the four targets, Azizi, the Iranian looking to buy Canadian training jets and American armored personnel carriers. The diplomats believed Azizi too hot, and probably under constant surveillance by the Iranian and/or the Emirati intelligence services. If the undercover American agents met with him, the diplomats reasoned, someone was sure to notice. At a minimum, this would irritate the Emiratis, who had not been notified of the undercover operation, creating headaches and embarrassment for the American diplomats. Worse, exposure to the Iranians might blow Cross International's cover, even endanger Lechleitner and Worley, or so the diplomats said. To emphasize their seriousness, the diplomats put their instructions in writing: *You are ordered not to meet with Azizi.* Lechleitner found this a little over the top, but he recognized the bureaucratic, cover-your-ass rationale. The diplomats didn't know him. For all they knew, he and Worley were arrogant cowboys, the kind of agents who nodded yes and then went ahead and did whatever the hell they wanted.

Lechleitner saluted and promised not to meet Azizi. But he was pissed. Azizi presented a righteous target, and Pensworth had created a hell of an opportunity by arranging the meeting. "I'd flown halfway around the world, worked on this for a year, and they'd taken the bat out of my hand," Lechleitner recalled.

A few hours later, Lechleitner gave Pensworth the bad news.

"Well," Pensworth replied. "They ordered you not to meet with Azizi. But they didn't say anything about me, did they?"

Lechleitner smiled. "That's true," the agent said. Pensworth was a British citizen. The American diplomats couldn't tell Pensworth what to do.

. . .

The following morning, Pensworth took a taxi to see Azizi.

The cab crossed Dubai Creek into the commercial section known as Deira. If new Dubai resembles Las Vegas, Deira is old

Dubai, a cross between Cairo and the Bronx—wide avenues, drab white apartment buildings, and bustling gold and spice souks teeming with tourists and traders. Deira extends north from the airport to the wharf where the Dubai Creek meets the Persian Gulf. Here, longshoremen pile boxes of embargoed American commercial goods—televisions, refrigerators, microwave ovens—atop modest wooden boats called dhows. The creaking dhows make short hops across the Gulf, following ancient trade routes from the Arabian Peninsula to Iran. The Iranian influence runs deep in Deira. Ten-story buildings are topped with the names of Iranian banks and anchored by Persian clothing stores, markets, and barbershops. Most Iranian brokers who contact American manufacturers use a front address in Deira.

At about 10:20 a.m., Pensworth stepped from a cab in the middle of a block lined with high-rises a short distance from the wharf. The Brit entered one of them and rode the elevator up to Azizi's office. After a brief wait, Azizi emerged and greeted him with a hug. The Iranian apologized for running late. He'd been on the phone with bankers, he explained. Annoying new restrictions were mucking up a $4 million deposit at a European bank, delaying a shipment of military parts from Brussels to Tehran. The deal would go through, eventually, but every day of delay was costing Azizi interest and time away from other business. Pensworth commiserated.

Over the next ninety minutes, the two elderly men batted around potential deals. Azizi brought up the idea of moving American armored personnel carriers and helicopters to Pakistan, and Pensworth offered South Asian shipping suggestions. Azizi mentioned that he was on the lookout for Russian-made fighter jet parts, and Pensworth passed along a contact in Cyprus. Azizi said he needed computer technicians willing to travel to Iran to install software upgrades, and Pensworth provided a trusted IT contact in the Mediterranean. They exchanged gossip and pricing related to an arms project in the Ivory Coast, as well as ways to transfer Canadian training jet aircraft to Iran. The trainers, Azizi emphasized, were a high priority.

Pensworth invited Azizi to join him at the airshow, where they could walk the exhibit floor, continue their discussions, and make more connections. Azizi declined, implying that it wouldn't be a good idea to be seen in public together. Instead, the Iranian invited the Englishman to lunch.

They dined leisurely at Sadaf, a high-end Persian restaurant near the wharf, mixing long moments of silence and mouthfuls of kebab and rice with careful queries about mutual acquaintances. At one point, Pensworth brought up the name of an American brokerage firm, Cross International, located in suburban Philadelphia.

Good, smart, creative blokes, Pensworth told Azizi. *Our kind of people. Not afraid to find ways to get things to Iran. The contact is a fellow named Patrick Lynch. His email is crossintl@aol.com.*

Azizi wrote this down.

Pensworth asked Azizi about an Iranian broker he might know, Alex Dave of SBC Technology Group in Shiraz. He passed along Alex Dave's email address and phone number.

Never heard of him, Azizi said. He promised to look him up. Pensworth was certain he would. Azizi liked to keep close tabs on the competition.

After the meal, the Iranian stood and excused himself. He had a flight to catch to Tehran.

Pensworth kept one more appointment that afternoon, hoping to cultivate another target for his American friends. He met with a Tunisian arms dealer with connections throughout Africa. Pensworth and the Tunisian discussed a potential deal that paired a Yemeni broker with a South African partner. They hoped to smuggle arms to the ruling junta in Myanmar. At the appropriate moment, Pensworth delicately brought up Cross International.

He explained that two Cross executives had traveled from Pennsylvania to Dubai for the airshow. Pensworth offered to arrange a meeting.

The Tunisian demurred. *Americans? Maybe some other time.*

. . .

Pensworth returned to the Metropolitan and briefed Lechleitner and Worley. Thus far, two of their four appointments—Azizi and the Tunisian—had not worked out as planned. And Alex Dave, the prolific Iranian who had promised to meet them in Dubai, had remained underground, declining or unable to answer his email. The Americans still had an appointment with Yasmin Ahmed, the Pakistani broker, but not until the following day. Frustrated, and apprehensive that their trip was fast becoming a bust, the undercover agents hit the convention, which was already well under way.

The Dubai Airshow attracted 575 exhibitors from thirty-seven nations that year. With so many industry and government executives on hand, the airshow offered a tremendous forum for announcing major deals. On the first day of the conference, Dubai-based Emirates Airlines signed a $9.7 billion agreement to buy forty-two B-777s from Boeing, an order that instantly made it the largest air carrier in the Arab world. Another $20 billion in announced contracts followed, but the Emirates-Boeing deal showcased the UAE's rising political and economic prominence.

Many factors contributed to Dubai's dubious reputation as an arms smuggling hub, and its close, complicated relationships with both the United States and Iran—natural resources, geography, economics, politics. The UAE held 8 percent of the world's proven oil reserves and was the world's fifth largest supplier of natural gas. Poised near the northern tip of the Arabian Peninsula, between the Persian Gulf and Gulf of Oman, the Emirates created one of the largest, most reliable, efficient, and tax-free ports in the world and the nation leveraged its economic connections to cultivate friends everywhere. The UAE was a rare OPEC member with close Western ties; ExxonMobil, BP, Occidental Petroleum, Total, and Shell held minority shares in Emirati companies, and U.S. corporations held a 45 percent market share in oil and gas field development. Politically, the UAE generally supported U.S. interests in the Gulf, including the war in Iraq; coalition forces used UAE air bases and ports for staging and for refueling tankers, surveillance aircraft, and pilotless drones; the Germans trained the Iraqi police force in the UAE; the Emirates pledged $215 million in Iraqi humanitarian and reconstruction aid, and, perhaps as important, promised to forgive Iraq's large outstanding debt. The UAE also acted behind the scenes. Government propagandists secretly drafted sermons supporting the new Iraqi government and distributed them to local mosques. In return, the Emiratis sought Western protection from its most likely predator, Iran. The ruling families of the UAE were among the richest people in the world, and they understood that the mullahs in Tehran considered Dubai the closest, fattest target of Western excess and godlessness.

The dramatic demographic change that the oil and gas trade boom had triggered in the UAE fed into Iran's jealousy and resentment, as well its economic envy. In the 1960s, the UAE population was 64 percent native Emirati. By the time Lechleitner arrived in 2005, it was just 21 percent. Most newcomers were from India, Pakistan, Bangladesh, and the Middle East. But more than 300,000 Iranians now lived in the UAE, as well, many middle-class immigrants. Their influence had to be respected by the ruling Emiratis, or at least carefully monitored.

The tension between Islamic culture and the Western economy forced the UAE to find compromises that kept everyone happy, at least on the surface, and commerce flowing. On a micro scale, it was the reason why you could legally buy liquor in Dubai, but only at a Western hotel.

The Emiratis took a similar view of arms smuggling. Careful to balance their reputation for trade with national security, they cooperated with the West in some cases, but not others. A classified diplomatic cable, sent not long after Lechleitner's visit, provides an example. When an HSI agent learned that an Iranian government-owned vessel docking in Dubai might be carrying American-made aluminum sheeting with potential use for nuclear and missile programs, U.S. diplomats called local Customs officials. The UAE officials declined to intervene, arguing they had no legal grounds to search a container merely in transit—though the ship had docked in Dubai to pick up more cargo, the suspect container had remained aboard the Iranian vessel, unopened. According to the U.S. cable, a senior Dubai official told the HSI agent, "Allowing searches like the one being proposed would be 'bad for business.'"

Iran wasn't the only nation exploiting Dubai's free-for-all ports. Other nations used Dubai as an arms and technology smuggling hub—Syria, China, North Korea, and Libya among them. Shortly before Lechleitner's visit, the American ambassador met with the Emirati foreign minister. According to a secret U.S. cable summarizing the meeting, the ambassador implored the UAE to do more to stop the North Koreans from shipping conventional and nuclear weapon technologies through Dubai. The foreign minister reportedly replied that the UAE was "well aware of the North Korean role in spreading weapons of mass destruction materials," but declined to do much about it. Perhaps as alarming, the foreign minister revealed, the Iranians and North Koreans often met in China to consummate deals, then shipped the arms and technology from North Korea to Singapore and Dubai to Iran. "China is a big dragon," the foreign minister told the Americans.

At the airshow, it was easy for Lechleitner and Worley to see the growing Chinese influence. And yet the agents couldn't ignore the largest influence of all: ninety out of the 575 exhibitors were American firms.

As they strolled the convention floor, occasionally handing out Cross International business cards, the agents found the exercise interesting but largely unsatisfying. As at almost any convention, the agents knew, the best deals were being made on the sidelines, behind the scenes, in private meetings. They'd traveled all this way, and so far they hadn't met with any arms dealers.

·   ·   ·

The following morning they got their chance.

Yasmin Ahmed met them in the lobby lounge of the Metropolitan Hotel.

Ahmed didn't fit the Hollywood stereotype of a black market arms dealer. The Pakistani woman, squat and perhaps fifty years old, unfailingly polite, was a naturalized U.S. citizen with kids in college near Philadelphia. To Lechleitner, her young male assistant looked more like an intern than muscle.

Yet here sat a woman convicted only three years earlier of trying to smuggle military radar and howitzer cannon parts. Obviously she was well versed in the munitions trade. Just minutes into the meeting, she began quizzing the undercover agents about MK19 automatic grenade launchers, sophisticated aircraft components, night vision and thermal imaging technology, and the Canadian unmanned aerial vehicle known as the Barracuda UAV.

She also asked about the FLIR project. *How are the inquiries coming along? What price point do you expect? Timing? Is it possible to get a discount on the grenade launchers?*

Lechleitner met her questions with his own. *How many will you really need? What about spare parts? Let's cut to the chase and make this easier: What's the ultimate destination?*

Ahmed ducked the last question. She had a contact in Lithuania, she said, who could transship almost anything. She had a special interest, she added, in an American company that made "high-reliability components," fuses and chips used in satellite and space programs. She pulled out her cell phone and dialed Karachi. Her husband-partner, Yusuf Khan, came on the line and she put him on speakerphone. The special fuses, he explained, were part of a redundancy system for satellites. They kept power continuously flowing to vital systems.

Can you get them? Khan asked.

I'll look into it, the undercover agent replied.

Khan hung up, and as the meeting wound to its conclusion, Ahmed asked Lechleitner if Cross International ever planned to open an office in Dubai.

Perhaps, Lechleitner replied. *Someday.*

Well, Ahmed said, *why not position someone from your staff inside our Dubai facility? We have plenty of room.*

Lechleitner said it sounded like an excellent idea.

. . .

On the thirteen-hour flight home, Lechleitner evaluated his targets, one by one, mentally drafting the report he'd write when he returned to Philly:

Esmaeil Azizi, Pensworth's Iranian pal, clearly presented the fattest target. Azizi was wealthy, sophisticated, connected, elusive, a Tehran arms broker tied to major deals on multiple continents. With a proper vouch from Pensworth, he might be willing to meet American brokers. Definitely worth pursuing.

Yasmin Ahmed also seemed promising. The undercover meeting with her had gone smoothly. Hopefully, they could take the next step and lure her to a friendly European country where they could catch her in a sting.

Pensworth's unidentified Tunisian contact carried a purported direct connection to Iranian government officials. But he had seemed reluctant to meet Cross executives. The Tunisia angle was looking like a long shot.

Finally, Lechleitner considered Alex Dave. The Iranian broker had been so prolific. He seemed to be in the market for military-grade electronics, radar, bulletproof gear, and radioactive material. Yet he never closed a damn deal, always proposing, negotiating, then moving on. And he'd failed to show in Dubai. On the flight home, Lechleitner decided it was time to close the file on Alex Dave and move on to pursue more likely prospects.

CHAPTER 7

Love and Profit

SHIRAZ, IRAN

As it turned out, Alex Dave, aka Amir Ardebili, was plenty serious. The week of the Dubai Airshow, he wired a $7,000 deposit to a New England broker for precision gyroscopes. The gyros represented just one of a slew of military-grade American, Canadian, and European products Ardebili purchased or received in late 2005, almost all of it smuggled through the Dubai mail-drop office. His purchases ranged from $11,060 spent on aircraft nuts and bolts to $1 million for a powerful sonar package. The sonar system—5,236 pounds of undersea tracking equipment packed into eight pallets—was loaded onto KLM cargo planes that flew from Montreal to Amsterdam to Dubai, and then to Iran.

Ardebili's work was far from glamorous. He toiled in a world of spreadsheets, RFQs, pro forma invoices, and shipping manifests. His deals fell into a familiar pattern: a state-controlled Iranian company—Iran Aircraft Manufacturing Industrial Company, for example—would send him a request for a product. He would turn to Google or Yahoo! to search for an American manufacturer or distributor, and send an RFQ. His inquiries during this period looked a lot like this one for infrared targeting systems: "Dear Sir/Madam: Hello. We visited your website and found a good mutual business possibility between both companies because of your presented brands and our products demand. We need a lot of parts in your field of activities and invite you to quote our inquiries . . ." If an American or European manufacturer responded, Ardebili began negotiating. As the years passed, his work improved in virtually every area—he became more efficient, his English matured, and he became more creative with the software he used to create the fake end user statements.

There remained many aspects he could not control. Wiring funds to Europe or the United States was still dicey, and the Tehran money exchange he employed to launder the money used an ever-changing network of banks in Switzerland, Germany, and Dubai. Rates varied; so did reliability.

Ardebili also struggled with the time element. Most deals took months to consummate and he did not receive his commission until the products arrived in Iran. The more sophisticated or specialized the product, the longer the lead time needed; some items made to order by the Americans took six to twelve weeks or more to manufacture and ship. In that time, it was always possible that the Iranian government might cancel the order, having found the product elsewhere or reconsidered its needs. A canceled order would leave Ardebili hanging and damage his reputation with the U.S. manufacturer. On the other end, it was always possible that an American company would figure out that he lived in Iran and, knowing he held no recourse, simply keep his deposit. On some large projects, the deposits involved advances from the Iranian government, funds for which Ardebili could be held responsible. "If I failed to get the part and lost the money, I would be on a blacklist for a while," he recalled. "If we owe big money to the government, I might have to go to jail." And if a U.S. distributor sent secondhand or defective material, Ardebili could find himself squeezed on both ends. American warranties and guarantees were unenforceable in Iran, and it was nearly impossible to win an argument with an unsatisfied Iranian government customer. "It's our duty to provide good parts," he recalled. "Sometimes you take chances. It's a very hard job."

Often enough, though, Ardebili's shotgun approach worked. According to financial records, Ardebili's company wired at least $1.8 million to European and American companies in 2005 and

2006. His smuggling partner in Dubai took a 5 percent cut to trans-ship to Iran, the money exchange in Tehran kept 1 percent for laun-dering the money to U.S. banks, and Ardebili aimed for a personal profit margin of 15 percent.

During those two years, Ardebili fulfilled a dizzying array of requests for the Iranian government. He bought bulletproof mate-rial, night vision equipment, and parts for Bell helicopters, F-14 fighters, C-130 cargo planes, and oil derricks. But he focused pri-marily on electronic components, precision pieces no larger than a car key. He bought thousands of them. Like the gyroscopes he sought, most American-made products were dual-use, designed for either commercial or military application. This included at least one order for microchips manufactured by an American company in Ari-zona. Known by the part number PIC16F84A, these were the tiny timing devices showing up inside IEDs in Afghanistan and Iraq.

. . .

Dual-use items like the PIC16F84A timing switches present one of the greatest challenges to U.S. export control agents. While the State Department regulates munitions—items strictly used for military applications—the Commerce Department issues licenses for dual-use products. Commerce processes 20,000 dual-use export license applications each year, and usually approves at least 80 percent of them. Manufacturers are responsible for complying with the arcane dual-use rules regulations. To determine whether a product requires a dual-use license, a manufacturer must consider four questions for each potential export, no matter the quantity or dollar value: Does the nature of the product itself require a license? Can the product be sent to the country in question? Is the foreign individual or company barred from receiving exports from the United States? How does the foreign end user intend to use the product? Each question must be answered by consulting and cross-referencing a series of Commerce Department lists, wading through a convoluted series of "commerce

control list categories," "product groups," and "commodity classifi-
cations." The Commerce rules are so bureaucratic that the department website offers a list of 101 "commonly used" acronyms, from
"AECA," the Arms Control Export Act, to "WA," the Wassenaar
Arrangement.

The regulations, as user-friendly as the tax code, have spurred
a thriving cottage industry of lawyers and database consultants.
Many U.S. corporations employ full-time export compliance officers. In a single month recently, exporters queried the online "Commerce Control" list 35,200 times. In the vast majority of situations,
exporters conclude on their own that they do not need a license for
a product and don't apply for one. Commerce officials insist that the
system works as intended, noting that they keep a keen eye on intelligence reports and stay in close contact with leading industry executives. But repeated government audits have found such self-analysis
lacking. Measuring actual data, the auditors concluded that $624 bil-
lion worth of dual-use products were subject to Commerce controls
in a recent year—yet exporters applied for a required license less
than 1.5 percent of the time. While most dual-use exports are harmless, others are not.

A triggered spark gap is a classic dual-use product, a device with
one common application for good and another for evil. The spool-
like product, the size of a grapefruit, is a high-voltage switch that
delivers a current over a very short period of time. It consists of three
electrodes in a hermetically sealed, pressurized ceramic envelope and
is filled with air or gas. As described in a U.S. manufacturer's specs,
the triggered spark gap offers "peak current capability of thousands
to tens of thousands of amperes, delay times of tens of nanoseconds,
arc resistance of tens of milliohms and inductance of five to thirty
nanohenries." In the civilian world, the device has several important
uses. Hospitals, for example, routinely use triggered spark gaps in a
device called a lithotripter, which crushes kidney stones by emitting
high-intensity sound waves. In military applications, the only use is

sinister. The triggered spark gap forms an essential part of the trigger used to detonate a nuclear weapon.

To prevent triggered spark gaps from falling into the wrong
hands, the Commerce Department declared the device a dual-use
item that required a license for export to certain countries, including Pakistan. The United States restricts such exports to Pakistan because of its growing nuclear program, its refusal to sign the
Nuclear Nonproliferation Treaty, and its reputation as a source of
clandestine nuclear exports. From the 1980s until the mid-2000s,
the Pakistani scientist A. Q. Khan notoriously supplied black market atomic bomb-making material and designs to Iraq, North Korea,
and Libya. He also tried to do business with the Iranians. The U.S.
government has never alleged that A. Q. Khan purchased American-
made products for potential use in nuclear weapons; he bought his
supplies in Europe. But in mid-2003, shortly before Khan publicly
confessed to supplying rogue nations, Commerce and HSI agents
received an anonymous tip that someone else was trying to smuggle
triggered spark gaps from the United States to Pakistan.

The tipster alleged that a man named Asher Karni, an Israeli living in Cape Town, South Africa, was trying to obtain two hundred
triggered spark gaps for a client in Pakistan. Under the scheme, the
switches would be shipped from a Massachusetts manufacturer to
a New Jersey broker, who would forward them to South Africa, a
nation for which an export license was not required. Karni would
then reship the triggered spark gaps from South Africa to Pakistan.
In a message to the American exporter, Karni identified a South
African hospital as end user for the two hundred switches. This was
a poor lie, as anyone in the business knows that hospitals generally
order only a handful of triggered spark gaps at a time. In a medical
setting, one triggered spark gap can be used repeatedly for years to
crush kidney stones. In a nuclear weapons setting, a triggered spark
gap can be used just once. A bomb maker will want dozens, if not
hundreds, on hand.

The U.S. agents who received the Karni tip obtained the confidential cooperation of the Massachusetts manufacturer. Federal agents directed the company to fulfill the first shipment of sixty-six triggered spark gaps, but only after secretly disabling them. The agents then watched as the precision switches, now inert, made the slow journey from Massachusetts to New Jersey to South Africa, and finally, to Pakistan. A short while later, U.S. and South African agents conducted nearly simultaneous searches of the New Jersey broker's and Karni's offices in Cape Town. Karni told South African agents that the triggered spark gaps had been forwarded to a Pakistani hospital and his paperwork showed that recipient in Islamabad to be an organization called the AJKMC Lithographic Society. The acronym alarmed U.S. agents because the initials are also commonly used by the All Jammu and Kashmir Muslim Conference, a political organization that supports jihadi groups linked to terror acts in disputed territory along the Indian border. After sifting through more incriminating seized documents, U.S. authorities filed sealed charges against Karni. Despite the search of his office, Karni apparently did not consider the matter serious. In his mind, it seemed like a regulatory issue, not a criminal case. On January 1, 2004, Karni departed with his wife and daughter for a long-planned ski holiday in Colorado. He was arrested at the airport in Denver and U.S. agents seized his laptop.

In many respects, the portrait that emerged from the emails and purchase orders agents found on Karni's computer was a familiar one—a successful businessman with no previous criminal record discovers that he can increase his profits by turning U.S. embargoes to his advantage, and so he does. "This is a tragic case of an otherwise respected, benevolent and pious individual who succumbed to financial temptations," his lawyers argued. Karni, born in Hungary in 1953, had moved to Israel as a child. After college, he earned an MBA while serving as an artillery officer in the Israeli army. In 1985, at age thirty-two, Karni moved with his wife and three daughters to South Africa. He became a leader in the Jewish community in Cape Town, where he served as synagogue cantor and tutored bar mitzvah boys.

Karni also became a successful businessman. Throughout the 1990s, he worked for an import-export company called Eagle Technology, where he first began transshipping U.S. products to embargoed nations. He left Eagle in 2002 to found his own import-export company and continued to help South Asian clients acquire U.S.-controlled dual-use products. In the laptop seized at the Denver airport, agents found evidence of at least seventeen export violations between 2002 and 2004, and another eighteen suspicious transactions dating to his tenure at Eagle. For the sixty-six triggered spark gaps, the records showed that Karni paid $33,000. The Pakistanis paid him about $60,000 after expenses, a profit margin of nearly 100 percent.

Karni's shipments of nuclear-capable equipment to Pakistan were not limited to triggered spark gaps. In spring 2003, he acquired three high-end oscilloscopes from an Oregon company and transshipped them to Pakistan. Oscilloscopes range in quality and sophistication and have many laudable medical and scientific uses—to determine heart rate in a cardiogram, for example. But oscilloscopes are also essential to calculate data during nuclear weapons tests. Two of the three oscilloscopes Karni purchased were received by the Al-Technique Corporation, a company on the U.S. prohibited list because of links to Pakistan's nuclear weapons and missile delivery industries. Karni's email records revealed that when he was arrested, he was negotiating to purchase thirty-six more oscilloscopes, valued at $1.3 million, for the same Pakistani network. Karni's supporters argued that he could not have understood the significance of the devices—and that, certainly, as a devout Jew and former Israeli soldier, he would not have knowingly helped radical Muslims build an atomic bomb. One thing was certain: Karni did not take sides in the politics of South Asia. During the period he sold nuclear equipment to the Pakistanis, he also sold electronics to Indian space companies with links to that nation's nuclear industry.

Karni cooperated with the U.S. agents, and a federal judge sentenced him to three years. U.S. authorities indicted the Pakistani buyer with whom Karni exchanged emails, but he remained at large, presumably in South Asia, and the case, though held out by authorities as a grand example of the threat posed by dual-use smuggling, concluded with a bit of a whimper. The White House rejected requests by the Commerce and Homeland Security agents to follow the trail to Pakistan in search of the true recipient of the triggered spark gaps. This left unanswered an important question: Were the switches destined for Pakistan's official nuclear program or for a rogue outfit? Either way, as a prosecutor in the case said, "The choices . . . are not comforting."

*   *   *

One warm evening in early 2006, the workaholic Ardebili put aside his laptop and invoices and grabbed a dog-eared book of poetry. He carried the book to a sacred spot in northwestern Shiraz, the Tomb of Shams al-Din Mohammad Hafez.

The fourteenth-century poet is one of the most spiritually influential figures in Persian culture. His poetry doesn't translate well into English—"You lose the harmony and beautifulness," according to Ardebili—and it is difficult for many Westerners to appreciate the grip Hafez still holds on the Iranian national consciousness. "Hafez reflected the life as it had been spun for the people of Iran for two thousand years," Iranian scholar M. A. Eslami-Nodushan recently noted. "He did so with such precision, that when, today, we drink of his lyrics it is as if we are drinking of history." Many Persians believe Hafez holds mystical powers.

Iranians come to the Tomb of Hafez to pay their respects but also to seek spiritual guidance. At the tomb, it is customary to open a book of Hafez poetry to a random page, blindly point to a passage, and divine one's future. Some visitors pay fortune-tellers toting Hafez anthologies to do this; others bring their own Hafez books.

On this evening, Ardebili carried his copy of *Divan-e-Hafez* to the pavilion where the great man is buried. Staring up into a dazzling turquoise and purple tile mosaic, Ardebili exhaled.

Was she the one?

Her name was Negin. A Tehran college student with intense brown eyes, full lips, a devastating wit, and unusual ambition. Negin came from a good family, the daughter of a schoolteacher and a bio-physicist, and granddaughter of a respected retired pilot and former Tehran government official. She loved poetry, played sitar, and liked to write. She was ten years younger, the same spread between Ardebili's father and mother. Though the couple had met in an online chat room, they told everyone they'd been introduced by mutual friends. People seemed more comfortable with that white lie.

Ardebili opened *Divan-e-Hafez*. The deck was stacked of course. Hafez wrote poems about love, courtship, and wine. Ardebili glanced down and began reading the poem on the page. He came to a line which read, *"Akhar ey khatame jamshide homayon asar gar fotad axe to bar laele negin am che shavad."* Very loosely translated, "If thy face relfects on my ring's gem, I would have love." In Farsi, "negin" is the word for gem. The poem contained his girlfriend's name! Coincidence or not, this removed any lingering doubt. Ardebili made plans to fly to Tehran to ask Negin's parents for permission to marry.

Negin hadn't planned to wed so young. She hoped to become a doctor or a writer and wanted to complete her studies before considering marriage. She didn't want to waste the opportunity. To be with Ardebili, she'd have to transfer universities, from Tehran to Shiraz, no small feat. Yet when Ardebili proposed one afternoon, Negin was startled by the quickness of her response. "There were a lot of boys around me," she recalled. "And a lot of girls around Amir, because he was in a good situation and a really nice boy. . . . He was a good package—not too handsome, but a good job, good family, very polite. In Iran, a lot of young boys and girls just like to have fun. But Amir was a deep person, and I was, too."

They married in Tehran that fall, the wedding a large, fairly rau-
cous affair. Later, Ardebili's parents threw a party for them in Shiraz.
Having a second party was slightly unusual, but it gave the Ardebili
family, still wounded by the loss of Amir's older brother, something
to celebrate. While the couple searched for a home of their own,
they moved into Ardebili's parents' house.

Both dove back into their work, Negin studying for the Shiraz
University entrance exams, and Ardebili buying American goods
for the government-controlled Iranian companies. The newlyweds
shared the worldview of many Iranians their age: they embraced
American culture, especially television shows like *Friends*, *Lost*, and
Prison Break, programs that could be downloaded online or bought
from counterfeit DVD street vendors. But they detested U.S. politics, espousing the widely held belief that the U.S. government
was prone to violent nationalism. America started too many wars,
they agreed, supplied too many dictators, and fueled its own economy with a massive military-industrial complex. What right did
the United States have trying to stop Iran from protecting itself
by building an atomic bomb? What hypocrisy. America is the only
nation in world history to unleash such a bomb. Tens of thousands
of civilians died in a flash in Nagasaki and Hiroshima. "When I see
the U.S. flag, I don't think of freedom," Negin said. "I think of war."

Negin didn't ask many questions about her husband's business.
But she knew enough to appreciate the irony: her man earned a living keeping the enemy at bay with its own weapons.

CHAPTER 8
A Warning

At Customs House, prosecutor Dave Hall looked his British informant in the eye. "How do I know you're not lying? How do I know you're not still in the business?"

Clyde Pensworth, visiting from London six weeks after the Dubai Airshow, grinned and gave a curt answer. "If I was, I could make more money than I am working for you."

Hall didn't laugh at the quip. His stomach churned. Pensworth hadn't answered the question directly, and Hall got the distinct sense that if he repeated the question, he'd get another evasive answer, or an out-and-out lie. As part of his arrangement with the Americans, the British arms dealer had pledged that he was retired and would not broker illegal arms deals while working as an HSI informant. His contract with the U.S. government specifically barred him from participating "in any unlawful activities without . . . express prior approval." Hall wanted to believe that his ace informant was living up to his side of the bargain. He was proving to be enormously valuable, first to Lechleitner in Dubai and now, as an advisor/teacher to agents in Philadelphia. But a new, vague query from MI5, Britain's internal security service, had troubled Hall.

"How do you know he's not just using you?" the MI5 official had asked Hall. "How do you know he's not still selling arms on the side?"

Hall didn't like the question. It made a strong insinuation—that Pensworth might be playing the Americans—without offering any facts to back it up. "I'm being told he's out of the business," Hall replied. "Do you know otherwise? All I need is for you to prove to me that he's back in business. If he's committing crimes, we'll help you catch him."

The MI5 man said simply that Pensworth was "under suspicion," further irritating Hall. Okay, fine, Hall replied. But is this just loose cop talk or raw intelligence? Do you have actual evidence? Specifics? Do you plan to arrest him? If so, we will back off.

Well, the MI5 official said, just be careful. Don't trust him.

No shit, Hall thought. Thanks for the great insight. Of course they couldn't trust him.

Pensworth was a professional salesman, a world-class bullshitter, a seasoned criminal, a loose cannon, potentially reckless and mercenary enough to brag to friends or prospective clients on the telephone about his "special relationship" with the American government. A Pensworth blunder could trigger a scandal, the kind that ruined careers. Worse, it might get someone killed.

The key to using Pensworth was to carefully mine him for resources, introductions, and ideas, borrow his reputation without getting sucked into his black hole of deceit and illegality. In the Americans' view, making introductions and training agents probably didn't rise to the level of violating British law. Then again, what Pensworth considered a mere introduction, the British might consider criminal.

Pensworth floated two such potential "introductions" to the HSI agents in early 2006. The first involved a Russian broker who planned to sell 100,000 Kalashnikov 47 rifles, better known as AK-47s, to the Libyan regime of Colonel Muammar Gaddafi. It was a $9.5 million deal. What if, Pensworth suggested, Cross International became involved?

The informant offered to swing it so that the HSI undercover company would help facilitate the delivery of the weapons from Russia to Libya. He argued that it presented a perfect opportunity for Cross International to establish credentials in the gray arms market—working on such a project was sure to open doors, leading agents to other illicit procurement cells. Sure, Pensworth said, we're talking about an astounding number of weapons. But the AK-47s are going to be shipped to Tripoli anyway—with or without HSI's participation. The weapons and money will never touch American or British shores, he argued. Why not exploit the opportunity?

The second Pensworth proposal involved sending military helicopters from Belgrade to Tripoli. Cross International would facilitate the sale of three used CH-47 Chinook cargo helicopters. The workhorse choppers, which debuted during the Vietnam War and continued to ferry U.S. troops and heavy gear in Iraq and Afghanistan, sold for as much as $32 million each. The CH-47s Pensworth hoped to broker were manufactured under license for Boeing in Italy and needed a lot of repair.

"My proposal," Pensworth told the Americans in an email, "is that we send the accepted orders to Cross International with all the sellers' details. Cross then can arrange for the [delivery] direct to Libya. This opens the way for Cross to know all the supply sources and the buyer sources which will add to your valuable knowledge base to use as future needs dictate. Of course, you will add a percentage to the costs to cover our costs."

The HSI agents knew they probably wouldn't move forward with either Libyan deal; indeed, they never did. And yet, as audacious and politically fraught as the proposals appeared, the agents didn't instantly discard them. They were trying to learn to think and act like smugglers, not law enforcement agents. They were trying to think creatively and find new ways to catch deadly arms traffickers. They knew they couldn't get there if they rejected each of Pensworth's proposals out of hand simply because they couldn't immediately envision a way to do it, or because the risk of a career-ending scandal was too great.

The Philly agents liked to bat around wild ideas in this manner, taking leads from foreign queries and seeing where they went. But given so many variables and obstacles, most prospective deals never got past the discussion stage.

At present, the most likely deals in the works involved the Pakistani broker Lechleitner had met in Dubai, Yasmin Ahmed, and her husband, Yusuf Khan. The Pakistanis were closing in on a deal with Cross International for cold-weather clothing and, separately, military-grade satellite fuses. Each set of extreme-weather gear—GORE-TEX boots, pants, parkas, and gloves, as well as thermal underwear, masks, gun holsters, ballistic goggles, and a hydration system—sold for $1,450. The gear was relatively easy to acquire and did not cause much concern for the U.S. agents. The satellite fuses were a different matter. Originally designed for use by NASA, the fuses were on the U.S. Munitions List and thus required a special license, impossible for Ahmed, a convicted felon, to acquire. Ahmed and Khan wanted to purchase 250 fuses for $40,000, and, once the initial deal was completed, another 1,000 for $160,000. Khan suggested that Cross International buy the fuses inside the United States under the guise that they were for domestic use, then ship them to Khan's office in Singapore. Lechleitner and his partner sent Ahmed and Khan the extreme-weather clothing samples—that was an easy call. The fuses were more sensitive, but the agents believed that Ahmed and Khan presented a window into a large, multinational arms procurement organization. In addition to satellite fuses, the Pakistanis were talking about buying a FLIR system, grenade launchers, attack helicopters, and refueling aircraft, purchases worth tens of millions of dollars. To whet the Pakistanis' appetite and gain their confidence, Lechleitner argued, the agents should send them a small shipment of sensitive satellite fuses. He understood that he would face resistance from other government agencies. The plan would require approval from HSI HQ, State, Justice, the Pentagon, and possibly NASA. But wasn't it at least worth considering? Lechleitner's bosses agreed to think about it.

As he pursued the Pakistanis, Lechleitner's list of other targets continued to contract and expand. Promising suspects vanished, often without reason, new brokers emerged, and old ones, thought long lost, reappeared. Alex Dave presented a prime example: when he'd failed to show in Dubai, Lechleitner had written him off; the Iranian broker never seemed to buy anything. But over the months that followed, Lechleitner slowly came to realize that he'd been wrong to dismiss him. The first clue had come when HSI colleagues in Boston had notified Lechleitner that Alex Dave had wired a $7,000 deposit to an undercover Massachusetts company to purchase gyroscopes. Intrigued, Lechleitner checked a larger confidential federal database called TECS, a collection of U.S. law enforcement notes from more than one billion records of people and companies suspected of criminal activity and designed to help connect what might appear to be otherwise random acts. The TECS search pulled up two more hits for Alex Dave. It turned out that he was also routinely negotiating with undercover HSI companies in San Diego and Chicago. That meant the Iranian was soliciting from *four* undercover HSI companies, repeatedly and simultaneously. The agents knew of no one else so prolific. It stood to reason, then, that he was querying an above-average number of real U.S. companies. Perhaps Alex Dave was more significant than he realized, Lechleitner thought. He put the Iranian back on his target list.

. . .

It was about this time that American troops in Iraq came across an unexploded IED with a remote control trigger. Following protocol, the troops delivered the device to Army technicians. These technicians autopsied enemy weapons the way coroners examined dead bodies. Dissecting this IED, they discovered a remote control device with a brand and lot number that could be traced to a manufacturer in California. This was hardly the first time the technicians had traced components found inside IEDs to an American factory. The trend stretched back at least as far as February 2004, the month

Lieutenant Seth Dvorin was killed by a remote control IED. One particular timing device—part number PIC16F84A—kept showing up inside unexploded IEDs in Iraq and Afghanistan. The $3 part discovered in Iraq included not only a product number, but serial and lot numbers, clues that could be used to trace its origin and path from the United States to the battlefield.

To re-create the trail, the military technicians forwarded their findings to federal agents at two tiny domestic law enforcement agencies, the Pentagon's Defense Criminal Investigative Service (DCIS) and the Commerce Department's Bureau of Industry and Security (BIS), which enforces dual-use export laws. DCIS and BIS agents began trying to reconstruct the overseas sales. Armed with search warrants, the agents followed an email trail that ultimately led them from a Phoenix manufacturer to a mom-and-pop distributor near Atlanta. A review of the distributor's records revealed the names of several Dubai customers. The agents obtained more search warrants, this time for the Dubai companies' email records, and spent months poring through them. This email trail led to the names of still more Iranian companies and email attachments containing orders and records of shipments from American distributors to Dubai and, ultimately, to Tehran. In 2004 alone, the agents found, the Iranian network had smuggled more than 23,000 American-made components. This included five thousand of the PIC16F84A microchips.

The Treasury Department issued sanctions against the foreign companies, but these were difficult to enforce without the cooperation of the Emirati or Iranian governments. And despite the good detective work, federal investigators in Florida could not very well arrest brokers living in Dubai or Iran without creating a sting. Although prosecutors ultimately indicted sixteen people and corporations in the case, and the case triggered leads against another seventy-five individuals, only one person, a low-level broker in England, was ever arrested. He was sentenced to one year's probation.

. . .

The Florida-based IED case was the kind of investigation that drove Malandra and Hall nuts. What was the point of indicting people and companies you couldn't arrest? The Iranian and Pakistani smugglers simply changed their names and resumed business. Malandra and Hall wanted to do more, make an arrest that would strike at the heart of the Iranian procurement network. By early 2006, nearly two years into their venture, Malandra and Hall believed they were making progress: Washington had granted formal approval to expand the scope of their project. Undercover bank accounts were set up in Delaware and overseas. Lechleitner, Michael Ronayne, and the other HSI agents, buoyed by the trip to Dubai and Pensworth's black-market-buyer-training seminars in Philadelphia, were feeling more confident in their undercover roles and had assembled a healthy list of prospective targets. Malandra had even moved the offices of Cross International from sleepy, suburban Yardley to downtown Philadelphia, making for a more convenient and efficient base of operation.

In the spring of 2006, the final, critical piece of deception—an overseas undercover platform—materialized. A senior HSI agent stationed in Frankfurt, Germany, offered use of a front company he was creating in Eastern Europe.* The Frankfurt agent was building the undercover storefront for another purpose, to try to snare a network of Kuwaiti and Saudi businessmen reselling stolen U.S. Army Humvees with ballistic glass, vehicles in short supply that were supposed to be protecting American troops from insurgent attacks. But the Frankfurt agent's fake business would suit any kind of international black market transactions. It carried the same kind of carefully manufactured legend as Cross International—backdated records, a physical office, the works. Malandra knew instantly that it was exactly the kind of overseas presence they had been looking for, an indigenous-looking European business with no apparent ties to the

---

* The location is intentionally vague.

United States. It was a stroke of luck, really. As a bonus, the veteran
undercover American agent in Frankfurt was already well positioned
and eager to help. He spoke Russian and enjoyed good relations
with national security services in two former Soviet republics—the
undisclosed country where he had positioned the undercover store
and Georgia, an unusually strong U.S. ally in the region. The American agent in Frankfurt was legacy Customs, a thirty-year government veteran who struck Lechleitner and Malandra as smart and
motivated, though also persnickety about his undercover persona.
When the agent spoke about the undercover craft, he used terms like
"magic" and "alternate reality," stuff you wouldn't find in training
manuals. A little intense? Perhaps. Everyone knew the best undercover agents were a little odd.

   This one called himself Darius.

CHAPTER 9

Propositions

SHIRAZ, IRAN

In early May 2006, Amir Ardebili opened an email from Clyde Pensworth. He knew Pensworth only through email and by reputation—British arms dealer, longtime friend of Tehran. In his message, Pensworth mentioned a Russian broker based in a former Soviet republic. The broker's name is Darius, Pensworth explained, and he has extensive contacts *inside* the United States through a company called Cross International. Darius uses this American partner to smuggle black market military gear throughout Europe and the Middle East, Pensworth said. Check out his website. He moves heavy gear, even Humvees.

Ardebili took a look. On May 11, 2006, he sent an email to Darius: My name is Alex Dave. A mutual friend referred me. Attached is an RFQ for American aircraft parts. Can you help?

Well, Darius replied, as you must know, it's impossible to ship directly from the United States to Iran. And in any case, you would need end user certificates. Impossible.

Maybe not so impossible, Ardebili wrote back. What if you shipped the stuff from the U.S.A. to a former Soviet republic where you have contacts? Then reship it to Iran. "Working via your company is very perfect way which long time we are looking for such a chance."

Darius replied quickly. "What you say can perhaps be good business, but I stress to you what we are doing is ILLEGAL in US. Question: Would original source of goods know they go on to Iran, or would original source believe all goods remain in Country X? With more discussion it is possible we do good business, but patience and good planning will keep us out of jail!"

Not to worry, Ardebili replied. "This is long time we are in the business and working in full security. Never know end-user are located in Iran. You should be capable to introduce us and get the parts, then change description and ship it to us."

Summer passed with no response from Darius, and Ardebili kept busy pursuing other deals. He also checked on a few wayward shipments, including one from the Massachusetts company for gyroscopes. It had been eight months since he'd wired a $7,000 deposit to the Boston company, directing his contact there, a man named Tom, to ship them to an address in Dubai. But instead of gyros, Tom sent excuses. The first attempted shipment, Tom told Ardebili, had been returned by Customs because of faulty paperwork. Ardebili had no way of knowing if Tom was trying to rip him off, and he had little recourse.

. . .

In early fall 2006, Ardebili reached out again to Darius, sending an RFQ for six electrical components. Darius emailed back a few days later, and when he did, he threw out a different kind of proposition. He explained that he sold American military gear obtained from black market sources in Iraq, Kuwait, and Saudi Arabia. The market for used or stolen Humvees and their ballistic windshields is high, he said.

"What I need to have is 'man on the ground' in Kuwait," Darius wrote. "It is not necessary that I have man that live there, but my representative must at least visit Kuwait City to walk into warehouse of my vendor. I need man who will look at merchandise and make on-scene determination that it is—or is not—what I need to buy. This job will actually be very easy. It is just a matter of having man with time/availability of being in Kuwait from time to time. Do you know any such man that can do such service for me?"

Ardebili had never been to Kuwait, but how hard could the work be? He'd recently obtained a passport in anticipation of a trip to Canada, where he planned to meet the sonar manufacturer, the one who'd sold him a $1 million system, looking to expand their relationship. But when he'd asked the Canadian embassy in Tehran for a visa, his application had been rejected by a form letter that stated in part, "You have not satisfied that you would leave Canada at the end of the temporary period if you were authorized to stay." The letter cited his lack of previous foreign travel. Ardebili figured a few trips to Kuwait for Darius would change that.

"I could do this job," Ardebili wrote to Darius. "Distance from Iran to Kuwait is 30 minutes by flying. But you should accept all costs of the trip and clarify what is the goods and merchandise."

The mysterious Darius did not write again for several weeks, and Ardebili found this frustrating, though not necessarily unusual. Darius's next email was long and somewhat rambling, and appeared to have been written from Georgia, the former Soviet state bordering Iran's neighbors, Azerbaijan and Armenia.

"I apologize for time that we have not communicated," Darius wrote. "Please understand that Georgia is very close to shooting war with Russia. There are already Russian soldiers and tanks in Georgia. Sometimes I am in danger of being shot for what I do. My business is not always convenient with regard to time. When my customer in Georgia tells me to wait because of various emergency conditions, I wait. Also, sometimes I am in a place where it is not safe for me to communicate. I should not have to say more than that for you to understand."

Darius promised to call soon, and Ardebili passed along his cell phone number.

A few minutes before noon on November 13, 2006, Ardebili's mobile buzzed.

"Hello," the caller said. "My name is Darius." The man spoke English with an East European accent, perhaps Russian.

"Hello, how are you, sir?"

"Yes, we finally talk."

Ardebili said, "I would like to know more information about your business."

"Well," Darius said, "my business is a trading company. We are just making deals as we can. Right now, I have a good client who is living in Georgia, and I tell you the truth, eighty percent of my business is him because he is paying the bills. This client has a need right now for American-manufactured military equipment, but obviously it is difficult for me to go to American suppliers because they have license requirements. I had a supplier in Europe who worked for the American government. This special friend is retired but was selling out of the side door. You understand?"

"Yes, of course."

"I have identified a man in Kuwait but he says I must travel there and I am saying maybe you, as speaking the Arabic language and living in that part of the world I'm thinking it's good that you could work as my representative, if that is what you are happy to do. I understand that you have made many deals with military equipment, yes?"

"Yes, I have done business with the military customers in Iran," Ardebili said. To begin, he asked Darius to send him a résumé on letterhead, and an East European address where American goods could be shipped. Such documents, he said, would help him convince the Iranian officials who placed the orders that Darius was a legitimate black market broker, loosening the purse strings. Ardebili did not add the obvious—that the documents would also help him determine if Darius could be trusted.

Darius promised to send something soon.

The Russian followed up a short while later, though he did not attach company letterhead or a résumé. Instead, Darius asked for more time. "My business, like yours, is against wishes and laws of the U.S. government, but U.S. government will never know about me because I am not buying from within U.S. If I can find U.S. property that is already outside U.S., law enforcers of U.S. will never find me. What you are proposing is more dangerous, as it would have property leaving U.S. with papers that identify where and who it is that is buying. Please be patient with me, as I am not ready today to commit to such a scheme with you. You yourself have say on the phone that this risky business. We must meet face-to-face eventually."

Face-to-face? Ardebili read on.

Darius threw out a tantalizing possibility. "I have relationship with cousin in U.S. who handles my banking. I am using Delaware U.S. company and bank for handle my monies. This is actually very common"—for tax and security reasons, he explained. He added that he used Georgia as a transshipment point because the former Soviet republic was not yet a member of the European Union, and therefore independent and generally unconnected to European police agencies. "I must still be careful. This is why my operation that I already do is so good. U.S.-manufactured military equipment, especially vehicles, ballistic armor, communications equip and light weapons, are all good. I ship direct to Georgia. If you are serious about this, I send you more info."

Ardebili considered this. He remained unconvinced that Humvee smuggling made much sense. The heavy vehicles would be expensive to ship and difficult to hide, and most important, were not in demand by his primary customer, the Iranian military. On the other hand, Ardebili was intrigued by the Georgian connection and Darius's relationship with the American broker. These were possibilities to be exploited.

Ardebili composed a short reply. To keep Darius's interest, he asked for more information about the Humvees. Ardebili also attached a new request for American-made gyroscopes and infrared cameras. "You are kindly requested to provide us your shortest delivery time and your quotation for following items urgently."

CHAPTER 10

The Magician

Darius lived on the twelfth floor of an apartment that overlooked Eschenheimer Turm, a medieval castle planted in the navel of modern Frankfurt. Seven hundred years old, the watchtower still stood sentry over the city center. At night, with Eschenheimer Turm lit in hues of gold and blue, Darius found the view magical.

Late one evening in early 2007, the undercover U.S. agent stretched his six-foot-five frame across a La-Z-Boy recliner in the apartment. He balanced a computer keyboard on his knees, slipped on reading glasses, and viewed the latest message from the Iranian Alex Dave. It contained a counteroffer for gyroscopes and infrared cameras. Rather than consider the new price point, Darius focused instead on the tone of the email. It pleased him. The Iranian appeared convinced that Darius was an East European arms broker. Alex Dave seemed to believe that Darius could offer special access to embargoed, American-made military products through his contact at Cross International in Pennsylvania. The illusion was on.

Darius was the name the U.S. agent used when working undercover. He picked it because it sounded vaguely East European and because he spoke Russian. A native of the American East Coast, Darius had spent much of his career in California before arriving in Germany. Politically, he was conservative, but held contempt for so many officials running The G that it would be a mistake to consider him a Republican. He was divorced; work consumed him anyway. His work ethic irritated less productive or inspired colleagues and his fortitude irritated pedestrian managers who considered him a pain in the ass. Darius liked to throw out one-liners about his frustration with the mediocrity within U.S. government: "There are too many small men in big chairs with very small agendas." "When ignorance becomes an excuse, stupid becomes a virtue."

Darius had spent thirty-five years working for the government. He was fifty-three now, and his posting at the Frankfurt consulate would be his last. He planned to retire within the year.

Like Hall and Malandra, Darius grew up in the mid-1950s. In high school, his height helped him star on the basketball team. But he was more interested in submarines and studied World War I and World War II sub commanders the way his teammates followed NBA players. In 1972, as the Vietnam War raged, Darius sought and won an enlistment at the Naval Academy, eager to become a submariner. But he failed the Navy eye exam and instead entered the Coast Guard Academy. He graduated in 1976 and was assigned to a big white boat in the Bering Sea. His crew spent a lot of time boarding Russian and Japanese fishing trawlers near the Alaska coast, enforcing fishing quotas. To augment the assignment, the Coast Guard sent him to school to learn Russian. He loved learning as much about the culture as the language; it offered invaluable insight into America's Cold War enemy. Following a two-year tour, he became a Coast Guard intelligence analyst, a job that eventually included law enforcement work. In 1979, Darius went undercover for the first time, busting a sailor for selling hashish. He enjoyed solving the riddles that police work presented and liked going undercover.

After a few years, he transferred to the Naval Criminal Investigative Service and became a full-time investigator. He made all kinds of cases for NCIS, from child porn to assault to forgery. In a major espionage case, he posed undercover as a drug cartel pilot seeking classified information about DEA and Coast Guard interdiction tactics. Darius did well, but he found the NCIS job generally buttoned-down and rote, hardly as glamorous or exciting as portrayed a decade later on the hit television show with the same name.

Friends suggested he consider the U.S. Customs Service. Good people are headed there, they said. Their cases are interesting and challenging. It's your kind of place, the friends said—unstructured, and freewheeling. Creativity is encouraged. Other agencies didn't suit him. The FBI was viciously well organized and formulaic, the IBM of law enforcement; the DEA had too many ex-Marines, chest-thumpers who liked to kick down doors.

Darius took a $27,000 pay cut to join Customs in 1991, but the agency gave him the freedom to do his job. "Customs was chaos bordering on anarchy. And that was perfect for me because the absolute lack of organization is ideal for initiative work." Darius spent the bulk of the next fifteen years in Southern California, mostly on drug cases. He developed expertise as an undercover agent, something he found matched his childhood obsession with submarines. Like submariners, undercover agents were often eccentric. They spent most of their time in another world, silently stalking prey. "The target never sees you coming, and the battle is over before the target knows it's begun." Darius enjoyed the gamesmanship, creating illusions and unraveling mysteries to catch bad guys. "Why wouldn't everybody want to do something that is interesting every day?"

Darius didn't drink or smoke anymore, but he found that performing undercover offered a similar heightened state of awareness, his body slowing, senses expanding. "You could say I got a warm buzz," he recalled.

Many undercover agents approach their work as actors might, studying roles and scripts. But to Darius, actors merely played parts on stage or in movies, scenes in which audiences willingly agreed to temporarily suspend disbelief. When he worked undercover, Darius considered himself a magician, an illusionist. Magicians created an alternate version of reality, one that played tricks on the mind. Working undercover, Darius had seen otherwise bright, sensible people become so bamboozled by a sting—so convinced they were participating in something that did not in fact exist—that their brains would create false memories. "Working undercover is a very cruel thing," Darius cautioned young agents. "You're raping someone's concept of reality."

While undercover work fulfilled Darius, it also brought stress and loneliness. Inevitably, many undercover agents become loners, misunderstood by colleagues. Tensions with supervisors are common. A supervisor can't feel the 24/7 pressure that an undercover agent does. A supervisor hasn't made the emotional investment—the personal, human connection—that an undercover makes with his target. An undercover agent sets out to make friends, knowing he intends to betray them.

"The undercover agent quickly realizes that everybody who likes him and trusts him is going to be destroyed, and everybody who hates him—management—is going to benefit by what he does, and worse, take credit because he can't go public," Darius recalled. "The undercover agent helps people who hate him and he destroys people who love him. What's he's doing is actually very, very hard, maintaining this alter ego. It's a Jekyll and Hyde experience. The personal life of an undercover dissolves and the facade becomes real."

Darius was a large, hardy man. But he pushed himself as an undercover agent and in the mid-1990s his body started to rebel. He was hit with spastic colon attacks and began vomiting in the moments before particularly stressful undercover meetings. At one point, while posing as a drug dealer, his hands began shaking so much he struggled to sip coffee. "Almost every day, something caused tension to the point where I could feel my heart beating." His supervisors seemed indifferent, a world away. The low point for Darius came as his mother lay dying in the hospital, an oxygen mask on her face. He received a page from the office, and assumed it was someone checking in to see how his mother was faring. Instead, it was someone from Human Resources calling with a question about one of his expense reports, a discrepancy that amounted to no more than a few dollars. It was the only call he would receive from Customs while his mother suffered. Not one coworker or supervisor reached out. A short while after the funeral, Darius recalled, he returned to the office, and a supervisor approached him. "Hey look, Bambi's back!" the supervisor said. Confused, Darius said, "Bambi?" And the guy said, "Yeah, Bambi—your mother's dead! Get it?" It was at once the stupidest and cruelest thing Darius had ever heard.

"He worked for the government for a long, long time, and as a consequence he became a lot smarter than most of his bosses," recalled a colleague. "He had to work for people who don't get it, and he had to carry more than his fair share; and his reward, quite often, was to get kicked in the teeth. It takes its toll. That's why you see inconsistent sides of him—frustrated with the government, but trying to stay disciplined and patient to do the counter-proliferation cases. It drove him nuts."

Darius tolerated pedestrian supervisors for another decade, but in early 2007, just as the email exchanges with Alex Dave began to pick up, he got a break. HSI headquarters sent Ronald Grimes, a sharp and worldly supervisor, to the Frankfurt consulate. Grimes carried a runner's lithe frame and an optimist's love of big cases. Here, finally, was a supervisor with an eye for challenging, significant investigations, not one looking to inflate his stats with easy cases. Grimes brought experience with complex international undercover investigations. He understood that they required uninterrupted focus, commitment, support, and a spot of luck. Grimes also understood the politics of working overseas inside the embassies—you were part of Team America: the CIA or State Department had to sign off on any foreign HSI operations, and, with the stroke of a pen, could quietly kill an investigation or arrest warrant for reasons of national security or diplomatic relations.

The small HSI shop Grimes inherited at the Frankfurt consulate had responsibility for twenty-three U.S. consulates scattered across Eastern Europe. The FBI boasted agents in most embassies and consulates, but HSI did not. Darius, Grimes, and their Frankfurt colleagues rode the circuit, traveling embassy to embassy, nation to nation, coordinating cases with colleagues based back in the United States. The Frankfurt agents got involved in a little bit of everything: drug and currency smuggling, human trafficking, arms trading, child pornography. Sadly, the child porn cases flowed in a torrent—the sheer number of file exchanges and websites was staggering, but so were the cyber-sleuthing capabilities of the American and German governments. Grimes instructed Darius to begin training a new agent to take his child porn cases. Knowing Darius planned to retire at summer's end, Grimes wanted him to spend as much time on the Alex Dave case as possible. "I immediately saw that this should be a priority, and that the only way to make a case like this was to keep the distractions away," Grimes recalled. "It was a special opportunity. You need ten cases in progress at one time to even get one like this to this point. These are quasi-business transactions and they can fail for any number of reasons. The chance of them going through is slim to begin with."

.   .   .

Although Darius had not known Malandra and Hall before they began investigating Alex Dave together, he shared their view that the best way to catch an arms dealer was to set up a foreign-based under-cover storefront. If properly created, the foreign storefront could be used to snare different kinds of criminals from different countries. The same business could be used again and again, recycled over and over for years, as part of any number of cases. Thus, months before he had even met Malandra, Darius had begun scouting for a pro-spective East European base for his undercover storefront.

In some nations, personal relationships are essential; local cops will help American cops once they get to know them. In other coun-tries, charms and diplomacy mean little; local cops will help only if their bureaucracies and laws permit it. Darius targeted a nation where personal relationships are paramount and, because he knew

Russian, a place where the language is common. (The precise location remains confidential.)

In any police agency, there's always a go-to guy, a worker bee undercover detective. Darius found his counterpart in this East European country, a mid-level detective in a national police force, and stalked him. The man carried the reputation as one of his nation's top detectives and, like Darius, appeared curious about other cultures. Leveraging his role as regional HSI attaché, Darius found ways to show up wherever he knew the detective would be. The third time Darius bumped into the man, he proposed setting up the joint undercover storefront. It was not a tough sell. "He was about what I was about—putting bad guys in cages," Darius recalled. The local police were astonishingly good at street-level undercover work, better, Darius thought, than the Americans, especially in terms of intrigue. They created deep, deep background and cover stories—the so-called legend an agent develops for his undercover persona. In this East European country, where organized crime was rampant, undercover cops built legends that stretched back to their teenage years. The two men bonded, in part, because they realized they could learn a great deal from one another. They sketched out their plan in a pub, agreeing to open a small local brokerage, one that specialized in American military and electronic equipment. Together, they set up an office in a busy downtown building, complete with backdated paperwork, website, and all the accouterments of an undercover site. The two agents also contacted their respective prosecutors and diplomats to hammer out the formal legal paperwork, including required permissions, frameworks, and rules to use any evidence gathered overseas in an American courtroom. Darius gave the storefront the nondescript code name UCSV.

In its first few months, the storefront garnered a few nibbles, and Darius traced some stolen American Humvees from Saudi Arabia to a German broker near Frankfurt, enough evidence, the HSI agent believed, to warrant undercover visits to Oman, Saudi Arabia, and Kuwait. "These Humvees were walking out the door at a time when there was a shortage of transport vehicles with ballistic glass," Darius recalled. "This was a matter of life and death to the troops in the field." But U.S. diplomats scuttled his plan, denying Darius permission to travel to the Middle East. No one told him why, but he speculated that one of the car dealer targets had a connection to a royal family. Darius began looking for an alternative approach, and it was a short time later that the Philadelphia agents approached him about Alex Dave.

The Philly agents hoped to lure Alex Dave from Iran, complete a sale for military material, arrest him, and bring him back to the United States. Yet now, after many months emailing Alex Dave, Darius was beginning to wonder if he hadn't been wasting his time. The HSI agent understood that the Iranians did not necessarily bargain in a linear fashion, the way Americans did, but that didn't make the asymmetrical negotiations with Alex Dave any less frustrating. Alex Dave would send a request, Darius would negotiate and ultimately agree to fulfill the request, and then Alex Dave would try to change the terms, price, or quantity. One moment, the Iranian would laugh off Darius's concerns about illegality, the next he would express worry. Darius couldn't tell if Alex Dave was changing positions as a negotiation tactic or because he suspected he was being set up.

In his Frankfurt apartment that evening in early 2007, Darius reread Alex Dave's latest email message: "As you know, purchase the military products for Iran is too risky work. We don't like to take in problems. We try to meet you in Iran to understand the situation in Iran."

Darius wasn't going to Iran. And, he figured, by this point a real arms dealer would have run out of patience with this punk. Enough dicking around, he thought. Time to push Alex Dave, hard. Darius typed a reply, writing as a Russian expressing himself in broken

English: "I do not understand. You do want to buy products for Iran, or do not want to buy products for Iran? You say the business is 'too risky.' If that is true, do not do it. Then you say you want me to come to Iran to learn the 'situation.' Whatever is this 'situation,' it is of not interest to me. If customer in Iran can pay money—not promises—I will sell to him. If customer cannot pay money, we have nothing to say to each other. I explain you why I am not coming to Iran. I had associate here in Europe who went to Near East Islam country to make business, and he never came back. If he is in jail or someone cut off his head I do not know, but I do not want to be the next story that people are telling. Iran is target of Bush and Israel and news is showing pictures of radicals. I do not need this." Darius reread his message, and sent it.

Alex Dave responded swiftly, again asymmetrically. "Thank you, I would be happy to be your co-operator and have friendly business for long time. I have ten years experience on working in Iranian defense organization . . . so I have a lot of information about them and their requirement." He urged Darius to be patient. Importing to Iran was not a problem, he wrote. "Here I can guarantee 100% security bringing equipment and people in and out of country! I then send units to Iran Air." As a sign of good faith, Alex Dave suggested, perhaps Darius could send a few "free samples" of the gyroscopes to show his customer, the Iranian military.

Nice try, Darius thought. He replied, "There is risk that your customer will take this one gyro, and then reverse-engineer the technology. This is not the worth the time and risk that my side takes. I want to build long-term relationship but I am not crazy. What kind of business is this?"

A few days later, Darius received another email from Alex Dave. This one contained a new request. It began, "This is urgent inquiry." Darius laughed. Yeah, aren't they all? "You are kindly requested to quote for us following urgently: MAPCGM0003 903218B, Phase Shifter, S-Bank, 6 Bit 2.3-4.1 Ghz, 1500, M/A-COM Inc." Darius looked it up and learned that a phase shifter was some sort of radar enhancer deployed for air defense.

Alex Dave followed up two days later, again urging Darius to move swiftly because his customer—the Iranian military—was negotiating with others for the phase shifters. "Our customer have receive offer from three company. One of them is us. Customer have very bad experience in purchase of parts and lots of companies did not have success deliver the parts, so they decided to ask three mentioned company to deliver the parts. Also, we will provide 12 percent prepayment in this matter. So please send me the official proforma invoice in your letterhead urgently."

Darius contacted Lechleitner in Pennsylvania for assistance, and by late April 2007, they had a proposal for 1,400 phase shifters ready for Alex Dave, this one written in Lechleitner's American business-man voice on behalf of Cross. "Total price $88,837. . . . Manufacture of said units shall begin within two weeks following down payment/cash deposit equal to 12% of total price. . . . Shipment of all 1,400 units is guaranteed within four months. The price quoted herein represents a total profit margin of 7.5%, and is offered in good faith for the purpose of establishing positive relationship with you and your customer."

Alex Dave quickly accepted the offer. Darius explained that his cousin in the United States, Patrick Lynch of Cross International, would be placing the order with the American manufacturer. He instructed Alex Dave to wire the money to Cross International in Wilmington, Delaware, USA. He forwarded the routing numbers. The Iranian promised to send the deposit immediately.

A week passed. And then another. No deposit. Three more weeks went by. Nothing. Darius decided to call Alex Dave.

The connection, from mobile phone to mobile phone, from Germany to Iran, was poor. Darius got right to the point: What's up with the deposit?

Alex Dave ducked the question. "Maybe you send me a correspondence in email."

"I'm not in the office right now," Darius said curtly. "Look, it's very simple. Are we going to have a deal?"

"Happy to hear your voice," Alex Dave said. "It's a bad connection."

"It's a very simple question: Are you going to send me money?"

"Yes, yes I tried two weeks ago but I was told the bank has returned the money. So I will send again today. Try to email me later."

"Yeah, but I sent you an email. I need money up front."

"You can provide with me with the bank number. We have a problem transferring money."

Darius didn't believe him and he didn't try to hide his contempt. "It should be easy. Don't you have a bank in Dubai?"

"Yes. It's more simple to transfer from Dubai."

"However you want to do it, I don't care but four weeks ago I tell you to send the money to the Delaware bank. It's easy to do. Why are you making this hard?"

"Darius, I look forward to future deals. I will transfer the money tomorrow. And I am waiting for your email."

Darius hung up and pounded out another email. He re-sent the routing numbers for the undercover Delaware bank account, as well as the phone and fax numbers for a branch office in Wilmington. "The only thing remaining is to make one deal happen, and we shall be on the road to success. Please notify me when you are sending the deposit."

Alex Dave replied three days later. "We could not do payment. We just can open the letter of credit. Please understand. Awaiting your confirmation."

Darius exploded. "I will admit it is temptation to deal with you because I very much am interested to have window in the Near East. But I must also think on how wishing something does not make it true. You have reversed your word on simple matter. In this business, a man's word must worth a million dollars. You are telling me now your word is not worth 10,000. I must ask. Can you even do a deal? Are you a businessman or are you driving a taxicab in Tehran? Are you capable of sending any money at all to my cousin? I do not mean informal transfer of money in a bag at the marketplace. Can you send any money by wire?"

"I am a serious customer," Alex Dave replied. "Why you do not want to believe? I want to open new window for your business. For sonars, night vision, distance finders, radars, aviation spare parts, underwater devices, C-130 upgrade project. We are the sole company in Iran which import sonar from the United States—there is no other company which does this."

Darius shook his head in disbelief. If all of the above were true, then why was Alex Dave having so much trouble coming up with the deposit? It made no sense.

The American had no way of knowing that, as implausible as it might seem, everything the Iranian had just boasted was true. Alex Dave was averaging $1 million a year in sales.

CHAPTER 11

"A Hero with the Ministry of Defense"

WILMINGTON, DELAWARE

A few weeks later, on a May morning during his short commute, Dave Hall's cell phone buzzed. The federal prosecutor recognized the overseas number. It was Darius.

"Hey there," Hall answered, and braced for the booming response.

"All hail Dave Hall!" Darius shouted from Germany. "Death to the enemies of Dave Hall! Victory!"

Hall didn't flinch. Passionate and cocksure, Darius was a workaholic and, some might say, an acquired taste. The undercover HSI agent seemed to speak his own language, an eclectic mix of Russian, English, Viking, and Vulcan. Darius's act grated on some agents, but Hall liked him.

"My friend, what's up?"

Their wide-ranging investigation, begun with the creation of the undercover storefront in Yardley, was stretching into its third year. They had undercover storefronts set up in Pennsylvania and a former Soviet republic—and a new promise from a second former Soviet republic, Georgia, to host an undercover operation should the U.S. agents succeed in luring an arms broker from Iran, Dubai, or Pakistan. The promise from Georgia was tentative and couldn't be finalized until the U.S. agents could present the Georgian police with a specific plan and specific targets.

Unfortunately, the most promising targets, Yasmin Ahmed and

Yusuf Khan, had vanished. For months, the Pakistanis had seemed poised to purchase FLIR systems and satellite fuses. Now they refused to return emails or phone calls and the Americans didn't know why. Other cases had soured as well. Pensworth's effort to draw his old friend Azizi—the Iranian he'd met in Dubai—into a deal with Cross wasn't working out. "To be honest, we didn't have a lot to show for our efforts at that point," Hall recalled. The prosecutor wasn't sure how much more time the HSI and Justice Department supervisors would give his team.

Alex Dave was one of several targets still lingering out there, mysterious, alluring, confounding. The Iranian had agreed to buy radar shifters from Darius—the deal now stood at one thousand units for roughly $90,000. But he still hadn't wired the promised deposit.

Without a deposit, the case against him was weak. Although the U.S. courts recognized a concept known as extraterritorial jurisdiction—the United States could enforce laws related to American-made technology *anywhere in the world*—the practice was controversial. To the average U.S. juror, it might not seem fair to charge an Iranian citizen for violating a U.S. law, when all he'd done was send an email from Iran to an American undercover agent located in Germany. The case would become much stronger if the Iranian made actual contact inside the United States—if he wired cash to a U.S. bank, for example. And, if Alex Dave used a Dubai or Zurich bank to skirt the financial embargo, Hall could charge him with money laundering. By instructing Alex Dave to send the money to a bank in Wilmington, the undercover agents were positioning the case to be heard in the U.S. District Court in Delaware, where Hall regularly appeared.

On the phone, Darius told Hall that Alex Dave was still driving him crazy with the mechanics of the deposit. Initially, the Iranian had agreed to pay a $9,000 deposit, the industry-standard 10 percent. A short while later, Alex Dave backed off, claiming temporary cash flow issues, and tried to negotiate it to down $6,000. When

Darius agreed to $6,000, Alex Dave countered at $3,000. The Iranian offered shifting excuses for the changing numbers. One day, he'd argue that Darius's deposit was too high, the next day he'd insist that there'd been a glitch with the wire transfer. Darius and Hall agreed that there were three possible explanations for Alex Dave's shifting excuses: one, he didn't have the money; two, the banking embargo was fouling up the wire transfers; or three, he was doing so many deals, he couldn't keep his lies straight. They thought the last explanation the most likely.

Darius asked Hall if the amount of the deposit mattered. In other words, he asked the prosecutor, how low could the deposit be?

Hall thought out loud. Theoretically, the deposit amount was irrelevant—it was as much a crime to wire $100 as $10,000. But an absurdly low deposit carried two perils, one legal, one strategic.

Legally, Hall worried that accepting a tiny deposit might open the door to an entrapment defense. A good defense lawyer would argue that such a low price was tantamount to a gift from the agents, and that they had seduced the Iranian into doing something he wasn't predisposed to do. It was a real danger.

Strategically, the European storefront, UCSV, and its Pennsylvania counterpart, Cross International, needed to maintain credibility. They had to act like real businesses. Hall worried that if Darius agreed to a negligible deposit, the Iranian might suspect this was all some kind of scam or law enforcement sting. If that happened, Alex Dave would report his suspicions to the Iranians or post them on Internet bulletin boards filled with gossip about American brokers. One posting could blow their cover and ruin all the work they'd done to create Cross and UCSV.

Hall told Darius he would review the latest report on the case when he arrived at the office. The prosecutor promised to call back shortly and rang off.

. . .

That spring, five thousand miles to the west, preparations were under way at the Honolulu courthouse for a little publicized national security trial. The remote locale probably had something to do with the lack of national media coverage, but it was one of the most significant counter-proliferation cases in a decade. Hall and Malandra knew of the investigation but had not followed it closely. The allegations bore similarities to the case against the plasma professor in Tennessee—the accused in Hawaii wasn't charged with smuggling anything tangible. But his indictment suggested that he helped the Chinese acquire stealth technology.

Born in Bombay, India, in 1944, Noshir Gowadia arrived in the United States in the summer of 1963. He trained as an engineer and was naturalized as a U.S. citizen six years later. A few years after college graduation, he won a coveted position at Northrop, where he would remain for nearly twenty years. At Northrop, Gowadia worked on a number of classified research projects, including development of stealth technology. From 1979 until 1986, he played a major role developing the B-2 bomber's revolutionary tailpipe, which made the plane nearly impossible to track using conventional radar. In 1986, at age forty-two, Gowadia learned that he had developed a genetic blood disorder, and doctors told him that he if didn't reduce his workload he would be dead within a few years. He quit Northrop and opened a consulting business in Albuquerque, New Mexico. In essence, he became a one-man defense contractor. He kept his top-secret security clearance and began teaching a classified course at the Georgia Tech Research Institute to government employees and authorized contractors. Gowadia consulted on several sensitive projects, including research for the next generation of CIA reconnaissance aircraft. He gave protection assessments for the new F-22 stealth fighter and for Air Force One, and began consulting on nuclear weapons at Los Alamos.

Gowadia enjoyed modest success, but in the early 1990s, one of his projects did not turn out as he expected and left him embittered.

This project was for DARPA, the Pentagon's shadowy Defense Advanced Research Projects Agency, which sponsors high-risk, high-payoff research. Like most of Gowadia's projects, the DARPA contract involved stealth technology—an effort to eliminate aircraft contrails, the telltale streak from a plane's exhaust, which from the ground appears to be white smoke. Gowadia submitted his report to DARPA and was paid $45,000. DARPA took this research and decided to proceed without Gowadia. He was stunned; he'd expected to advance to the more lucrative phase of the project, one he expected was worth a $2 million contract. To ensure that the scientist could no longer participate, DARPA officials raised the classification of his study to a security level for which he was not cleared. Gowadia became incensed that he could no longer legally access his own work, writing angry letters to the secretary of the Air Force, members of Congress, and family members.

"I was one of the fathers of the U.S. Air Force Northrop B-2 Stealth Bomber and its entire propulsion system was conceived and conceptually designed by me," Gowadia wrote to a relative. "My bosses, who had very little to do with the design, got the awards and large bonuses. My reward was that the long, hard hours ruined my health for good. After 27 years, I am looking forward to leaving the defense industry. There are several classified, top-secret inventions I have given to this country for no compensation. Well, in the commercial world, you and I are both going to get back what we have deserved all along."

Gowadia turned his attention to international clients. He also opened Swiss and Lichtenstein bank accounts and created European charities, financial moves prosecutors alleged were part of a scheme to avoid taxes. In 1999, Gowadia bought property on a cliff in Maui that overlooked the ocean and, with the help of a large construction loan, began building a $1.8 million home. But he struggled to keep up with the monthly mortgage payments, and soon, prosecutors said, he crossed the line, leveraging his classified knowledge for profit. Gowadia began touting his expertise in stealth technology, specifically infrared heat suppression, to potential overseas clients. As part of this effort to market himself, he faxed information promoting his stealth abilities to the Swiss defense ministry, a European aircraft company, and an Israeli businessman—data he maintained was inaccurate marketing gibberish but that the government insisted was classified. At about the same time, Gowadia also began talking to the Chinese. He made five visits to China over the next several years, and was paid $110,000 as a consultant, including on a project to reduce the heat signature from a cruise missile's exhaust nozzle.

FBI and Air Force security agents had been monitoring Gowadia and his trips to China, though they did not act until the fall of 2005, when they arrived at his Maui home armed with a search warrant. Gowadia was outside tending his garden when the feds arrived, and he began to tremble as agents started carting off records. The agents did not arrest him immediately; instead, they engaged him in a series of extraordinary interviews that stretched for nearly a week. Foolishly, Gowadia believed he could explain himself to the agents—and without a lawyer present. Perhaps because he was an engineer and valued precision, Gowadia insisted on providing written statements. In them, he acknowledged providing classified information about stealth technology, a 1960s-era CIA reconnaissance plane and a 1970s-era cruise missile. He made frank admissions. "What I did was wrong to help People's Republic of China make a cruise missile," he wrote. "What I did was espionage and treason, because I shared military secrets." He was arrested and charged with espionage. At trial, Gowadia argued that the FBI had twisted his words. He insisted that he had given the Chinese nothing of value—he had simply made harmless adjustments to the Chinese cruise missile exhaust data and taken their money.

The jury convicted Gowadia on nearly every count. The judge sentenced the scientist, age sixty-six, to thirty-two years in federal prison. That same month, the Chinese unveiled their first stealth fighter jet.

In Wilmington, Hall reached his desk and opened the new reports from Darius. The bulk of them contained excerpts of emails between Darius and Alex Dave during April and May 2007. The exchanges followed a familiar pattern.

> Darius: "My side is taking huge risk to start this relationship. If your side cannot take a small step towards us as well, then your side is not made of substance for big deals. 12% deposit for black market deal is nothing. . . ."

> Alex Dave: "Darius, please be patient . . . I am doing my best. I should pay under the table in this project."

> Darius: "A real customer can pay this easy. An amateur cannot."

> Alex Dave: "So you want to be sure that we are amateur or real customer."

> Darius: ". . . In this business, a man's word must be worth a million dollars. I must ask, can you even do a deal?"

> Alex Dave: ". . . What will happen if I pay US $10,000 for you and then you say, sorry cannot provide, or sorry cannot ship. . . ."

> Darius: "If you think $10,000 is a big risk, then you are not the customer we need. I spend $10,000 entertaining clients."

Hall felt discouraged. He closed the file. Was this case going anywhere?

Reluctantly, Hall shifted to the most pressing item in his queue, the local corruption case against the two former New Castle County officials. Three years after indictment, the county case still dogged him and had devolved into a political and legal circus. The elderly trial judge was growing more irascible by the day. The defendants, prominent Delaware Democrats, had seized upon recent allegations in Washington that the Bush Justice Department had fired eight U.S. attorneys nationwide for failing to aggressively prosecute cases against Democrats in their districts. Democrats in Delaware tried to tie the local corruption case to this political conspiracy. Hall's boss, U.S. Attorney Colm Connolly, categorically denied it, but it was tough to prove a negative. The sideshow only increased the pressure on Hall to succeed.

The corruption trial was scheduled to begin the following month and last six weeks. With dozens of witnesses, the small-town saga threatened to consume Hall's summer, forcing him to put Alex Dave aside. Already, Hall was working nights and weekends with Connolly, prepping witnesses and drafting final motions.

And then, suddenly, a week before trial, the judge eviscerated the government's case by barring key evidence. The prosecutors were forced to strike a weak deal. Hall got his summer back.

A short while later, the prosecutor received a new series of transcripts from the exchanges between Alex Dave and Darius. They were still negotiating for the radar microchips called phase shifters.

Darius: "When you send the $ to my cousin's bank in Delaware US, we will have factory configure phase shifters. I expect about two months after receipt of money we can deliver. How long after customer receives the merchandise will you provide total payment for these units?"

Alex Dave: "Max. 2–4 weeks, but what about the next 4,000 pieces? Should we wait two months for each 1,000 pieces?"

Nothing will happen, Darius replied, until the first deposit is made. Not to worry, Alex Dave replied. "I have the formal agreement with my customers in Iran." The problem, he said, is that the wire transfer bounced. "We just can open a letter of credit."

Hall laughed when he read that. A letter of credit? Was he kidding?

"Letter of credit from Iran bank is garbage," Darius replied. "If bank refuses to pay, what do we do? Ask the U.N. to help us? We are violating the law by selling you these devices. What court is going to help?"

Hall turned to the final exchange in the reports, a series of Yahoo! instant messages about the phased array microchips.

Darius: "You know these parts are used in missiles. My cousin has tell me that People's Republic of China tries to buy often but cannot."

Alex Dave: "Maybe. But our customer do not need to use in missile. They need it for radar, I think."

Darius: "Will this deal make you a hero with the Ministry of Defense?"

Alex Dave: "Not directly. We have the purchase order from one of the companies which are a subsidiary of the Ministry of Defense."

Darius: "It is still good."

Yes, Hall thought as he closed the file. It is still good.

CHAPTER 12

Shakespeare

They were squeezed together into a bright-orange plastic booth in a strip mall, polishing off Wilmington's best burritos, when the call came. Malandra, the HSI group supervisor, took it on his cell. It was Lechleitner, calling from the offices of Cross International in Philly. Malandra listened intently for a few moments, nodded once or twice, and said, "Roger, thanks." He returned the phone to its holster and smiled to his colleagues at the table, prosecutor Hall and agents Michael Ronayne and Harry Ubele. It was July 23, 2007, more than three years since they'd launched their investigation of Alex Dave, and the guys were still debating whether the Iranian was a true arms broker or an Internet con man.

"That was P.J.," Malandra said. "Three grand just showed up in the Cross undercover account." Wired from a bank in Dubai by a Tehran company, a deposit from Alex Dave. "Looks like we're going to Georgia," Malandra said.

. . .

Back at Customs House, the agents pulled together an op plan, a formal proposal for their overseas sting against Alex Dave. If all went according to plan, Darius and his "American cousin," Lechleitner, would meet Alex Dave in Tbilisi, the Georgian capital, in late September or early October. Posing as Patrick Lynch of Cross International, Lechleitner would deliver the radar microchips to Alex Dave in a hotel suite as hidden cameras rolled. Lechleitner and Darius would also discuss prospects for future deals with Alex Dave, a feint designed to get him talking as much as possible about the Iranian procurement process—what their military sought and how they ultimately acquired it. After several hours, the Georgian police would enter the room, arrest Alex Dave, and he would be extradited to the United States. At least, that was the plan.

Three elements took priority: finding ways to expand the potential charges beyond the single count of smuggling radar; confirming the arrangements with the Georgians, particularly extradition; and, no small matter, coming up with the radar microchips Alex Dave expected to see in Tbilisi.

Expanding the criminal charges. Whenever possible, prosecutors like to charge a person with multiple acts of similar crimes—three drug deals or six instances of money laundering instead of one. It helps eliminate the defense that the crime was some sort of misunderstanding or a single lapse in judgment. It also provides redundancy; if one charge gets tossed because of a technicality or unforeseen error, the other charges remain, and the case isn't a total loss. As the Alex Dave investigation unfolded, Hall believed that Ardebili was bombarding the agents with so many RFQs for products—they continued to arrive on a weekly basis—that he was bound to request something else, sooner or later, that they could also deliver to Tbilisi. The agents also brainstormed ways to link the separate Massachusetts transaction—the $7,000 Alex Dave had sent to the undercover HSI agents in Boston—to their case in Delaware. They considered what Alex Dave's reaction might be if Lechleitner claimed to know Tom, the Boston undercover agent, and offered to deliver his gyros in Tbilisi. Would that work? Or make Alex Dave suspicious?

Extradition. The sting would be pointless if they didn't make plans to extradite Alex Dave. The Georgian police might have agreed to cooperate with a U.S. sting but the nation's courts, not the police, would ultimately decide whether he could be extradited to the United States for trial. In recent years, U.S. law enforcement agents had run stings against Iranian arms dealers in Hong Kong,

France, Germany, and Austria, making arrests, only to have foreign judges refuse to extradite the accused. Most of those arrested had been freed and returned to Iran. To try to avoid that kind of embarrassment, Hall and Lechleitner flew to Tbilisi in August, and Darius took them to meet top Georgian officials. The United States did not have an extradition treaty with the former Soviet republic, and, thus without any formal, established mechanisms the two countries agreed to create a specific agreement for the Alex Dave case. It was a bureaucratic but critical step.

The radar chips. Alex Dave would arrive in Georgia expecting to receive one thousand phased array radar chips from Darius and Lechleitner. The dime-sized microchips allow an antenna to scan the sky at lightning speed, tracking incoming fighter aircraft and missiles in a manner that traditional radar cannot. The agents felt compelled to present Alex Dave with real microchips—at least temporarily—if they hoped to get him talking about other potential deals and provide insight on Iranian procurement. But this specific microchip, known by its serial number MAPCGM0003, proved difficult to acquire, even for the agents. Unlike other devices, these were not so easily borrowed from the Pentagon. The chips the U.S. military owned were already installed inside weapon systems, not stored separately, sitting on some shelf. The agents realized they would have to acquire them elsewhere. But the state-of-the-art microchips took months to manufacture and even longer to order through routine channels. Plus, they were expensive.

The agents considered whether to approach the manufacturer directly. From time to time, certain U.S. corporations agreed to quietly lend a hand with undercover investigations. Some loan trucks or uniforms emblazoned with company logos for undercover surveillance. Others provide office space or specialized expertise. The FBI has even solicited celebrities to help them with stings, famous people playing themselves, lending their aura to help catch crooks. Some companies are happy to help law enforcement. Others demur, citing legal, philosophical, or liability concerns. There is always a danger, of course, that an agent might query the wrong company, one run by criminals or people who hold a grudge against the government. As always, the more people who know about an undercover operation, the greater the risk.

Here, the Philadelphia agents decided to reach out to the nearest radar chip supplier, which was based just north of Boston. The task fell to Lechleitner's colleague, Michael Ronayne, in part because he spoke with a thick Boston accent but also because he was the newly designated agent of record, or "case agent," for the Alex Dave investigation.

Ronayne was a Malandra protégé, steady, street-smart, though relatively new to HSI. Most agents were veterans or ex-cops. Ronayne formerly bused tables and worked the door at Planet Hollywood. Thirty-eight years old, he still carried the frame of a bouncer—six-foot-two, shaved head, and 225 pounds of muscle. Ronayne considered himself a quintessential blue-collar guy from southeast Boston. Growing up, he had expected to become a firefighter, like his father and grandfather, but hadn't scored well enough on the entrance exam to earn a slot. After college, he'd worked a soul-crushing job as a car insurance adjuster for eighteen months and quit after a close friend his age died; it made him realize he wanted to do more with his life than earn a living. He moved to Florida and took temporary jobs while he searched for something meaningful. He worked for a financial firm, then for a few months as an aspiring actor/model and finally for Planet Hollywood in Orlando.

In the spring of 2001, on the advice of a friend of his father, Ronayne applied to U.S. Customs and was invited to take the special agent's test. He studied every day for two months and passed the written portion. His oral session was going well, too, he thought, until the agents interviewing him began to snicker. Each time he spoke, the agents giggled, and Ronayne figured he'd probably blown it. Assuming he had little left to lose, the South Boston native finally confronted the agents. "What's so damn funny?" One of the agents replied, "We're all just wondering how that Southie accent's going to go down on the Southwest border." Relieved, Ronayne laughed with them, thinking, *A bunch of ballbusters, nice.*

Ronayne arrived at the academy the first week in September 2001, and by the time he graduated the priority had radically shifted from drugs to terrorism. Customs assigned him not to the southern U.S. border, but to Philadelphia. When he reported for duty, the boss issued him a pager, a phone, and a car—and immediately put him on a temporary surveillance detail, a group of agents assigned to follow a suspected terrorist on the East Coast. Ronayne spent the following four years working for a squad stationed at the Philadelphia airport, mostly making drug cases. Like an athlete in training, Ronayne recalls, "I got my reps, learned the system." He wrote investigative reports, testified on the witness stand, and wrote affidavits for search warrants. In 2004, Malandra arrived from Washington to run the airport squad and they bonded. When Malandra took over the counter-proliferation squad, he brought Ronayne with him. Arms and technology smuggling presented new challenges—airport drug cases were fairly straightforward—and Ronayne relished the work. It meant making fewer arrests, but it gave him a tangible opportunity to protect people, in this case, U.S. troops deployed overseas.

Ronayne dialed the microchip manufacturer in Massachusetts and, with his Southie accent, asked to speak to someone in charge. He was transferred to a woman who answered curtly, "How can I help ya?"

Ronayne identified himself and, somewhat clumsily, began describing the Shield America program, the business outreach project designed to prevent military technology from falling into enemy hands. She cut him off. "Yeah, yeah, I know all about that. How can I help ya?"

The agent explained.

Yeah, the lady agreed, that is a problem. The microchips are constructed of gallium arsenide and built to order. It would take three or four months to manufacture the one thousand chips the agents needed. The wholesale price for one thousand units is about $100,000, she added.

This is important, Ronayne said. He didn't have three months or $100,000. The agent began to explain that American pilots' lives might someday hang in the balance, that any air force using phased array radar holds a great advantage—but she cut him off again. She understood and promised to check into it. A few hours later, she called back with a plan—one of the oldest tricks in the book.

"I can sell you ten real radar shifters," she said, "and make you 990 blanks that look and weigh the same. Put the real ones on top, and the buyer won't be able to tell the difference. Will that help?"

"Yes," Ronayne said. "I think it just might."

. . .

As the former national chief of counter-proliferation, Malandra carried considerable influence inside HSI. But now that he was back on the streets as a mere group supervisor, he needed someone to run interference for him, push headquarters to fulfill the mission's needs, and, most of all, trust his instincts. Fortunately for Malandra, his direct boss, Andrew McLees, was both a friend and someone wise in the ways of the bureaucracy. McLees was an assistant Special Agent in Charge and a rising star within HSI. In a few years, he would be named chief of staff to the director in Washington. A trim man with neatly parted salt and pepper hair, McLees had met Malandra during the mid-2000s, when Malandra had run the airport squad and McLees had supervised the squad at the docks. Neither squad was large enough to cover a target on stakeouts twenty-four hours a day and so Malandra and McLees had covered for each other. McLees and Malandra were both Philadelphia natives, intense Flyers fans, and connected to the Philadelphia police—like Malandra, McLees's uncle had been a Philly cop. Perhaps most significantly, McLees embraced Malandra's aggressive investigative philosophy. He also understood that cases like this one could be crapshoots: time-intensive, expensive, and far from certain. In a government environment where efficiency was often measured by cold statistics—number of arrests and deportations, pounds of dope and dollars seized—McLees shared Malandra's willingness to take risks.

Years earlier as a street agent, McLees had risked his life undercover during a drug case in Central America. Yet the Alex Dave case intrigued him like no other: A sting in an exotic locale on the other side of the world. A target lured from a refuge in Iran. A potential secret extradition and extraction. A chance to crawl inside the Iranian procurement process.

Part of McLees's job was to keep all the bullshit out of the way, to deflect any bureaucratic hurdles, so Malandra and his guys could do their job. Now that they were headed overseas, the stakes, stresses, and hassles were sure to increase.

One afternoon, McLees stopped by Malandra's office for an update and raised a key administrative point: They would need a code name for the operation. A case generating so much paperwork and expense would require it. The name needed to be original, but generic enough to be politically correct—and, for security reasons, it should not make any reference to Iran, weapons, or Alex Dave.

They bounced around a couple of names. Most were lame. Finally, Malandra said, "How about Shakespeare?"

"Shakespeare?" someone said, confused.

"Yeah," Malandra said. "This guy has so many quotes"—requests for quotes—"he's like Shakespeare."

No one objected. The Alex Dave sting became Operation Shakespeare.

. . .

As expected, Alex Dave continued to bombard Darius and Lechleitner with requests for military equipment, from sonar to communications gear to night vision technology. One of his more
intriguing requests was for something called a DADC-107, a digi-
tal air data cockpit computer for the F-4 fighter. The updated computer increases the accuracy of a jet's weapons systems, air speed,
and angle of attack. "Could you supply?" Alex Dave wrote. "This is
too urgent." The undercover agents said yes, as a matter of fact they
could. Hall began preparing new charges related to the DADC-107.

By summer's end, as the meeting in Georgia drew closer, Alex
Dave dropped his online moniker. "Amir Hossein Ardebili, this is my
real name," he told Darius.

"Very nice to meet you," Darius wrote back.

The Americans couldn't know if Ardebili was his real name or
not. They had no sources inside Iran, and Amir Hossein Ardebili
did not pop up in any Interpol databases. Alex Dave had used other
names in the past, but Amir Hossein Ardebili struck the agents as
more genuine than the others. They shifted to using this name.

In mid-September 2007, a few weeks before the meeting in Georgia, Ardebili unwittingly handed the Americans a gift. He asked Darius if he could help with two problem shipments. One involved a lost
deposit in New York, the other a lost deposit in Boston. The Boston one, Ardebili explained, involved a set of gyros. He had sent this
company $7,000 several years ago but they had struggled to smuggle
the items. Twice, Ardebili said, shipments from Boston to Dubai had
been returned by Customs. The manager of the Boston company, a
man known only as "Tom," had expressed interest in meeting Ardebili in Eastern Europe. Well, Darius told Ardebili, if you trust Tom,
perhaps he can join us in Tbilisi. Ardebili assured him that Tom was
trustworthy.

The U.S. agents celebrated their dumb luck. The agents could
lead Ardebili to believe that Tom would be coming, until the last
minute, then substitute his "assistant," to be portrayed by under-

cover agent Harry Ubele. They contacted the HSI office in Boston to coordinate the paperwork, and Hall began drafting more charges against Ardebili.

·   ·   ·

International undercover operations are nearly always filled with diplomatic, bureaucratic, and political obstacles. In the weeks before Operation Shakespeare unfolded in Tbilisi, these dynamics became exacerbated as relations between Iran and the United States quickly deteriorated.

First, President Ahmadinejad declared to reporters in Tehran that the United States was losing the war in Iraq. Once American troops pulled out, he said, Iran planned to exert its influence. "The political power of the occupiers is collapsing rapidly. . . . Of course, we are prepared to fill the gap." President Bush responded almost immediately. During a speech before the American Legion Convention, he leveled his most direct warning to Tehran to date. He said that Shia extremists inside Iraq, "supported and embodied by the regime that sits in Tehran," were responsible for most of the attacks against U.S. troops. "Iran has long been a source of trouble in the region." Bush said. "It is the world's leading state sponsor of terrorism. Iran backs Hezbollah . . . Iran funds terrorist groups like Hamas and the Palestinian Islamic Jihad, which murder the innocent, and target Israel, and destabilize the Palestinian territories. Iran is sending arms to the Taliban in Afghanistan. . . . Iran's Islamic Revolutionary Guard Corps are supplying extremist groups with funding and weapons, including sophisticated IEDs. The attacks on our bases and our troops by Iranian-supplied munitions have increased in the last few months. . . . The Iranian regime must halt these actions. And until it does, I will take actions necessary to protect our troops. I have authorized our military commanders in Iraq to confront Tehran's murderous activities." The last line—obliquely authorizing a military strike against Iran—became the day's news headline.

The Iranian foreign minister, Manouchehr Mottaki, fired back the following day. "Bush's remarks showed indecision, lack of wisdom and political despair," he intoned. The exchange of barbs continued throughout September 2007. Western and Middle Eastern media began to speculate that a U.S. attack against Iran might be imminent.

In the last week of September, as the Operation Shakespeare agents prepared to depart for Tbilisi, Seymour Hersh of *The New Yorker* reported that the Pentagon, pushed by Vice President Dick Cheney's allies, was busy refreshing war plans for Iran. "There has been a significant increase in the tempo of attack planning," Hersh wrote. He quoted a former CIA official, who drew parallels to the run-up to the Iraq invasion: "They're dragging in a lot of analysts and ramping up everything. It's just like the fall of 2002." Hersh appeared on CNN and said, "The strategy is a targeting change. We're threatening Iran. We've been doing it constantly. But instead of saying to the American people it's about nuclear weapons . . . it's now going to be about getting the guys that are killing our boys. We're going to hit the facilities we think are supplying some of the explosive devices into Iraq." A short while later, CNN's Christiane Amanpour broadcast a special report, *Ahmadinejad: Soldier of God*, analyzing the growing tensions and the Iranian leader's messianic beliefs. She concluded, "There is now a full-fledged war of words between the presidents of Iran and the United States." Also, during the final days of September, Ahmadinejad headed for New York, where he planned to address the United Nations General Assembly and give a speech at Columbia University.

. . .

As these political tensions swirled, Hall submitted the final draft of his formal Operation Shakespeare memo to the Department of Justice's director of international affairs. The six-page document laid out the investigation, the sting, and the still tenuous plans for extradition:

Ardebili is a notorious Iranian arms broker, who has negotiated with numerous undercover storefronts over the years. The phase shifter is the tip of the iceberg. In the negotiations with the storefronts, Ardebili has requested price quotes for thermal weapons sights, F-4 and F-14 fighter aircraft parts, UT-2000 underwater communications systems, image intensifier tubes for night vision goggles, and a marine radar surveillance system. He has been communicating with the undercover agents involved in the phase shifter transaction for three years, during which time he has requested quotes on over 600 items. He attempted to get the undercover agents in the phase shifter deal involved in a $2 million sonar transaction and has recently sent quotes for Bell military helicopters. Ardebili has also solicited quotes for a digital air data computer for an F-4 fighter aircraft and a $3 million airborne mine countermeasure device. The phase shifter deal itself gives rise to a number of adverse inferences about Ardebili's intentions and capabilities. Phase shifters are used in phased array radar, satellite communications and electronic warfare. A request for thousands of copies is extraordinary in that it suggests he has a customer with enormous military requirements, such as the government of Iran.

Overseas stings by U.S. law enforcement agents are rare, and Hall knew he would be expected to include a few lines to justify this one. "Ardebili is extremely elusive," Hall wrote. "He will not travel to the United States for a meeting with the undercover agents and his willingness to travel to Georgia likely may be the only opportunity to effect his detention and arrest."

Hall added a few important lines about the risks of extradition, reiterating that Georgia and the United States do not enjoy a formal extradition treaty. Hall reported the results of his preliminary trip to Tbilisi to meet senior Georgia officials, including the ongoing effort to complete a "memorandum of understanding" that would serve as the legal mechanism for Ardebili's extradition. To underscore his belief that the Georgians would cooperate, Hall wrote the following in bold text: "This matter had been raised to the highest political levels in Georgia and the Prosecutor General"—the equivalent of the U.S. attorney general—"has briefed the Georgian president."

Hall added that Ardebili was expected to arrive in Tbilisi on October 1, 2007.

In six days.

CHAPTER 13

Contagious Enthusiasm

SHIRAZ, IRAN

A few days before Ardebili's scheduled departure from Iran to Georgia, he opened a new message from Darius.

"I am already here in Tbilisi," Darius wrote. "I have Georgian bodyguard who can drive everywhere where we need to meet. It will be no problem. We will only be in Tbilisi two nights. We will leave together the morning of Oct. 3 for the Black Sea. There we will stay at private resort. It is not hotel. It is spa that is used only by government officials here. It is also close to my warehouse. The weather is beautiful right now. You come at good time!"

Ardebili looked forward to finally meeting Darius and his American cousin Patrick, and he was pleased that Tom had agreed to fly from Boston to join them in Tbilisi. It had been nearly two years since Ardebili had wired $7,000 to Tom for the set of military-grade gyros. As important, Darius and Patrick had come through on the DADC-107, the two digital air cockpit computers for the F-4. They'd be bringing them along with the radar microchips. It would be a bountiful trip.

Ardebili tapped out his reply. "We will together relax beside Black Sea! I really need to relax. This is five months hard working without any rest. Thank you for your reservation. . . . It is important to have good meeting together and long term business together. I will get the purchase order for the two systems of DADC-107. The customer will test and then will place the order for 50."

Darius's response came quickly. "Something I have not yet tell you is that my sister is wife to a Deputy Minister of Ministry of

159

Internal Affairs—and you are his guest also. In Georgia MOIA is organization in charge of all police and security matters. It is their spa where we will stay." Darius asked about the deposit for the DADC-107. "Will your side send money to Delaware bank before you come? Sooner you send money, sooner we deliver units."

Ardebili promised to send 10 percent shortly. He also asked Darius and Patrick about a $30,000 infrared guided missile counter-measure device. Could they obtain it in time for the Georgia meeting?

Ardebili turned to focus on a few unrelated deals he hoped to complete before he left for Georgia. He sent emails about obtaining stealth cloaking material from Belgium, inertial navigation technology from Germany, and armor-plated fabric from Holland. He wired $56,000 to Dubai—along with a document titled "Top Secret Quote"—as partial payment for military-grade U.S. electronic components. And he made progress on a $68,000 deal to obtain underwater homing beacons from a California company.

Ardebili carried a thin pocket calendar in which he kept notes on various orders. The English-language pages contained weekly, Western-style affirmations. This week's read, "Nothing is so contagious as enthusiasm." On the eve of his trip, he stepped out to buy presents for Darius and Patrick, tins of pistachios, a specialty of Shiraz. The irony of such a gift—pistachios were among the handful of items exempt from the U.S. trade embargo—was lost on Ardebili.

He packed a few dress shirts, a pair of black slacks, and a pair of blue jeans. He stuffed five American $100 bills and a stack of large-denomination Iranian rials into his brown wallet, walking-around money. He charged up his cell phone, and, wondering whether it would work in Georgia, shot Darius a quick email.

"I have a lot of customers may need to call me in duration which I will be there," Ardebili wrote. "I should check about the different projects which I have with you. Can I have the mobile card to send for customer to call me with this number?"

"Good thinking," Darius replied. "I will get you local phone that work so you can receive calls. I try to have number for you tomorrow. I will also find time when you can use the Internet. I want you to bring your ideas and knowledge."

Ardebili promised to do so. With their new partnership—Cross International ordering from inside the United States, Darius forwarding everything to Georgia, Ardebili arranging for Iran Air to transfer the products to Tehran—the future appeared limitless. Darius had written in a recent email, "Our future is going to be big. I sometimes believe you do not know how big will our deals be."

Darius reminded Ardebili to come prepared to discuss any number of potential deals. Bring your laptop, he wrote.

Good idea, Ardebili thought. With the laptop handy, he'd have his whole office at his fingertips. He could access any invoice, any request from the Iranian government, the names of three hundred U.S. companies he'd been negotiating with. Files going back four years.

Darius was sure to be impressed.

PART TWO

The Sting

2007

CHAPTER 14

Mother Georgia

TBILISI, GEORGIA

Perched like a wedding cake on a cliff overlooking the coffee-colored Mtkvari River, the Old Tbilisi Hotel stands opposite the city's signature attraction, the fourth-century Narikala Fortress. Beside the fort rises Mother Georgia, a sixty-foot-tall aluminum statue that celebrates the city's founding in AD 458. From a distance, Mother Georgia resembles the Statue of Liberty. On closer inspection, Mother Georgia carries neither a torch nor an inscribed tablet. In one hand, she lifts a welcoming goblet of wine; in the other, she carries a sword. The mixed message is unmistakable: Georgians are hospitable; cross them at your peril.

Despite the name, the Old Tbilisi Hotel is not old. Ten years earlier, the speck of land was a municipal park. Speculators bought it from the city during the mid-1990s, when economic chaos followed the fall of the Soviet Union and Tbilisi was desperate for cash. The speculators erected a hotel and the Old Tbilisi opened in 2001, modest but formal. The entrance boasts eight marble columns and from the center of the lobby grows a grand ivory marble staircase covered with an oxblood-red carpet. The hotel windows are draped in the same Soviet red; so, too, are the bedspreads. The Old Tbilisi offers twenty-four relatively spartan rooms—most with twin beds, a couple of chairs, and a wooden desk. A few suites include a sitting room, large enough for small, discreet business meetings. Fancier and larger hotels can be found in Tbilisi—the Marriott, the Sheraton, and the Radisson, to name three—but they are busier and tend to attract Westerners, their lobbies rife with intelligence operatives and electronic eavesdropping.

On the afternoon of September 30, 2007, the day before the Iranian arms broker was expected to arrive in Georgia, two unmarked cars departed the Ministry of Internal Affairs, zigzagging in the direction of the Old Tbilisi. The cars paused at the Tbilisi Sheraton long enough to pick up members of the U.S. Homeland Security team from Philadelphia, a crew led by supervisor John Malandra. Still groggy from the eighteen-hour journey, Malandra joined the car that carried the senior Georgian officer, Archil Pavlenishvili. A compact, bald man who spoke in the same rapid-fire manner as Malandra, Pavlenishvili headed a "special tasks" division at the security branch of the Ministry of Internal Affairs.

In many ways, Pavlenishvili represented the great changes to Georgia and to its national police force during the previous decade. When Pavlenishvili joined the national force as a crime scene technician in 1996—five years after independence from the Soviet Union—rampant violence, crime, and police corruption held Georgia in a vise grip. Traffic cops routinely stopped cars and demanded bribes for invented infractions. Victims of more common crimes were often reluctant to call the police for help—afraid that officers would round up suspects, innocent or not, and torture them. Pervasive corruption and mafia influence infected virtually every area of government. Georgians expected to pay bribes to register property, obtain a driver's license, and gain admittance to university. Combined with the armed conflicts in post-Soviet border regions, the culture of corruption fueled already chaotic economic conditions. Few Georgians paid taxes and the government struggled to provide basic services. On a good day in the late 1990s and early 2000s, the electricity in Tbilisi flickered on for seven or eight hours. According to a World Bank study on the post-Soviet era, "The two most pressing problems facing the new government were a plundered treasury and a failed state in which criminals and government officials were indistinguishable." Reforms implemented by 2003 were not enough and late that year, when the ruling government's reelection was proved a fraud, tens of thousands of demonstrators, many carrying roses and backed by the United States and nongovernmental organizations, staged twenty days of massive but peaceful street demonstrations. The protests culminated in the resignation of the president and new elections, and a new Georgian government closely allied with the United States. The so-called Rose Revolution, a bloodless coup, brought dramatic reforms, especially to the national police force.

With such a sordid history, most Georgians over forty could not be trusted to serve in the government—inevitably, they would have ties to the Communist Party or the corrupt post-Soviet regime. And so, in 2004, the new president began a great purge. He fired more than 80 percent of the police force and thousands of other civil servants. Promising young men like Pavlenishvili, many with Western educations, were promoted to prominent positions throughout the government—from the electric utility to the tax collection agency to the universities. The old guard had warned that putting so many young people in charge would prove to be a mistake, but so far, buoyed by $2 billion in U.S. aid and European guidance, things seemed to be running fairly well. By October 2007, the city streets were relatively safe to walk, and crime victims felt comfortable calling the police for help. In a symbolic step, the government demolished old-guard police stations across the nation and in their place built modern glass structures with giant windows—a metaphor for the new transparency.

Georgia, however, could only reform so quickly. Legacies of autocracy and corruption lingered. Shortly before the Homeland Security team arrived from Philadelphia in October 2007, the Georgian president and defense minister publicly traded corruption allegations. The defense minster resigned to lead an opposition party, and afterward the police arrested him at his party's offices, and

charged him with taking kickbacks. A local television crew video-
taped the arrest but the police confiscated their footage. To the U.S.
ambassador, who supported the president, it wasn't immediately
clear if the minister's resignation and arrest were legitimate or political. The week Malandra's team landed in Georgia, the ambassador
filed a discouraging report to Washington. "The Georgian government's image has taken a huge blow."

The young Pavlenishvili tried to avoid politics. At age thirty-
two, he commanded a unit that specialized in counter-proliferation.
His officers tracked arms smugglers and would-be nuclear terrorists who tried to peddle radioactive material stolen from old Soviet
military sites. The job kept Pavlenishvili in close contact with the
FBI agent stationed at the U.S. embassy in Tbilisi. For Operation
Shakespeare, Pavlenishvili considered his chief task to be logistical,
not investigatory—the Georgians expected to arrange locations for
the undercover meetings and provide armed backup in case anything went wrong. Senior Georgian officials selected Pavlenishvili's unit for the task because his team was among the nation's most
elite undercover squads, a handpicked group of officers who could
be trusted. It was critical, his superiors had stressed, that his men
follow Georgian procedures precisely; a deviation from procedures,
no matter how minor, could jeopardize the case in the American
court system. Though Pavlenishvili had been briefed by his bosses
on Operation Shakespeare, he looked forward to hearing about the
case directly from Malandra. It was always better to talk street cop
to street cop. Besides, he spoke English better than his bosses. As
the unmarked police car pulled away from the ministry, Pavlenishvili
asked Malandra about how he expected the meetings with the Iranian to unfold.

"Well," Malandra said, "we're going to meet in a hotel room,
drive around in a car a little bit, have a lunch, maybe dinner. I'll need
to wire all those places because you never know what's going to be
said spontaneously."

No problem, Pavlenishvili said. The car pulled up to the Old Tbilisi Hotel, only a few blocks from the agents' hotel. The Georgians discreetly escorted Malandra and a few American agents through the marble lobby up to suite 22, a top-floor suite with a sitting room.

Pavlenishvili pointed to three chairs. "He will sit there. Your guys will sit here and here."

"Okay, fellas," Malandra said. "Where're we going to put the cameras?"

The Georgians snickered. Pavlenishvili pointed to a Utrillo-style painting on the wall. "Camera is already there."

The Georgians led the Americans next door to a room with surveillance gear connected through the wall to the hidden camera in the painting. Malandra laughed. To him, the setup looked permanent, a residual mind-set from KGB days. So he said, "Okay, looks great. Where are we going to eat?"

"We know a great place," Pavlenishvili said.

They returned to the car and sped off, snaking down a hill to a popular restaurant beside the Mtkvari River. Designed to mimic a small Georgian village, the restaurant's courtyard was busy with chefs grilling beside a large outdoor hearth. The Georgian police led the Americans into a set of private dining rooms on the edge of the property, snug spaces with warm light and local portraits hanging on redbrick walls. "You will eat here," Pavlenishvili said. Malandra nodded. A local policeman pointed to a microscopic camera embedded in one wall, then guided the Americans to the room next door to see the surveillance gear. This, Malandra assumed, must have been a former KGB haunt, prewired with hidden cameras.

Finally, Pavlenishvili explained, the Georgians would provide a Mercedes SUV and two of their undercover agents, who would pose as Darius's driver and bodyguard. Malandra thanked him and suggested that it might be a good idea to plant a video camera in the Mercedes.

Pavlenishvili grinned. No problem, he said. There's a hidden camera in the Mercedes's rearview mirror.

.   .   .

Given the time squeeze, the Philadelphia agents' briefings on Georgian history, politics, and culture had been quick, delivered by way of State Department background papers, travel guides, and anecdotes from Darius. A country of 4.5 million people, and slightly smaller than South Carolina, Georgia is located at Europe's eastern edge, between the Black Sea, Russia, Turkey, Armenia, and Azerbaijan. Georgia's varied topography can be compared to California's: flat, arid, desertlike sections; lush vineyards and beaches along a seacoast; and also snowcapped, Alpine-like mountains.

In terms of history, Georgia's current independence is something of an anomaly. Except for periods during the eleventh and twelfth centuries, outsiders have ruled Georgia for most of the last two thousand years—the Persians, the Romans, the Byzantine Empire, the Arabs, the Turks, the Russians. During the early years of the Soviet Union, Georgia received favored status—Stalin was a Georgian—but now the two countries mocked and resented one another. Russia posed the only threat to Georgian independence.

Briefing fellow Americans, Darius explained the national psyche this way: "Georgians are a combination of Klingons and Apaches. They are warriors, men from another millennium who get along very well with the United States because they think the rest of Europe are a bunch of wimps." The prominent highway between the airport and downtown Tbilisi, he noted, is named George W. Bush Street in honor of a 2005 visit by the American president. "They love Bush. He mispronounces words and starts wars. What's not to like?"

Since the fall of the Soviet Union in 1991, Georgia and the United States had emerged as strong allies, and during Bush's second term these ties deepened. For the Bush administration, Georgia represented a success story. It was a young, relatively stable democracy, at least when compared with Iraq. From a geopolitical perspective, Georgia presented the United States with an opportunity to develop a strategic foothold at important crossroads between Russia, Europe, and the Middle East.

Wary of Russian aggression, especially in the separatist South Ossetia and Abkhazia regions, Georgia knew that U.S. support helped keep an enemy at bay. In recent months, border skirmishes between Georgia and Russia near the disputed regions had escalated. In August, a Russian jet dropped a dummy bomb inside Georgia—a not so subtle reminder that the Russian air force could attack virtually unopposed from the air. On September 20, ten days before the U.S. agents arrived in Tbilisi, Georgian forces exchanged gunfire with a group of ethnic Abkhaz soldiers and killed two Russian military advisors. The border incident had triggered a tense, closed-door session of the United Nations Security Council in New York, one in which an enraged Russian diplomat accused the Georgians of murder. Most Georgians—and much of the world—believed a Russian invasion inevitable. (Indeed, the following summer Russian tanks would cross the border, triggering a five-day war, and South Ossetia and Abkhazia, now occupied by Russian troops, would become "independent" states. Then, shortly before the 2014 Winter Olympics in Sochi, staged less than an hour's drive from the Abkhazian border, Russian troops would extend an eleven-mile "security zone" into the Georgian territory. Weeks later, just up the Black Sea coast, Russia would "annex" Crimea from the Ukraine.)

"This is Georgia," Darius told his American colleagues in Tbilisi. "These are people living on the edge. Tomorrow is not guaranteed."

. . .

The weekend the Americans arrived in Tbilisi, they continued to receive reports of rising tensions between Washington and Tehran. Echoing the alarming piece in *The New Yorker* about a possible U.S. air attack, a headline in *Newsweek* cited "Whispers of War."

That Sunday, Bob Schieffer of CBS News opened *Face the Nation* with grim words, citing the bellicose speeches given that week by President Mahmoud Ahmadinejad while visiting the United Nations and Columbia University in New York. "The Iranian president has gone home," the anchor said. "The drawdown of American troops has begun in Iraq. But is the war moving now toward Iran? . . . The administration may be planning air strikes into Iran. Could that happen? . . . In Washington, when you talk to people in the intelligence communities, in the foreign policy communities, in the consulting firms around town, there's this talk going about that something is about to happen in Iran."

And, as the U.S. agents made final preparations for the sting against the Iranian arms broker, new reports surfaced about the dangers facing American troops in Iraq and new evidence that the Iranians were involved in a systematic effort to supply Iraqi insurgents. In *The Washington Post*, Pulitzer Prize–winning reporter Rick Atkinson began a definitive series on IED attacks against American troops. "More than 81,000 IED attacks have occurred in Iraq, including 25,000 so far this year," he wrote. "The war has indeed metastasized into something completely different, a conflict in which the roadside bomb in its many variants . . . has become the signature weapon in Iraq and Afghanistan, as iconic as the machine gun in World War I or the laser-guided smart bomb in the Persian Gulf War of 1991." Thus far, IEDs were responsible for nearly two thirds of the 3,100 U.S. deaths to date in Iraq, Atkinson wrote, and approximately eighteen thousand wounded.

The *Post* stories did not cite the American-made remote control IED triggers found on the Iraqi battlefield—that link would not be made public for years—but the report raised an alarm, noting that 70 percent of recent deaths could be traced to armor-piercing devices supplied by Iran and a so-called "underbelly" bomb. Underscoring this danger and the links to Iran, U.S. officials in Baghdad convened a press conference that Sunday to announce the capture of an Iranian operative in northern Iraq. The Iranian belonged to Tehran's elite Qods Force, a military unit suspected of shipping surface-to-air missiles to Iraqi insurgents. Though the HSI agents caught reports about the press conference from the televisions in their rooms at the Sheraton they felt no need to discuss them. Everyone understood the stakes.

. . .

On the morning of October 1, 2007—a Monday—the American team gathered for a final briefing at the Sheraton. On the outside, the 140-room hotel resembled an ugly mid-twentieth-century cruise ship. Inside, it offered the muted ambience and cuisine of almost any Sheraton found in the United States, a familiarity and blandness some of the U.S. agents found comforting.

Following operational security protocol, the American team had booked rooms at three hotels—a suite at the Old Tbilisi for the sting, a room at the Iliani Hotel for the target, and a bank of rooms at the Sheraton, where the agents and prosecutor would actually sleep. They did this to avoid counter-surveillance: the U.S. agents didn't want to be seen by Ardebili or any of his potential associates congregating at the Old Tbilisi. They did it for safety, too. It's never a good idea for an undercover agent to actually sleep in the hotel room where a meeting with a target takes place. Targets have been known to bust back into the room during the middle of night and try to rob or kill an undercover agent.

At the Sheraton, Malandra began the briefing, reiterating roles and the op plan. Three agents were undercover: Darius, as an East European arms broker; Lechleitner, as Darius's cousin, "Patrick Lynch," from Philadelphia; and Harry Ubele, as the Boston arms broker who worked for Tom and who would bring the gyroscopes. Malandra was team leader and coach. Ronayne was case agent and quarterback. Hall was legal advisor. Grimes, the HSI supervisor from Frankfurt, was tasked to coordinate with the Georgian police. The

final member of the team was Bob Lerario, an agent from the Pentagon's Defense Criminal Investigative Service who had been working
side by side with the HSI agents in Philadelphia for years. Lerario's
assignment was to install and monitor the surveillance gear.

Amir Ardebili was scheduled to arrive from Iran that afternoon,
around 2:30, on a connecting flight from Baku, the capital of Azerbaijan. The Americans planned to have Darius meet Ardebili at
the airport. Two undercover Georgian policemen posing as Darius's bodyguards would drive them into the city. On the ride, Darius
would offer Ardebili a choice: they could drive directly to Darius's
hotel, the Old Tbilisi, to discuss business; or, if Ardebili wished to
rest up, they could drop him off at his hotel, and return to pick him
up several hours later.

During the first meeting at the Old Tbilisi, Darius planned to
introduce Ardebili to "Patrick Lynch." "Lynch" would deliver a shoe-
box-sized package with the promised M/A-COM radar microchips—
the string of ten authentic chips on top and 990 counterfeit ones
underneath. To keep Ardebili from dashing back to Iran before the
agents could engage the Iranian in a long discussion, they planned
to tell him that the American broker bringing the gyroscopes—
Harry—had been delayed until the following afternoon.

At the Sheraton, Hall went over his legal wish list one last time.
He focused on the elements of the crimes as detailed in the sealed
U.S. court document charging Ardebili. It was not enough to merely
get Ardebili to accept the contraband military components on tape,
he reminded the agents. To win a conviction in an American court,
it would help immeasurably if the agents could steer the Iranian into
making certain admissions on tape, statements that would convince
a judge and jury that he hadn't been entrapped. Hall wrote the elements out in shorthand on a legal pad:

Delaware. The $3,000 deposit for the radar chips had been wired
to a Delaware bank, creating legal jurisdiction there. But it would
help a local jury identify with the case if the subject of Delaware

came up casually during the sting. That way, the charges wouldn't seem so foreign.

Nature and use of the contraband. It was important to get Ardebili to admit that he understood that what he was buying carried a military purpose and that he intended to deliver it to the Iranian government. If possible, the agents needed to lead Ardebili into admissions that would preclude him from later arguing that this had all been some sort of misunderstanding, that the goods carried some civilian application, or that he was merely a delivery boy, that he hadn't been the person sending the emails, making the requests, or wiring the money.

Smuggling. Under U.S. law, the agents needed to demonstrate that Ardebili understood that he was violating the American embargo. In court, it wouldn't be good enough to show that he merely planned to smuggle goods from Georgia to Iran. The agents would have to get him to say that he did so in violation U.S. export laws.

Conspiracy. The sealed U.S. charges against Ardebili included conspiracy, an allegation that required prosecutors to prove that he'd worked with at least one other person to smuggle the goods. The case would be stronger still if they could get Ardebili to name names in Iran.

The wire transfer. The document trail showed only that the $3,000 deposit wired to the Delaware bank account had arrived from a German bank. The U.S. agents held no evidence that Ardebili had actually authorized the transfer from Iran to Germany to Delaware. They needed to get him to admit this.

Money laundering. Likewise, the agents did not have definitive proof that Ardebili had wired the $3,000 deposit from Iran to Delaware via Germany *in order to circumvent the financial embargo,* an act considered money laundering under U.S. law. Prosecutors liked to bring the money laundering charge whenever possible. It carried stiff penalties—ten years or more.

Finally, Hall reiterated: Beyond the four corners of the indictment, remember to elicit as much intelligence as possible about the Iranian procurement network.

The agents didn't ask many questions. By now, everyone understood what to do, and besides, jet lag still dulled their senses. Ronayne, tense, wondered if he still had time to get in a workout. Ubele felt physically ill. Nauseated and sweaty, he left to lie down.

A bunch of the guys went down to lunch, among them the undercover stars, Darius and Lechleitner. Darius, so persnickety in preparation, couldn't relax, worried they might have missed something. At the meal, he kept throwing out contingencies and hypotheticals. Role playing, he assumed his Russian-accented, broken-English character and said to Lechleitner, "Okay, Patrick, how much for Bell helicopter?"

Lechleitner was drinking a large soda. He stuck the straw in his mouth and mumbled. Darius was the senior agent, but P.J. found the constant drilling ridiculous. There were only so many figures he could recall and so many things he could worry about. It was more important to keep calm, Lechleitner believed. He'd be fine, if Darius would just chill out. Lechleitner said, "I dunno, $10 million."

Darius snapped. "You got to say more than that. You're not taking this seriously enough!" The other agents suppressed smiles.

"Okay, okay," the younger man said. "Sorry. Ask me again."

Darius resumed his Russian accent. "How much? How much for helicopter?"

Lechleitner smiled mischievously, mimicking Mike Myers's Dr. Evil. "A helicopter? I'd say it's worth $40 gazillion dollars!"

Darius stood, fuming. "This is bullshit. I'm not working with you." He pushed his chair back and walked off.

Lechleitner rolled his eyes. "Go ahead. Go to your room. I'll meet with him without you."

No one else said a word.

CHAPTER 15

Arrival

BAKU, AZERBAIJAN

That afternoon, Amir Ardebili's connecting flight to Tbilisi departed Baku. From a window seat, he gazed out over the Azerbaijan capital, the Caspian Sea vanishing as the jet pushed west toward Tbilisi. A flight attendant from Azerbaijan Airlines moved down the aisle, offering drinks: water, soda, beer, wine. Ardebili did a double take. Openly selling alcohol! Booze could be found in Shiraz and Tehran, of course, but on the black market. He let the flight attendant pass without ordering.

It was a little past 3 p.m., and already this was Ardebili's third flight of the day, a succession of hundred-minute hops—Shiraz to Tehran, Tehran to Baku, Baku to Tbilisi. He'd left home for the Shiraz airport before dawn to catch the first flight. Traveling with him was a last-minute companion, his seventy-year-old father, now napping in the next seat. Ardebili intended the trip as thanks for the nice wedding reception his father had arranged the year before. It would do his dad some good to take a vacation from his mother. She worried too much. That morning, as Ardebili had escorted his dad to the waiting taxi outside his parents' home in Shiraz, she'd gripped her son's wrist and pleaded, "Don't go." She told him she'd had a nightmare, a premonition. "Something bad will happen," she'd said. Ardebili had kissed her and moved swiftly to the taxi.

Ardebili peered through the oval airplane window, the plane chugging over swaths of forests. His thoughts turned to Darius. What did he look like? How would their meetings unfold? Ardebili hoped the trip would mark the beginning of a lucrative, long-term relationship. If Darius and his American partner came through—if they brought the radar microchips, gyroscopes, and F-4 computers as promised—Ardebili hoped to spend the bulk of their time in Tbilisi discussing future deals. Already, the Iranian military had instructed him to purchase fifty more F-4 computers from Darius. The military also wanted him to buy night vision equipment and missile guidance parts. Ardebili carried specific part numbers in his daily calendar and on his laptop.

The whine of the propellers faded, and the plane began its descent, approaching Tbilisi. In the distance, a curling river split the capital. The plane buzzed over Bronze Age burial mounds and a Georgian military factory, then put down at a gleaming new airport of glass and steel.

The flight from Baku pulled to the gate at Tbilisi International Airport. Joined by his father, Ardebili swung his laptop bag across his shoulder and followed the other passengers shuffling to Passport Control.

.   .   .

Inside Suite 22 at the Old Tbilisi Hotel, Lechleitner and Bob Lerario, the DCIS agent from the Pentagon, scurried with last-minute preparations. For security reasons, the agents could not communicate securely with colleagues at the airport, and thus had no sense of when Ardebili might arrive. According to the airline schedule, the plane should have landed by now, and the ride from the airport to the hotel usually took about fifteen minutes. For all the agents knew, the car ferrying Ardebili was already en route.

Lechleitner and Lerario began aligning the chairs in the suite so that at least two of them were facing the hidden camera in the wall painting. To test the setup, Lechleitner sat in one of the chairs, while Lerario ducked into the adjoining suite to check the monitor. The picture looked clear and the sound levels were fine. Lechleitner tried sitting in the other chair, and again everything seemed good. But

Lerario wasn't satisfied. He returned to the room and reconsidered the setup.

The camera in the painting was hardwired to an outdated analog recorder in the next room. The view on the monitor seemed okay, but what, he wondered, would the actual recordings look like? The meetings might last hours and stretch across two days. What if the battery or tape unexpectedly failed? The pinhole camera was stationary—what if Ardebili turned his back to the painting or moved the meeting to the bedroom or bathroom? What then? After spending three years trying to lure Ardebili out of Iran, the Pentagon agent concluded that he could not risk recording their best evidence with only one dated, stationary system.

He dug into the black bag he'd brought from Philadelphia and told Lechleitner to peel off his shirt. Lerario pulled out a pocketknife, needle, and thread and began replacing one of the shirt buttons with a tiny, remote control button-camera. Lechleitner put the shirt back on, and both agents winced. The button-camera didn't match the other buttons on the shirt. It looked ridiculous. Lechleitner left to look for another shirt.

The Pentagon agent studied the room again. He grabbed a wicker wastebasket from a corner and moved it closer to the door. He knelt with a pocketknife, bore a small hole in the wicker frame, and inserted the remote control button-camera. He stood and headed for the door, eager to check the reception next door. On the way out, he glanced over his shoulder and caught himself—where he'd drilled his hole, telltale white-wicker shavings were scattered along the crimson carpet. Lerario fell to his knees with a roll of Scotch tape. He tore off a piece and began patting the carpet to collect the shavings.

. . .

The line for Passport Control was short, and within five minutes Ardebili and his father arrived at baggage claim. The carousel was on the ground floor, in the belly of the airport's open glass and steel concourse. Above, Ardebili could see the shops and offices of the upper floors, and through thirty-foot windows, a fading and gray afternoon sky. His view of the lobby was blocked by ten-foot-high billboards and sliding exit doors. As passengers claimed bags, the doors hissed open, and Ardebili could catch quick glimpses of expectant faces. He scanned the crowd outside for signs of a tall, East European–looking man. Nothing. Maybe Darius was sending a driver. After a few minutes, Ardebili's bags appeared, and father and son moved toward the doors. They paused for a moment when they reached the other side, but in the moment before a gypsy taxi driver could pounce, Darius emerged from the crowd and called out Ardebili's name. They patted each other on the back, pleased to meet at long last. Ardebili introduced his fellow traveler. "Nasrollah Ardebili, my father."

Darius shook the man's hand. The agent couldn't tell if Ardebili was telling the truth. He might be his father or his might be an Iranian intelligence operative. But at the very least, Darius thought, he looked to be seventy years old and weak. He wouldn't pose a physical threat.

Darius led Ardebili and the old man outside to the idling, black and boxy Mercedes SUV. The undercover Georgian policemen posing as Darius's henchmen helped the Iranians load the bags into the rear compartment. Ardebili climbed into the right rear seat, cradling his laptop on his knees. His father squeezed into the middle, between his son and Darius. The Mercedes pulled out onto George W. Bush Street, the modern six-lane expressway that connects the unremarkable ten miles between the airport and downtown Tbilisi. The camera hidden in the car's rearview mirror captured their conversation.

Darius chose his words carefully, aware that he was playing to two audiences, Ardebili and a possible jury back in Delaware. If the case went to trial, Darius would find himself on the witness stand, explaining video of the conversation, facing cross-examination from a defense attorney. With the tape rolling, he needed to walk a fine line—playing up his role as an international arms dealer, but in such a way that didn't alienate jurors. So while a real arms dealer might let f-bombs fly or make sexist or racist comments, Darius could not.

To begin, Darius laid the foundation for his broken English, offering in advance an explanation should he should slip up and offer an American idiom. "I tell you secret," Darius said. "I learn English in America when I spend one year there in school."

About a minute after the Mercedes pulled away from the airport, Darius's mobile phone rang—right on cue. He glanced down at the phone, pretended to be annoyed, and sent the call to voice mail. Then he said, "Oh, this reminds me. I have for you a SIM card for your phone."

Ardebili wedged the card into the back of his phone, oblivious that the Americans would now be able to monitor his every call and movement in Georgia. "You are kind," Ardebili said.

Darius waved his hand and, feigning politeness, asked Ardebili to tell him how he got started in the import business.

"I was in this business when I was with the government, eight years," Ardebili said. "I got a lot of knowledge in the government and decided it is better to work private, on my own."

This was news to the Americans. They had not known that Ardebili had once held a position *inside* the Iranian government. He would know more than the average arms broker. Darius nodded nonchalantly and said, "Today, we will talk and I will explain you all my situations—what I can do, what I cannot do. I hoping we will come together for a very profitable relationship."

"You know," Ardebili began, "I have a lot of friends in Iran. Some of the goods, they just touch my hands and I forward to them. I think in the near future it would be good if you came to my country and I introduce you. In Tehran and Shiraz, you can see the possibilities . . ."

"Yes, we must lay the groundwork," Darius said.

"Your cousin is here now?" By cousin, he meant Lynch/Lechleitner. "The goods are here?"

The radar microchips, yes, Darius said. But because Tom had

been unavoidably delayed, his assistant Harry would be bringing the gyroscopes instead, Darius explained. "You will see Harry
tomorrow."

Ardebili's face was impassive. "We have been trying for three years
for these gyros." He had sent a deposit to Boston, he told Darius,
but had never received any merchandise. "I think he's a professional,"
Ardebili said, "but we have a bad history and we want to do business."

Darius assured him that Harry would show up. Then he asked
Ardebili, "These gyros are military gyros, yes?"

"Yes."

The Mercedes approached the Hotel Iliani. The inn was located
at the foot of a city neighborhood known as the Hill of Dreams,
steps from the State Philharmonic, Opera, and Drama theaters,
walking distance to Parliament and the city's museums and Supreme
Court. The Iliani had twenty-four guest rooms, about as many as
the Old Tbilisi, though it was far less elegant. The Iliani looked like
a Soviet-era concrete apartment building and was crammed onto a
narrow street. A concrete wall shielded the lobby from the constant
drone of traffic from Kostava Street, an extension of the city's signature boulevard, Rustaveli Avenue.

Darius wished the ride hadn't been so short. As the car pulled up
to the hotel, Ardebili began talking about how he'd made arrangements to have the gyros shipped through Azerbaijan to avoid
Customs.

The bodyguards unloaded the bags, and Darius asked Ardebili if
he preferred to take a break or proceed directly to the Old Tbilisi to
pick up the microchips. Ardebili said it would be good to get a quick
nap, refresh, and meet again in a few hours. Darius promised to send
the car around again at 7:30 p.m.

Minutes after he checked into the hotel, Ardebili pulled out his
cell phone, the one with the new SIM card. He dialed his wife and
boasted about his grand reception.

CHAPTER 16

The Magic Show

TBILISI, GEORGIA

At 8:04 that evening, Darius escorted Ardebili and his father into the Old Tbilisi Hotel and up the central staircase to Suite 22. Ardebili carried a small white plastic bag in one hand and his laptop in the other. Darius introduced Patrick Lechleitner as the Pennsylvania arms broker Patrick Lynch.

Lechleitner stuck out his hand. "A pleasure," he said. Ardebili was dressed in a purple dress shirt and blue jeans. His father wore a tweed blazer and arrived with his fingers clasped. Darius directed his guests to a pair of chairs that framed a window—and also faced the hidden cameras. "Seats for the guests of honor," he said.

Darius opened with a joke. "Patrick is my cousin, but he is more like brother to me. What does this mean? If I die, I don't know if he will cry, but he gets to wear my shoes."

Ardebili translated for his father and both men laughed politely. Darius offered refreshments. "Tea, coffee? Whatever you like. We will have the people downstairs make for you." The Ardebilis and Lechleitner asked for tea and Darius stepped out briefly to place the order.

"So," Ardebili said to Lechleitner, "you are living in the United States?"

"Yes, living in the United States." Lechleitner spoke with his regular, flat, mid-Atlantic American accent. "Business is in Delaware and Philadelphia. You know the area?"

"No, I've never been to the United States."

"Delaware is a small state. Maybe one million people. Very small state in the U.S. Close to Philadelphia."

"Near the sea?"

"The coast," Lechleitner said. In the room next door, where agents Ronayne and Lerario were huddled watching via hidden camera, Ronayne consulted his notes and put a check mark next to the word *Delaware*.

Darius returned to the suite and the elder Ardebili spoke in Farsi, gesturing with his right hand for emphasis. It was the most animated Darius had seen the father. His son translated. "My father say you look similar."

"Well," Darius said, pointing to his partner/cousin. "We have the same blood but his side of the family married into Irish. I am all Eastern Europe. His mother is Irish blood. But he still gets to wear my shoes when I die."

They laughed again.

Darius studied the father, tanned and tiny, a white-haired old man nearly swallowed by his chair. He looked exhausted from the journey and seemed to strain to understand English. The old man probably *was* Ardebili's father, Darius concluded. That didn't make Ardebili any less dangerous. As tradecraft, some crooks and spies brought innocent-looking family members along as distractions, something to soften the edges. Darius recalled American drug dealers who'd bring a baby or a toddler with them, deploying a child as some sort of human shield, figuring it would lower the odds of violence.

Ardebili reached into his plastic bag, removed two small tins, and placed them on the coffee table. "This is a gift from Iran. Pistachios. For you and for Patrick. I hope you enjoy."

The undercover agents dug in. "Delicious," Lechleitner said.

Darius stood and retrieved a small white box from a table against the wall, inches from the pinhole camera. "We brought something for you," he said, "but I don't think you are going to eat it." He handed the box to Ardebili, and the Iranian lifted a thin plastic package of ten microchips from the top row. Each chip was black, the size of a quarter, and the name of the manufacturer, M/A-COM, was stenciled on the top in large white letters. Ardebili checked the front and rear of the package and broke into a wide grin.

Lechleitner caught his eye. "Hard to get."

"Yes, I know," Ardebili said. He turned the package around to examine the back side. Darius and Lechleitner watched to see if the Iranian would delve into the counterfeit row of microchips. He did not. He put the box down and said, "This shows that you have the capability. I've been working to get these for two years now. We have a lot of correspondence together, but because we didn't know each other, we couldn't trust each other." Ardebili pointed at the box. "How many chips?"

Lechleitner said, "One thousand." As ordered.

Ardebili promised to wire the balance shortly. "I think they will be buying fifteen thousand more."

"Why are they buying so many?" Darius asked.

Ardebili scratched his chin. "They are making a special radar." He mumbled the last word and it came out sounding more like "rudder," not "radar." Lechleitner cocked his head.

"Phased array," Ardebili said.

"Oh, radar," Lechleitner said, repeating the word slowly. Ardebili spoke English with a thick accent, and there would be times throughout the day when the agents would have to get him to clarify his words. They could not depend on microphones to pick up everything precisely. And though Darius was wearing a third hidden microphone on his belt for backup, it was always possible that inadvertent background noise—a horn from a passing car, the soft crack as Lechleitner munched a pistachio—might muffle something important the target said. The language difference mattered, too. Ardebili's English was decent, but there were gaps. If the case ever went to trial, a defense attorney might argue that something important Ardebili had said was misunderstood or lost in translation. This meant there would be times during the meeting when the agents would want to break the conversation down to an elementary, almost childlike level.

Darius jumped in. "Radar? For looking in the sky for airplane?"

"Yes, for protection," Ardebili said. "Antimissile, I think. I don't know because our customer never tells me what the purpose is. But I know they are manufacturing this system." Each phased array radar system, Ardebili explained, required five thousand microchips. His customer, he said, is the Iranian air force.

Lechleitner handed Ardebili a M/A-COM document filled with technical specifications, a tactic designed to confirm for a jury that Ardebili understood precisely what he was buying and what it would be used for. Ardebili skimmed the page and asked Lechleitner to tell him more about the manufacturer, M/A-COM. Lechleitner obliged, sticking to the truth, stuff easily found on the Internet. He couldn't know if this was some sort of test, to see if he really had a contact on the inside, or if Ardebili was genuinely curious about M/A-COM. As the younger agent spoke, Darius studied the Iranian's eager face. A military-trained interrogator, Darius searched for clues that might betray a lie: Did Ardebili's neck muscles tense? Did his eyes flicker? Did he pick lint from his clothing?

When Lechleitner finished describing M/A-COM, Ardebili said, "I have a question because I really don't like to have risks for you. Are you protecting your inquiries? Because I'm going to send a lot of inquiries to you. Are you sure about your channels?"

"My channels in the United States?" Lechleitner said. "I am 100 percent sure. They are trusted people, and we have arrangements to get goods here."

There was a knock at the door. The tea. A young waitress in a white blouse and dark trousers entered, placed a tray on the coffee table, and ducked out.

Next door, Ronayne, watching on a monitor and listening through headphones, continued to scribble notes. The agent was amazed at how well the sting was working: *The undercover agent describes his special access within M/A-COM and Ardebili's reaction is to remind the American to be careful. Ardebili so believes the three of them are working together to commit crimes he's offering advice on how to avoid getting caught.*

Back in the suite, Ardebili took a sip of tea and announced, "I am going to say more about myself." He went to work for the Iranian government when he was twenty-three years old, he said, and spent seven or eight years there, procuring electronics and weapons systems. "My father always told me, 'Don't leave the government.' And I think that parents never believe what their children can do. My father thought I would not be successful. Because it's really hard to work in Iran privately without special channels. All persons need special contacts to get the work. It is special rules in Iran." At IEI, Ardebili had created these "special channels" throughout the government, he said. Now, he was exploiting them.

"You were working for the Iranian Ministry of Defense?" Darius asked.

"No, no. I was working for IEI, Iran Electronic Industries. It is a company with five sub-directorates. Shiraz Electronic Industries is the biggest. Before the Iranian Revolution, when Iran had a good relationship with the United States, General Electric came to Iran and helped establish Shiraz Electronic Industries. This is a really big company. There are seven subsidiaries: aviation, submarine, automation, radio, and others. I know all of them, and have a chance with other Iranian government companies. One of them is SPO—this is the Ministry of Defense. They purchase a lot of inquiries directly but I didn't have a very good result dealing with them because I think they have other good sources. When I called them, they said your prices were very high. Maybe it's because they can purchase directly from their subsidiaries they have in Armenia and in India."

Darius leaned in to clarify. "So the Ministry of Defense has components and is run like a company, with offices in other countries?"

"Yes."

"And they are doing the purchasing, which is keeping the Iranian companies from getting business?"

Ardebili nodded. "IEI is a company that's a subsidiary of the Ministry of Defense."

"IEI is organized by the government?"

"Yes, yes, of course." Ardebili continued his story. "So after seven years at IEI, I had a lot of experience—general manager of company liked me and I did good work there. I was expert and I could have a good job there—for example, supervising groups of people. But the job wasn't satisfying me. I wanted to come out and work for myself."

"Now, your function in this company, IEI, you were purchasing, making acquisitions?"

"Yes. First, I was in quality assurance." He tested smuggled samples, confirming their reliability in advance of a final sale and shipments. "For example, night vision. We wanted to buy it for the military forces. But before that we should check it." The SEI lab did more than test samples—it tried to reverse engineer them. "They're really experts. For example, during the Iran and Iraq War, we took many parts from the Iraqis, their radars and night vision. IEI opened them and reassembled them and then tried to make them from that. They are making a lot of American products in this section." Some American products, however, could not be reverse engineered, he said. "For the night vision, remember I sent a request for tubes? This is only part they cannot manufacture."

Lechleitner: "So they've perfected the others, but the tubes they can't?"

"Yes, this is a very professional part. And they will also like to have, for example, the ALQ-144." This was the infrared guided missile countermeasure system for U.S. Army helicopters. "I have purchase order for one sample."

"Very hard to get," Lechleitner said.

"For two years."

"Two years and they are still trying? Because of the embargo?"

"Yes, they can't get it. Iranian aviation is really grounded. They don't have spare parts. They don't have them because the planes are all from the United States. But the United States won't sell any parts to them. There is the same problem with civil aviation, Boeing airplanes and Bell helicopters."

Ardebili's contacts inside the Iranian government varied, he explained. "For Shiraz Industries, SEI, my relationship is very, very close. . . . Come to Shiraz and I will provide a meeting for you with them."

Darius said, "You know someone who is knowledgeable in the company or powerful?"

"Both." SEI executives trusted him enough to advance him cash for large purchases, he said.

Lechleitner and Darius took Ardebili's opening on finances to segue to money laundering. "Is the transfer of the rest of the money for the chips going to happen the same way as the deposit?" Lechleitner said. "Because you remember we had trouble with that transfer. Is it through the same bank? I think we have the paperwork."

Darius walked over to the bureau, directly in front of the hidden camera, and fetched a piece of paper. It was a copy of the wire transfer for the MA/COM deposit, and it showed the money flowing from Germany to the Delaware bank. He handed it to Ardebili.

The Iranian read the document. The wire transfer was sure to become an exhibit against Ardebili at trial, and a prosecutor would be required to prove its authenticity and relevance. If the agents could get Ardebili to do it himself on tape, all the better. Ardebili scanned the page and said, "This is the payment I did for you."

As helpful as the admission was, it offered evidence only of the second half of the money laundering scheme—the transfer of funds from the German bank to Delaware. The agents didn't have records or proof from the first half of the transaction—the transfer of funds from Ardebili to his friend in Tehran and from this man to the German banks. They tried to maneuver Ardebili into admitting that he'd made all the financial arrangements, laundering the money from Shiraz to Tehran to Germany to Delaware.

Feeding Ardebili's ego, Darius said, "Help me understand . . . Whose money did you send? Your money or the customer's?"

Ardebili pointed at himself. "My money."

"Your money? Your money was in Iran."

"Yes."

"Then you take it to an exchange in Iran?"

"Yes."

"And they send it to these people that you don't know?" Darius asked.

"Yes, I don't know them. I think this is a bank in Germany. They have different channels. I don't know. I don't ask."

Lechleitner said, "Because I am the one sitting in the United States, I want to make sure if they trace this back it goes to the German bank and so . . . it's arranged so they can't tell the money came from Iran."

"Don't worry about it," Ardebili said. "I've installed this method to provide you the money. My friend is an expert."

Next door, Ronayne made another checkmark—*money laundering*.

Ardebili returned to his theme: selling himself and the benefits of a three-way partnership with Darius and Lechleitner. As it happened, Ardebili had separated from his Shiraz partner, Sina Tavokoli, whose sloppy organizational skills were alienating clients. Ardebili needed a new partner and a new trading hub. "It's really hard to work by myself," he told the undercover agents. "And I think I have received you from the gods."

Ardebili paused to gauge their reaction, but the Americans resisted the impulse to fill the silence. Lechleitner rubbed his eyes. Darius sat still, hand curled under his chin. Ardebili continued.

He explained that competition inside Iran was fierce. Whenever quasi-government entities like SEI and IEI sent him requests, they also sent the same RFQ to three or four other Iranian middlemen. SEI and IEI waited for all the bids to arrive and then weighed them against each other. This was one reason the whole process took so long.

Darius asked Ardebili if he knew who his competitors were.

No, he said. They kept that from him for strategic reasons.

Darius asked about competitors. "Do you know if they are providing real MA/COM parts?"

"Unfortunately, they have good contacts."

Lechleitner was dubious. He pointed at the MA/COM chips on the table, and asked Ardebili if was sure his competitors had really been able to acquire the same items. "These are very, very difficult to obtain and I have a very good source. These are very high-tech. Could they be buying counterfeit?"

Ardebili laughed and said that the Chinese certainly sold counterfeit electronics. "I received an offer for $1 each." Lechleitner laughed with him.

Next door, Ronayne remained thrilled. Ardebili was voluble, more comfortable talking than listening. Sensing a tremendous opportunity to work with Darius and Lechleitner, Ardebili was playing salesman, eager to prove the value he could offer—his extensive knowledge of, and access to, the Iranian military procurement network. Ronayne thought the agents were playing it well, letting him talk, interrupting only to clarify. But Darius and Lechleitner also looked drained, Ronayne thought, exhausted from stress, jet lag, and the residual tension from their dustup at the hotel that morning. There was still a long way to go. They planned to stretch the meeting over at least two days, plenty of time for something to go wrong, a slipup, a double cross, or something they'd failed to anticipate.

As if on cue, Ardebili's father opened his eyes and began speaking in Farsi to his son as he moved toward the door. Ardebili said, "My father is going to take a walk outside, around the hotel."

This was not a good idea. If something happened to the old man on his nocturnal stroll, it could wreck the case. Or if the man were truly an agent of Iranian intelligence, he might be leaving to deliver a signal to colleagues. Darius and Lechleitner also needed to react in such a way that the father's restlessness would not compel the son to cut the meeting short.

Darius stood. "Wait one minute," he said. "I tell you what: I can find for him a companion, and there will be no problem." He offered to fetch his bodyguard.

The father snapped in Farsi and the son translated. "He says it's not necessary."

"Well," Darius said. "I would feel better." Tbilisi was growing safer, but the city could still be dangerous after dark.

Lechleitner jumped in. "Uh, not so nice out there." He drew his hand across his throat in a slashing motion and winced. The father saw it and sat back down. Darius stepped out to fetch the escort. He returned with one of his bull-necked bodyguards, and Ardebili's father shuffled out with him.

That settled, Ardebili returned to his pitch. He explained that he had a good contact in Dubai, a partner who helped him forward products from the United States and Europe to Iran. "Dubai is a short flight from Shiraz—thirty minutes." The guy can transship almost anything—electrodes, microchips, weapons, car radios, refrigerators, airplane parts. Commercial market, gray market, black market, you name it. But lately, Ardebili said, the United States had been putting more pressure on Dubai to inspect products headed to Iran. Which was why he was eager to find a new transshipment point, like Georgia.

Ardebili laid out his proposal: whenever he received an order from the Iranian government for American military goods, he would offer the sale to Darius and Patrick first. If they could supply the item, they would ship it from the United States to Georgia, where Ardebili would take delivery. If Darius and Patrick could not locate the goods inside the United States, Ardebili would find another American supplier. Even under this second scenario, Ardebili would give Darius and Patrick first crack at smuggling the goods from America to Georgia. To Ardebili, getting the stuff out of the United States was the hardest part.

Darius acted intrigued. He reminded Ardebili of the source of his prowess in Tbilisi. "My sister is married to a very important man in Georgian government."

"Yes, you mentioned this in email."

Darius nodded. "Right, okay, so Georgia is having amazing political problems with little regions that are maybe trying to break away to independence or go back to Russia. So in these regions, there are partisans who want to buy weapons. The Russians are helping them. And it's best if they have American weapons. This way, it does not look like Russia is helping. So my brother-in-law, married to my sister, comes up with incredible idea. We have a system of selling things out of America as if it's scrap metal, but in big containers we have real military equipment."

Ardebili knew how to falsify shipping manifests. "You change the descriptions—"

"Now, with my brother-in-law," Darius continued, "I have total trust with him and him with me. There is never a question. So he sends me 50 percent down payment, which already covers our costs. When he receives container, it goes to partisans and Russians pay— or I should say someone pays, but I don't know who, but I think it is Russians. Who is more evil than Russians? Then I get paid again. This is very lucrative. So we are very strong sending things to Georgia because we have"—and here Darius deliberately used Ardebili's phrase—"special channel." Darius had contacts in other countries, he said, but nothing so secure as Georgia. "As you know, black market is great profit, but also great risk."

Ardebili gestured at Lechleitner. "Especially for Patrick, living in the United States. I'm in Iran. If the government of the United States learns of this, I am protected, but Patrick, no. In the United States, they don't joke."

Darius held up his right hand, like an exclamation point for the jury. "I'm glad you understand the situation."

Ardebili reached down and took the black case from beneath his seat. He pulled out the computer and flipped it on. "It's better to demonstrate something for you," he said.

As the laptop booted, Ardebili said, "It's good to meet face-to-face, learn more about each other. I believe that the most important matter is trust."

Ardebili tapped a few keys and swiveled the screen to reveal a scanned document. It looked like some sort of purchase order. Darius put on his reading glasses and hunched over the screen. The document, written in English, appeared to show Ardebili relaying a price of $950,000 to some Chinese company, almost assuredly a front company for the People's Liberation Army, for the purchase of some sort of American electrical components. Darius and Lechleitner didn't recognize the part number or its purpose, but the purchase order/letter made clear that it was of the highest quality and, most significantly, American-made. Lechleitner read a few lines aloud, for the camera.

In the next room, Ronayne did a double take. China? Ardebili wasn't just *buying* military-grade technology from China for Iran, he was *selling* American-made stuff to the Chinese.

Ardebili clicked on another file and asked again about F-4 cockpit computers, the DADCs. How quickly could Darius deliver them? As soon as a deposit is received, Darius replied. Ardebili promised to send 10 percent as soon as he returned to Iran.

"This is a very, very urgent inquiry," the Iranian added. "Because they are going to launch the F-4. If you can provide the DADC, they are going to ask for other subsystems. All of the systems are diminished after seven years of the war with Iraq. None of them are flying."

"None of them are flying?" Darius said.

The problem is spare parts, Ardebili confirmed. The Iranian air force can't acquire enough of the tiny electrical and computer components it needs to keep the F-4s aloft. "Sometimes they are making devices and they are missing one part, or it is broken," he said, adding that this has created a golden opportunity. "This is a good time to get a good margin because they have lost a lot of time and money. They need to launch the planes. They will pay anything to get the parts. We won't have any competitors."

Fine, great, Darius said, repeating his bottom line: "If you can provide the money . . ."

The elder Ardebili strolled back into the suite and took his seat, but the son barely acknowledged him. He stayed on task, assuring Darius and Lechleitner that his primary customer always paid its bills to trusted suppliers.

"The Iranian government has never stolen my money," he said. "If I get the part, and the part is original, I get the money. You will not lose your money. Be sure about this matter. They will pay very fast." He dropped the name of the second-ranking person at SEI. "I have his cell phone number. I told him I am coming to Georgia to get the MA/COM chips. He assured me he is going to pay fast. They know I going to bring very hard parts to find. Don't worry about it."

They were ninety minutes into the meeting now. It was past 9:30 p.m. Lechleitner rubbed his eyes. Darius's foot throbbed from gout. The old man kept nodding off. But Ardebili kept talking, bouncing from subject to subject. "You know, there is real profit for helicopters . . ."

Darius said he knew where to find good used helicopters, but warned that they were expensive and bulky to ship, not the kind of item easily returned. "It flies but it is not brand-new helicopter," he cautioned. "It is used. I don't want to bring to Georgia and then have your customer say, 'Well, it is not good enough, not new.' So will your customer send a representative to America to look at the helicopter? That could be dangerous for him."

"They couldn't come to the United States," Ardebili said.

"Well, not legally, but they could go to Mexico and drive across the border like everyone else."

Maybe, Ardebili said. "You send a proposal and pictures and specifications, and I will send it to the customer. Another dealer I know purchased Bell helicopters and paid cash. If they are sure about the offer and trust the dealer, they will pay." It's all about trust, he emphasized. "They trust me," he said, "and we will say we are same company. They will trust you then same as me. We should be team."

The potential is unlimited, Ardebili added. The Iranian military, SEI, IEI, and others send so many inquiries each week he can barely keep up, he said. He fished his appointment book from his pants pocket, pointed to a page with part numbers scribbled in black ink. "My customer called me yesterday when they heard I was going to Georgia. And I have here inquiry." He jotted down a part number and handed it to Lechleitner. It was for a specialized kind of American-made, military-grade gyroscope, a device manufactured by Honeywell and designed for altitude reference, mid-course guidance, and turret and sight stabilization. The device could be used to help fly a plane or direct a missile. "There is good market for these gyros in Iran."

Darius said, "Are you getting RFQs from all parts of this IEI pyramid? How many components are there ten, fifteen?"

"Yes, let me show you." Ardebili turned the screen to face the agents, clicked an icon, and began pointing out various files. "These are my customer files. Okay? IEI is here, this is SEI, this is the optical company, and there are others here and here, and here." He opened a few files, and found an Excel spreadsheet filled with inquiries. He read off various column headings: "This is an offer sheet. This is quotation. This is customer reference. This is the description. And this is the price." He showed them several new and old projects, each in various stages of completion. The undercover agents strained to keep poker faces.

Ardebili said his customers were especially interested in obtaining electrical testing equipment, basic things like oscilloscopes. He told them about a $115,000 Hewlett-Packard testing system he had arranged to have smuggled from the United States. An American, a black market broker like Lechleitner, had made all the arrangements, he said.

"Very big risk," Lechleitner said.

Ardebili shrugged. He told them about a different kind of gyro, and began searching for a picture of it on his computer. Ardebili asked Darius and Lechleitner if they recalled the part number. It was one of the gyros Ardebili had once emailed Patrick about.

The undercover agents exchanged knowing glances. Ardebili had just handed them an opening to launch their next sleight of hand: Darius pretended to jog his memory for the part number, and after a few seconds Lechleitner pretended to have an epiphany. "Well," he said, "I have the quote sheets right here!" He reached for a series of spreadsheets he happened to have handy and started flipping through the pages. "This is a list of all the RFQs you sent us," he told Ardebili. Several years' worth. Lechleitner scanned one document and found the part number.

Then Darius, as if the idea had just hit him, said to Ardebili, "I tell you what we like you to do with this document right here that Patrick has. This is list of what we think you have sent to us. We would like you to review and make sure is correct. We are going to give to you, and anything you no longer want, you scratch out. If something is special importance, please make little star next to it."

Ardebili seemed distracted. He was still searching for the gyro picture on his computer. But he took the document and agreed to look it over. The Americans hoped he would—if he did as directed, Ardebili would unwittingly hand them an intelligence coup, a sense of what military components the Iranians had already acquired, what they still needed, and which American companies might be helping them.

Darius moved to the next gambit—getting Ardebili to confirm that he was the one who had in fact sent each of the incriminating emails to Darius and Lechleitner. Darius handed Ardebili another document, an email he had sent months ago. The undercover agent posed his question as innocently as possible, as if he were merely curious. "When I send an email, it only me, Darius, sending you email. Is it same with you?"

"Yes, only with me," Ardebili said, still half distracted, still searching for that gyro picture on the laptop. "And same with you? Always you?"

Darius nodded. "Yes, and you? Every Yahoo! Messenger conversation—only you? Even when I am angry with you?"

"All of them, yes," Ardebili replied, so unaware of the setup that he added a joke: "And when you made an angry message to me, I shut down the computer."

The three men laughed. Next door, Ronayne, listening through the headphones, made another check mark, *emails authenticated.*

Back in Suite 22, Ardebili said, "I have one more inquiry." He asked if they could help him find 200,000 bulletproof vests, or, even better, the technology and equipment to build their own factory to manufacture vests inside Iran. "There's a lot of demand. Could be a very big contract."

"If it's possible, I will see," Lechleitner promised.

It was late, nearly 10 p.m., and Darius began going over the agenda for the next day—a morning meeting, a traditional Georgian lunch, a special tour of Tbilisi for Ardebili and his father, then a final meeting where Harry would arrive from Boston and deliver the gyros. The day after that, Darius said, they'd tour his warehouse in Tbilisi, and then drive down to the Black Sea beach resort, where they could relax for a few days.

Ardebili started to pack up. As he did, he said, "Patrick, do you know how I met Darius?"

Lechleitner stalled. "Um . . ."

Ardebili smiled. "I think even Darius forgets."

Darius, unsure were this was going, said simply, "A long time ago."

"If you remember," Ardebili said, "I received an email from England . . ." This was from Pensworth, the British arms dealer who'd vouched for the Americans. "And I received an inquiry from Iranian government for radioactive material."

"Radioactive material?" Darius said. "For medical?"

"No, no," Ardebili said. "For other."

Ardebili packed the agents' spreadsheet into his case, and bid them good night.

Next door, the unexpected reference to radioactive material startled Ronayne, and he removed his headphones and repeated it to Lerario, the other agent in the room. He put the headphones back on and listened some more. Lechleitner and Darius seemed to be handling it well, reacting with relative nonchalance. Best to let Ardebili end the meeting on his own terms, and avoid suspicion by asking too many questions. Besides, Ronayne and Lerario were anxious for the meeting to end. They had just been alerted to an alarming development, one that threatened to ruin all their hard work.

CHAPTER 17

"They Think the War Is Coming"

TBILISI, GEORGIA

A few minutes after Ardebili and his father departed, the agents met Hall and Malandra in the courtyard of the Sheraton to discuss the new development. Incredibly, a critical piece of legal paperwork, the official Georgian authorization for the hotel sting, had yet to be signed by a Tbilisi judge—or, according to a conflicting account, had been signed but wouldn't be delivered to the Americans or filed with the court until the following morning. The delay wasn't the Georgians' fault, Hall was told. It was an American miscue. An obligatory U.S. document—the diplomatic memorandum of understanding for the case between the two nations—had not arrived in Georgia until that very afternoon and had only recently been presented to the Tbilisi judge. Hall had drafted the document six weeks earlier, following a meeting with Georgian prosecutors. The memorandum, once signed by a Georgian judge, would grant the Americans official authority to conduct the sting, make recordings, take the recordings back to the United States, and use them in an American court. It would also grant the Americans authority to seize evidence, including Ardebili's laptop, and introduce it during U.S. court proceedings. Apparently, State and Justice Department bureaucrats had dithered for weeks editing Hall's original draft, as one agent recalled, "making mindless changes, like changing the word *happy* to *glad.*" The oversight was no minor matter. Without the local judge's signature, the sting was not yet legally authorized in Georgia. And if the sting wasn't formally authorized in Georgia, a U.S. judge might bar any evidence collected so far in Tbilisi. Hall sighed. The inestimable forces of The G had created a snafu—Situation Normal, All Fucked Up.

There was only one solution. Once the Americans received the signed Georgian order—presumably the following morning—the undercover agents would have to try to get Ardebili to repeat all of his incriminating statements about money laundering and smuggling. The process would be laborious and somewhat perilous. But with the loquacious Ardebili, it certainly seemed possible.

. . .

Shortly before ten o'clock the next morning, the Mercedes arrived for Ardebili at the Iliani Hotel. He emerged a few minutes later, alone, and greeted Darius in the lobby. He said his father would catch up with them for lunch. The old man was tired, he explained. He'll be fine on his own, the son said.

During the ten-minute ride to the suite at the Old Tbilisi Hotel, Ardebili began talking politics. "I think the United States has a propaganda against us," he told Darius. "As you know, the world propaganda is under the control of the United States, and showing that the Iranians are terrorists."

"Uh huh," Darius said, treading carefully.

"But I don't think so," Ardebili said, his words recorded by the microphone in the rearview mirror. "Maybe, for example, our government has good contacts with Hezbollah in Lebanon and supports them with products."

"Uh huh."

Ardebili mentioned Iranian president Ahmadinejad's trip to New York the previous week. "I don't know if you've seen the latest news about his visiting of Columbia University . . ." Western press accounts had focused on Ahmadinejad's sensational remarks in New York about homosexuals and the Holocaust—that Iran had

no gays and that the Nazi extermination of six million Jews ought
to be researched "from different perspectives." But in less-reported
remarks, Ahmadinejad had also discussed Iran's effort to obtain
material and fuel for its nuclear effort, remarks certain to be of interest to arms brokers. Look, the Iranian president had said during his
speech at Columbia, the West won't even sell us spare aircraft parts.
So why would Iran expect the West to sell us nuclear materials on
the open market? The West, the president told the university audience, had forced Iran to use the black market.

Darius said simply, "Yes, I am aware."

"What was the feedback?" Ardebili inquired.

Darius ducked the question. "I am here in Europe. The news that
I received, really, is that he was there and he left. There was no opin-
ion offered. You must understand: my little country is like leaf in the
wind. We don't control things. The world controls us. We are not
concerned so much about fighting between America and Iran. You
can ask Patrick, perhaps his insight will be better."

"Yes," Ardebili said as the Mercedes pulled up to the Old Tbilisi.

They stepped out of the car and strode past the fountains that
framed the hotel entrance. At the front desk, Darius ordered tea and
they headed up the central staircase to Suite 22. Lechleitner was
waiting for them and steered Ardebili to the same seat as before, the
one facing the cameras hidden in the painting and the wastebasket.
The Iranian set his laptop bag on the floor. In the next room, agents
Ronayne and Lerario followed the action on a monitor. By now, they
had the Georgian judge's signed order in hand.

In Suite 22, Ardebili crossed his right leg over his left and said to
Lechleitner, "I was just telling Darius about the meetings which Mr.
Ahmadinejad, the president of Iran, had at Columbia. Did you hear
about this? Did you read in the newspaper?"

The reference struck Lechleitner as an odd way to begin. He,
too, played dumb. "I haven't heard. Sometimes it is difficult to get
news when traveling."

Darius jumped in. "Does Mr. Ahmadinejad know you are with us here today?"

Ardebili deflected the question with a laugh. Then he said, "This is important matter. All the governments affect our work. At the present, it's the worst situation for Iran—all the rest of the world is against Iran. Mr. Ahmadinejad is really looking for a new route to make a quarrel with the United States and Mr. Bush really hates Mr. Ahmadinejad. The United States is going to push Iran. I think this is good for us. If our government cannot purchase the normal way—"

"More profit for us!" Lechleitner said.

"Yes, there are many companies with me," Ardebili said. "It's good." He pulled out his cell phone and said he needed to make a quick call to Tehran.

While Ardebili dialed, Darius excused himself and slipped into the hallway. He knocked lightly at the suite next door. An American colleague let him inside. Sensing that Lechleitner's chair was too close to the center of the room, partially blocking Ardebili's face from the camera, Darius lowered his voice to a whisper. "I'm concerned that you can't see him," he told agent Mike Ronayne, who sat before the monitor.

"Yeah, good catch," Ronayne said. "If he moves back just a little bit, it would be better."

"Give me a pen," Darius said, and someone handed him one. He wrote a quick note, put it in his pocket, and dipped back into Suite 22.

Ardebili was still on the phone, so Darius discreetly flashed the note in front of Lechleitner and the younger agent pushed his seat back a bit. Ardebili hung up without reaching anyone. He said his contact had probably been out late the evening before, celebrating Ramadan.

There was a soft rap at the door. A waitress brought the tea and set it on the coffee table. Darius poured tea from a pot, and used the

opportunity to pull the table back in such a way that it forced Ardebili to scoot even closer to the center of the room. With the view of
Ardebili's face now unobstructed, Darius asked him to tell him more
about the sonar possibilities he'd written so much about in emails.
"The sonar," Darius joked. "For fishing?"

Ardebili looked him in the eye. "For the protection of the oil
tanker." The sonar system was designed to detect submarines, divers, and anything else that might pose a threat to Iran's lucrative
Gulf oil platforms and shipping tankers. The systems Ardebili purchased had worked well for two years, he explained. "It was a good
deal for us." But then things began to break down and develop
software hitches. Like any tech customers, the Iranians found
themselves at the mercy of a company's help desk or repair service. Unlike other users, of course, whenever the Iranians called
the help desk, they had to pretend they were phoning from another
country.

"This is a very, very comprehensive product—it's not cheap—
and there is no way to ask the manufacturer to come to Iran and
fix it," Ardebili said. So far, he said, they'd managed to fix forty-five
computer and electrical bugs by email and phone, but at least ten
chronic problems persisted.

Darius wondered whether the sonar company's ignorance was
willful. "I think they must know they are dealing with Iran," he said.
"For them to not know they are dealing with Iran, they are stupid
like a potato. I understand why they will not say so in an email or
a phone call, because they think someone might be listening, but
surely they must know?"

Ardebili sipped his tea. "I think they know but not show that they
know. They are very wise."

"They are still building more sonar for the Iranians?"

"Yes, before I come here I speak with the general manager of the
submarine industries," Ardebili said. The general manager, he said, is
anxious to find a shipping route other than Dubai.

"Well," Darius said. "I was thinking the company could ship the sonar to Patrick, and Patrick could send that out of America as scrap metal and it comes to Georgia." From Georgia, the sonar could be driven eight hours to Baku, the Azerbaijani capital. In Baku, it could be loaded onto to an Iran Air cargo jet. "Can it go air freight?" Darius asked.

"When we did it from Dubai, we used a ship," Ardebili said. "Here's another way: we could bring the parts to the Iranian embassy in Azerbaijan or Georgia."

Lechleitner cocked his head. "Dealing with the embassy? They may think you are a spy. That's a whole new thing."

"Yes," Darius said. "It's similar to espionage."

"So that's dangerous in your mind?" Ardebili said.

"Yeah," Lechleitner said, genuinely surprised. "You know this can be done? Is it possible? Has it been done?"

"It is not necessary to knock on the embassy door," Ardebili said. "We could meet in a hotel room, for example. You can give a hotel name and room number and a time for me. Or you can have a meeting at a warehouse."

"This we can do," Darius said. "We have a warehouse. If the diplomat comes to the warehouse, I can give him the keys to the truck. Does this really work?"

"Yes, yes."

The undercover agents pressed for more details. Ardebili sat silent for a moment, scratching his chin. He picked up his cell phone. "Let me try another number. This is a very powerful man in the Iranian army."

Darius stretched. "Tell him Darius and Patrick say hello."

Again, no answer. Ardebili set the phone down. He said, "I have another person inside the United States that can help."

"When you say United States, this is an Iranian gentleman or American?" Darius asked.

"American." A New Yorker in the high-tech electrical components business. "He was powerful and expert in this matter. I was his agent. I sell his products to Iran. I got 10 and 15 percent commissions."

"So this American," Darius said, "he was receiving money directly from the Iranian government, and then paying you your commission?"

"Yes, yes." But he was a thief, Ardebili added. After a few deals, the American kept Ardebili's deposit for radar microchips, and cut off all communication. "He should pay the money. We had a contract." Ardebili asked Lechleitner if he might help him collect on the debt when he returned to the United States. Lechleitner said he'd have to know more about the guy.

Okay, Ardebili said, and took out his laptop. He clicked on a recent purchase order and turned the computer screen toward Lechleitner. "You can find his picture on his website and his résumé. I have here is his mobile." Ardebili wrote out all the contact information.

"Good," Lechleitner said, collecting the details.

Yes, very good, thought Ronayne, sitting next door. We'll be sure to follow up.

Darius decided that it was time to revisit the startling question Ardebili had left hanging the night before: his interest in radioactive material.

"Now on the nuclear issues," Darius began, "you said a couple of years ago, you were looking for radioactive something or other."

"Yes."

"Is that still something that people are trying to find?"

"I can check it," Ardebili said. "Are you are able to provide?"

"I don't know," Darius said. "In the former Soviet Union, there is much nuclear technology that people are losing and finding, you know? The best equipment is always from USA. Are you interested in what they are calling 'proliferation' equipment?"

"Yes," Ardebili said. "I can purchase whichever parts you can provide."

Darius said, "But are you looking for the nuclear weapons making, or just the nuclear power? Or all, everything?"

"Everything," the Iranian said. "I am a dealer as you are a seller. I can do anything. I can make a contact." He paused, then added. "Sometimes I think maybe it's not good to work on the parts that kill people."

"Yeah," Lechleitner said.

"I prefer to work in defense, not parts which kill people," Ardebili said.

Not parts which kill people? The comment struck the undercover agents as absurd, given all the military equipment Ardebili had discussed thus far.

Lechleitner asked Ardebili to tell him more about reverse engineering.

"We have good engineers and specialists in the technical end now in Iran," Ardebili said. "If you provide a part or schematic, we can make."

"Like you did with the Iranian missile, the Toofan," Lechleitner said, referring to the surface-to-air weapon. "It's very similar to the American TOW missile. Same principle."

"You have very good information, yes."

While it might seem counterintuitive, Ardebili added, reverse engineering could be lucrative for them. Because the Iranians cannot completely re-create everything in their labs, they often find themselves falling short by one or two parts. These parts are usually the most complex, expensive, and essential. A clever and connected arms broker who can supply that final part can make a serious profit. Iran can reengineer every aspect of night vision, except one, he reminded Lechleitner. "They have trouble with the tubes. We can make a good profit, because I know they have good demand."

"These tubes," Darius said. "What kind of profit are we looking at? What is the demand? How many do they want in one year's time?"

About two thousand, Ardebili said. "A thirty percent markup. The price is more than $1,000 for each."

Lechleitner calculated the potential profit. "That's $300,000."

.   .   .

So far, the Americans thought, they were getting pretty good stuff on tape.

Ardebili had admitted to most elements of the crime: He sent the email orders. He laundered the money through German or Swiss banks. He used a dummy company in Dubai to avoid the embargo. He accepted the delivery of the MA/COM radar chips and the agents planned to hand him the gyroscopes that afternoon. Most important, Ardebili had stated repeatedly on tape that he understood he was breaking U.S. laws. But there was one criminal charge that they had addressed only indirectly—conspiracy. With the language difference, the agents wanted to be sure they hadn't left anything to interpretation.

Darius believed it was time to push things a bit—be direct, explicit, take a chance. Ardebili appeared primed, deeply entranced in an alternative reality, one in which he, Darius, and Lechleitner were perfect partners—an Iranian, a European, and an American together, beating the embargo, on the cusp of great fortune. Even so, Darius understood that his next move was so audacious, it might well break the spell, causing Ardebili to become suspicious, snap out of his trance, and realize that he'd been had, forcing the Georgians to make a premature arrest. On the other hand, if it worked, the gambit would cement the conspiracy charges and generate a bounty of new intelligence about the Iranian procurement network.

What the hell, Darius figured. It was his last case.

"Let's talk about planning," Darius said to Ardebili. "There are different ways we can, on our side, prepare to be your partner. One way is to look at demand: What is Iran planning buy in the next five years? Another way to look is your connections. What is called in

English? You have all people together . . ." Ardebili listened closely. Lechleitner kept his mouth shut.

Darius put on his reading glasses and picked up a pocket Russian-English dictionary. He thumbed through it for a few seconds and finally pointed to a page. *"Conspiracy!"* he announced. "When all are agreeing . . . You have big *conspiracy.*"

Ardebili nodded. "Yes, yes." Next door, the U.S. agents suppressed laughter.

"So," Darius said, "we can look at what Iran is going to buy in next five years. We know mines are problem for them. The sonar they are buying. If we think of mines in sea as problem for Iran, we can focus on this. Maybe in next half hour, we can write down problems that Iran has that we can work to solve. We can also look at your conspiracy. Are you mainly aviation or mainly small technical components or communications?"

"All of them," Ardebili said.

Darius stood to retrieve paper and a pen. He lay them on the coffee table.

"We want to see where we can make the most profit," Lechleitner said.

Darius said, "Can you sketch diagram of who and what kind of knowledge and expertise you are connected with and that you are working with?"

Ardebili picked up the pen. He understood: his new partners could make more efficient queries inside the United States if they knew precisely how the process worked and what Iran desired in the long term. For the next ten minutes, he drew the undercover American agents a detailed sketch of the Iranian arms procurement network—*the conspiracy*—writing down the names of Iranian front companies, American companies they'd done business with, and the various Iranian subsidiaries, which could be trusted and those which could not.

Ardebili peppered his lecture with facts, analysis, salesmanship, and gossip. He claimed to have fifty customers, all of them owned or controlled by the Iranian government. Some Iranian companies were more influential than others, of course, but 90 percent of what they ordered was manufactured inside the United States. It was impractical to try to predict what the military would request, he said. "For example, each year, I receive different demands for Kevlar material . . ."

Ardebili wrote down the names of two dozen government-controlled companies acquiring U.S.-made gear, each with its own specialty—body armor, night vision, gyroscopes, marine automation, communications, aviation optics, electronic warfare, radar, jet parts, and so on. He lined them up by category and drew important connections. IEI companies were best, Ardebili advised. They were the biggest, they paid on time, and they sold mostly electronic equipment, small stuff that was easier to smuggle and offered better profit margins.

At one point, Ardebili stopped writing, looked up, and said, "This is a very secret list, please. Have it in your pocket. Or customer will kill me." He laughed as he said it, but he wasn't joking.

"You can trust us," Lechleitner said. "No worries."

"I trust you."

Ardebili told them about another secret Iranian project, a plan to upgrade the C-130 aircraft, the jumbo American cargo plane known as the Hercules. Like almost all of its other aircraft, Iran's fleet of C-130s, purchased by the Shah during the 1970s, were hobbled by a lack of parts and upgrades. "One crashed into an apartment building in Tehran two years ago. A lot of people burned. It's really bad. I received documents and secret information that in next five years they are going to upgrade the Hercules."

"This is valuable information," Darius said. "Let me tell you why we asking so many questions. I describe Patrick as a magic man, like man who finds the unicorn horn. But it is very hard for him. You cannot just knock on door and buy these things in America. These phase shifters were a side-door deal through a special relationship. He cannot waste time making relationships. Now, quotes are coming to you slowly. He cannot just get the prices quickly for you. He has make sure the deal is kept quiet. Since this 9/11 in America, many American companies are crazy patriots and this *so* illegal, what we are doing. And you know this is against the law, but I tell you, in America this is dangerous . . ."

Ardebili nodded. "Yes."

"So we only make our special relationships in America that are worth the time. So more we know your customers' needs, we can start relationships today. You say in the next five years, Hercules aircraft will be upgraded. Okay, now Patrick can start making relationships about this airplane. He finds people willing to sell. . . . He must very gently see if they are willing to sell out side door or under table." For emphasis, Darius waved his hand beneath the coffee table. "Because we are right now under the table. Black market."

Ardebili smiled.

"It may take him six months but Patrick can build relationships, all under table"—Darius rapped the bottom of the coffee table again—"right here." Darius jumped up to the light switch by the door and flipped off the lights. "Black market!"

Ardebili laughed. "Good demonstration."

"I want no misunderstandings," Darius said.

Lechleitner said, "Good profit, but dangerous."

Ardebili agreed. "A dangerous business."

Lechleitner and Darius looked at each other as if to say: What more could they accomplish this morning? Not much, it seemed. The agents felt mentally whipped, though satisfied that they had backtracked enough, more than making up for not having the Georgian judge's signature on the paperwork the day before. Lechleitner slumped in his chair and massaged his left temple. Darius slouched, shoulders hunched, the pain returning to his foot. It seemed like a good time for lunch. Darius reminded Ardebili that he had arranged for a guided city tour for Ardebili and his father after lunch, and then they would reunite in Suite 22 to meet Harry, who would deliver the gyros. Ardebili had other things on his mind. He wasn't quite ready to quit for the morning.

He leaned forward, animated. "A very powerful person in the government turned on the green light for me two or three weeks ago for the DADC," Ardebili confided, referring to the F-4 fighter cockpit computer he expected to receive from Darius and Lechleitner the following day. But this important Iranian official also sought a great deal more, Ardebili said, opening his laptop again. The Iranian air force, he said, hoped to rapidly upgrade every aspect of the Islamic republic's fighter jets—from the tip of the nose cone through the cockpit to the rear engine exhaust.

A sense of urgency drove Tehran, Ardebili explained. In the last five years, the United States had invaded Iran's neighbors, Iraq and Afghanistan. Now, with rhetoric between Tehran and Washington escalating, Iranian officials increasingly believed a U.S. attack to be imminent.

Ardebili said, "They think the war is coming."

CHAPTER 18

"Very Rich Men"

TBILISI, GEORGIA

The Mercedes ferried Ardebili to pick up his father and then to an upscale restaurant about a mile from the Old Tbilisi, between a busy avenue and the river. A wall of stone shielded the place from the buzz of traffic, and the best tables overlooked the river. In the central open-air courtyard there were gardens and traditional outdoor ovens. Darius escorted his guests to a private dining room. It was a snug rectangular space, with warm redbrick walls and shelves filled with antique plates and cooking utensils. Diffused light filtered through a pair of foot-high stained glass windows. On the walls hung Georgian paintings of raw meats, spoons, and ladles. In the far right corner was an easel with a Renaissance-style oil painting of a young woman. In the near right corner stood a golden lamp. Behind the lamp, a pinhole camera and microphone in the wall gave the Americans in the next room an excellent view.

Lechleitner was waiting for them and he guided the Iranians to seats facing the camera. The waiter arrived and they ordered plates of chicken kebabs, veal, rice, and potatoes, plus a round of Pepsi Light. At the waiter's suggestion, they added mushroom soup and *khachapuri*, the traditional and ubiquitous Georgian cheese bread. None of the four men had slept well, drained from their meetings and lingering jet lag. They joked about it, and then Ardebili said, "What do you know about Iranian culture?"

"Very little," Darius said. "And what I do know is probably not true. Educate us."

"Iran is an old country," Ardebili said. "Shiraz is the center of culture in Iran." He handed them his mobile phone to show them a picture of the poet Hafez's grave. He spoke of the great king Darius, who oversaw the construction of the ancient city of Persepolis. The ruins were one of Iran's most popular tourist attractions, he explained, about an hour's drive from his home in Shiraz. He held up a picture of Persepolis on his cell phone and compared it to Egypt's pyramids, with one important distinction: "Darius was a good man because he never rushed people to make his buildings and he paid them. The Iranians were not slaves. They found salary cards 1,200 years old to prove this."

"Sounds fascinating," Lechleitner said, genuinely interested but also exhausted from the stress of role playing.

The father began speaking in Farsi and Ardebili translated. "It's a great country, Iran. Good people. Seventy-eight million people. Iran has a lot of younger people—I think the third youngest country in the world. But the war with Iraq really, really damaged Iran. The war wasn't just between Iraq and Iran because the U.S. and Russia, the Arabs, and all of the world helped Iraq. Iran was alone, and only able to purchase goods from China and North Korea. It was a very bad time in Iran." The younger Ardebili added, "When I was eight, the war started; when I was sixteen, it finished. It's not good to have war again."

Lechleitner, hungry, pointed to the plate of flat bread on the table. "Have some," he told the Ardebilis. "Dig in." A waiter delivered the *khachapuri* and Ardebili's father resumed his history lesson, the son translating. "Afghanistan and Azerbaijan used to be part of Iran . . ."

After a short while, Darius steered the conversation back to business. "Did you get chance to look at spreadsheets we showed you last night? Your prior requests for quotes."

"Yes, and we should push for projects where we are sure," Ardebili said. They could save money by cutting out middlemen whenever possible, he said. "I think it's best I work directly with the end user."

The kebabs, rice, and veal arrived. They ate in silence for a few moments. Eventually, Ardebili struck up a discussion about cultural and culinary differences between Iran and Eastern Europe. The discussion segued to soccer.

As they finished the meal, Darius returned to business. "Patrick here has found another unicorn for you—helicopters."

"And filters?" Ardebili asked. Helicopters without filters were worthless in the desert.

No problem, Lechleitner said.

"I think it's a good team," Ardebili said, gesturing at Darius and Lechleitner.

"We'll work well," Lechleitner said.

"I think God really takes care of me," Ardebili said. "I really believe he was good to introduce Darius and Patrick to me to make a business."

"Sometimes you get what you need when you least expect it," Lechleitner said.

Ardebili's father spoke and the son said, "My father say, 'You have good future. May God have more for you.'"

The elder man spoke again and Ardebili grinned some more. "He say, 'You are rich men and soon you will be very rich men.'" They all laughed.

"Ready for your tour?" Lechleitner said.

The waiter cleared the plates, and Darius left to fetch the drivers. Ardebili's father stepped out for a smoke.

When Darius returned, he said, "And so now we go back your hotel, where, as soon as you ready, we have guide who take you and your father on tour of city. And when you are done, you go back to your hotel and relax, and I call you, and you meet Harry and get gyros."

The check came, and Darius said, "Patrick, you want to take picture?" Lechleitner pulled out a disposable camera.

The Ardebilis lined up against the wall next to Darius, smiling, leaning close, friends now.

Lechleitner lifted the camera to his eye. "Say cheese . . ."

CHAPTER 19

Takedown

Late in the afternoon, the third undercover American agent rose from his hotel bed, walked to the bathroom mirror, and winced. Harry Ubele looked awful, like he had the flu—puffy eyes, sweat trickling through this thick brown beard. He splashed water on his face. This would be his first undercover mission. What a way to break in, he thought.

He'd been awake much of the night, the undercover script bouncing around in his mind. When he had managed to nod off, he'd been haunted by nightmares—in one of them, Iranian agents crawled through his bedroom window. He needed to pull himself together, he told himself. In a few hours, he would meet Ardebili, deliver the gyroscopes, and minutes later, if he didn't screw up, Ardebili would be in handcuffs.

Ubele knew the other guys were worried about him, concerned he was too sick or nervous. Throughout the day, he'd stayed behind at the Sheraton, eager to be alone, hoping to catch a few hours' sleep. It hadn't come.

Ubele wasn't worried about physical danger. Before joining Homeland Security, he was a Navy rescue diver, a daredevil who leapt out of helicopters and yanked downed pilots from the sea, risking his life on virtually every mission. Operation Shakespeare presented a different kind of pressure. He didn't want to disappoint his fellow agents, or the American pilots counting on him to keep the surface-to-air technology away from the Iranians. Ubele looked at himself in the mirror again and said out loud, "Don't screw up."

Takedown 217

. . .

A few minutes after 6 p.m., Ubele stood outside Suite 22 at the Old Tbilisi Hotel, in character as a courier for Tom, the Boston arms courier. He gripped a black leather bag that held the gyroscopes.

Lechleitner joined him by the door. Darius was already inside with Ardebili.

This was it, the final play. The room next door was now crowded with Americans and Georgians—prosecutor Hall and agents Ronayne, Lerario, Malandra, and Ron Grimes huddled around the video monitor, and in a smoke-filled corner, four local plainclothes policemen, none of whom spoke English. Once Ardebili accepted the gyros, Darius would give the silent takedown signal on camera and the Georgian policemen would make the arrest.

Lechleitner rapped twice on the door and Darius let them in.

Ardebili, full of confidence, stood to greet Lechleitner and smiled as Ubele strode into the suite. Lechleitner introduced them and everyone sat down. Ubele said he was glad to finally make it. Heading off questions about his baggy eyes, he told Ardebili that he'd arrived in Tbilisi at 4 a.m.

There was an awkward pause.

Darius filled the silence with a joke. Looking at Ubele, he pointed to Ardebili and said, "This man is thinking that if you did not bring his gyros, he's going to be very upset."

"I brought the gyros—wouldn't be here if I didn't bring the gyros," Ubele said.

Ardebili welcomed him warmly into the conspiracy. He laid out the new business venture with Lechleitner and Darius, and explained how they planned to smuggle American products to Iran through Georgia, instead of Dubai.

"Yeah, that's good for all of us," Ubele said.

As with the microchips, the American agents needed to steer Ardebili to confirm on tape that he'd been the one behind all the emails and payments for the gyros. Ubele offered a simple ruse: Since I'm just the courier, he told Ardebili, my boss says I need to verify that you are indeed the buyer. To do that, I'll have to ask you a set of questions.

Ardebili shrugged.

Ubele: "When did you first request a quote for the gyros?"

Ardebili: "About three years ago."

"You sent money? How much?"

"Seven thousand," Ardebili said. "And we had a problem with the export license. We listed the description as MP3 players but Customs got it."

Ubele apologized again. "Look, I don't want to insult you. I just want to make sure it's you. Because you know, I had to take a big risk taking these out of the United States, smuggling them out, you know. Makes me a little nervous to hand over."

Ardebili offered to speed things up. He opened his laptop and clicked on a file and said it contained copies of email messages between Ardebili and Ubele's boss. He tilted the laptop toward Ubele, offering it as proof of his identity.

Ubele scanned a few nonchalantly and said, "That's fine." He fished the box of gyros from his bag and laid them on the coffee table.

Ardebili opened the box and pulled a few out. He handed one gyro each to Darius and Lechleitner to examine.

As he did so, Ubele pulled out paperwork. "Now this is the original order you sent," Ubele said. "If you don't mind, I'm going to have you sign for it." He needed a receipt for his bosses, he said. And for the jury.

Ardebili took the receipt and signed it.

There was one last move—get Ardebili to confirm he'd laundered the money for the gyros from Iran to Europe to Boston. As the Iranian admired one of the long-sought gyros, turning it over in his hand, Darius gave it a go. "Did you have trouble sending him the money to the U.S. for these gyros?"

"Oh, no."

"Well, then why did you have trouble sending me money to the U.S.?" Darius made it seem like a joke between friends busting each others' chops. "You like sending him money and not me?"

Ardebili laughed at Darius's persistence. "It was three years ago. And we sent it from a different country. . . . We use my contact in Iran, and he transfers money to Germany and after that to U.S."

Satisfied, Darius stood and stretched. He walked over to the painting on the wall and looked directly into the pinhole camera. He nodded twice, the signal.

In seconds, there were two knocks on the door. Darius left to answer it.

Ardebili was too busy talking to Ubele about sonar to notice, until four Georgian policemen burst into the room and pinned him to his chair.

PART THREE

The Secret Prisoner

2007–2012

CHAPTER 20

Coups and Complications

"Don't let them fucking do it!"

John Malandra circled Dave Hall as he fumed, his face unchar-acteristically flushed. They stood in a corner of the Sheraton lobby, ninety minutes after Ardebili's arrest. It was evening in Tbilisi, lunch-time in Washington. Hall pressed a BlackBerry to his ear, on the line with a Justice Department superior in the States. Hall swiveled, try-ing to break eye contact with Malandra so he could concentrate. But Malandra wouldn't let up, weaving like a boxer, whispering, "Don't fucking let them! Those fuckers! Don't let 'em do it!"

The initial euphoria from the Ardebili arrest had vanished. Hall had called superiors at Justice with the good news, but instead of an attaboy, he'd received a sucker punch. Officials in Washington were so elated that they were considering using the Ardebili arrest as the centerpiece for a long-planned press conference on a new counter-proliferation initiative. To get good play in the media, the Justice officials needed a hook, something sexy; the Washington beat reporters would yawn if offered "news" of the creation of a govern-ment task force. But the Ardebili sting—that would be fresh, excit-ing, enticing.

Hall and Malandra didn't object to the task force concept, or let-ting superiors take credit for the agents' hard work—that happened all the time and was simply how the system worked. But they were apoplectic that Justice officials might take Operation Shakespeare public prematurely, spoiling potential spin-off investigations. At this point, the agents couldn't know whom Ardebili might implicate

223

while in custody or where the leads he had provided during the sting might take them. Just as important, the agents couldn't know what they might find inside Ardebili's address book, cell phone, and laptop. Thorough searches would take time—months, maybe longer. Hall and Malandra believed they might not get another opportunity like this for years.

Malandra continued buzzing around Hall. "You tell them we didn't do all this to make a single arrest, like this is some kind of traffic stop," Malandra said. "You fucking tell them that."

Hall didn't need any encouragement. "Unbelievable," the normally composed prosecutor stammered into the phone. "Simply unbelievable. Do you fucking understand what's at stake here? Do you?"

The official on the line didn't budge. "The press conference has already been scheduled."

"You've got to tell them not to do that," Hall said.

"No."

"Well, then tell them they can expect me to be testifying in Congress," Hall said, his words slowing, becoming more deliberate. "They can expect me to be complaining to the IG and OPR"— the Justice department's inspector general and office of professional responsibility.

"You don't want to make threats," the man said.

"I am making threats," Hall replied. "Feel free to quote me on that."

.   .   .

After the arrest, the Georgians hauled Ardebili from the Old Tbilisi Hotel and brought him before a magistrate. The judge ordered him held in Georgia's most notorious jail, Prison No. 5, pending extradition proceedings. A facility routinely cited by human rights organizations as unfit for human habitation, the prison had been constructed a hundred years ago. The ceilings and floors sagged; holes in walls revealed exposed electrical wires; stuffed cell blocks reeked of sweat, excrement, and cigarette smoke. With roughly 3,500 inmates and half as many beds, prisoners slept in shifts. As a foreigner, Ardebili rated a cell with political prisoners, rather than thugs. Still, it was rank, Ardebili recalled. "We washed in the toilet."

And yet as degrading and dangerous as Prison No. 5 might be, Ardebili feared extradition more. He believed that if the Georgians turned him over to the Americans, he would be shipped to Guantánamo. No one would ever hear from him again.

During his first days in prison, Ardebili learned that the Georgians had placed his father on a plane back to Iran but little else. With no contact with the outside world, and nothing but time in his cell, he struggled to reconstruct what had happened. At the hotel, the Georgian police had also arrested Patrick, the American. Ardebili wondered if was being held in another cell. Ardebili also considered the fates of Darius and Harry. Were they here, too? Or had one of them been an informant? If so, which one?

.   .   .

The U.S. agents returned to Philadelphia, and within days an HSI forensic team began extracting data from Ardebili's laptop. The agents quickly broke his passwords and recovered a treasure trove of intelligence—40 gigabytes, 101,000 files, 26,000 email messages, almost all of them related to smuggling U.S. military technology. The laptop contained four years' worth of correspondence with U.S. manufacturers and Iranian procurement officials—PDFs of brochures from American companies, Excel spreadsheets of price quotes, PowerPoint presentations from U.S. and Canadian weapons manufacturers, Word documents with correspondence and shipping information. A search of the word *missile* on Ardebili's computer returned 1,498 files. The files incriminated him in ways the agents had not expected, suggesting that he'd bought millions of dollars' worth of military-grade technology. More important, the files revealed what the Iranian military desired—what the Islamic Republic needed in order to upgrade, resupply, and expand its army, navy, and air force. For example, agents discovered evidence that the Iranian navy planned to wrap forty vessel hulls with stealth technology designed to avoid U.S. radar. And they discovered a deal with an Arizona firm for at least 124 microcompressors, the very make and model of a component used to trigger IEDs in Iraq and Afghanistan, creating an indirect but startling link between Ardebili and roadside bombs responsible for so many thousand U.S. troop deaths.

Overwhelmed by the torrent of information, the agents brought in specialists from Boston, San Diego, El Paso, and the Pentagon. Raw data flowed to Washington and intelligence officials visited Philadelphia. The Department of Energy's rapid-response team sent people trained to spot someone assembling the seemingly innocuous parts needed to construct an atomic bomb. Although the Energy team found no evidence of nuclear or chemical weapons in the laptop, the scientists reported surprise at the sheer volume of military-grade trading going on.

The agents and forensic analysts soon traced thirty-three bank transfers, money sent from Tehran via Germany and Switzerland to the U.S. accounts of American manufacturers. They found transactions involving seventy American companies, sixteen of which held large Pentagon contracts. The agents identified two dozen additional Iranian procurement agents—men like Ardebili—as well as fifty Iranian government subsidiaries buying weapons and components for the Islamic Republic. The agents identified a Singapore front company shipping military electronics for the Iranians, and a California fax-forwarding company that Ardebili used to make it appear that he was operating from inside the United States. By late October, the agents were cross-referencing the names of companies and individuals they'd found in the Iranian's laptop with the massive electronic database of shipping exports maintained by Homeland Security.

The data in the laptop didn't reveal arms trading in the manner of the Hollywood cliché—Ardebili wasn't a Bond villain, sailing the

Persian Gulf in a big yacht, henchmen and bikini babes by his side. But in many ways, the laptop data revealed something as significant: the Iranian playbook for deploying scores, if not hundreds of procurement agents just like Ardebili, to fortify their army, air force, and navy with American products.

In Philadelphia, the HSI agent coordinating everything, Michael Ronayne, marveled at the speed with which Operation Shakespeare seemed to be expanding. Ardebili's computer would keep U.S. agents around the world busy with investigations for years. Now all they lacked was the man himself.

. . .

Despite the laptop coup and Ardebili's arrest, the agents still faced four formidable obstacles. They needed to keep the case sealed and out of the public eye so they could pursue the new leads; they needed to successfully navigate the Georgian legal system to win Ardebili's legal extradition to the United States; they needed to find a secure way to fly Ardebili from Tbilisi to Philadelphia; and they needed to do all of the above before either the shaky Georgian government fell to revolution or the Iranians found a way to free Ardebili—or murder him in prison.

Keeping the case secret proved to be the quickest complication to resolve. Hall and Malandra managed to raise enough of a ruckus that the Justice Department officials agreed not to reveal the Ardebili case during their press conference. Later, the Washington officials insisted that the intercontinental argument had all been a misunderstanding, one that could be chalked up to time differences, stress, and distance—they would never jeopardize an ongoing case for publicity purposes. Malandra and Hall didn't see it that way, and the rift caused by the dispute would poison relations between Justice headquarters and the field agents and prosecutors for years to come.

Securing Ardebili's extradition and transfer proved much harder than expected. It required constant pressure on the Georgians as well as colleagues inside Homeland Security. By then, Darius had retired, and Malandra struggled to convince other Homeland Security agents in Europe that they ought to station an agent in Tbilisi to provide firsthand reports from the Georgians on Ardebili's status. That initial resistance evaporated when word came unexpectedly in early November that Ardebili wanted to meet with the Americans. If Ardebili wanted to talk, he probably wanted to cooperate. HSI dispatched agent Glenn Spindel from Frankfurt.

Unfortunately for HSI, Spindel arrived in Tbilisi in early November, just as a tide of protests against the ruling Georgian government turned violent. Seventy thousand Georgians jammed the streets, and as the riot police swarmed, the capital shut down. Tear gas wafted up into Spindel's hotel room. "Things are pretty crazy here," Spindel emailed to Malandra at one point. "However, if the prosecutor can get me into the prison I'm going to go." The situation turned worse the next morning. The Georgian president declared a state of emergency, closed the highways and schools, shut down the opposition television news station, and expelled all Russian diplomats as presumed provocateurs. Spindel anxiously waited several more days, and then gave up. The senior Georgian officials, so supportive a month earlier, were now too preoccupied to facilitate a prison visit. Their government was teetering. It might not survive the year.

As the Americans pushed the Georgians for extradition, the Iranians pressed just as hard for Ardebili's release. The Iranian ambassador met with Georgian president Mikheil Saakashvili and warned that if Ardebili was extradited to the United States, the Iranian government "would not be responsible" for the safety of Georgian citizens living in Iran or Georgian troops serving with coalition forces in Iraq. The Iranians also threatened to cut off a vital natural gas line that ran from Iran through Azerbaijan to Georgia and provided a critical source of heat in the winter. The Iranians appeared to be using whatever leverage they could to prevent the Georgians from sending Ardebili to the United States.

At one point, the Iranians even tried to kill him. According to Georgian intelligence, officers uncovered a plot in which the Iranians sent a diplomat to the prison and slipped Ardebili some sort of a pill. The diplomat told Ardebili that the pill would make him appear deranged, and that as a result of his "crazy" condition, the Georgians would be forced to move him to a lower-security prison hospital, where Iranian agents would help him escape. In reality, the pill was cyanide. A suspicious Ardebili wisely chose not to swallow it. When the Americans learned of the failed assassination plot from the Georgians, it increased their anxiousness to extradite him. If the Iranians wanted Ardebili dead, they reasoned, he was even more valuable than they thought.

The Iranian pressure grew so intense by December 2007 that the Georgians urged the Americans to be prepared to take Ardebili off their hands the moment the final extradition ruling came down, whenever that might occur. To that end, Malandra and Ronayne began searching for a swift and secure way to fly Ardebili from Tbilisi to Philadelphia. This, too, proved much more difficult than expected.

The proposed prisoner transfer was too sensitive to risk using regularly scheduled commercial flights, so Ronayne and Malandra quietly put out the word to other U.S. agencies that they needed a government plane for a special mission to Tbilisi. The response was disheartening. Several sister Homeland Security agencies expressed reluctance or claimed impotence. Enforcement and Removal Operations, which operated a small fleet of jetliners to conduct large-scale deportations from the United States, reported that Ardebili could catch a ride on one of its regularly scheduled flights from Moscow or Islamabad, but couldn't be picked up in Tbilisi. U.S. Customs and Border Protection told HSI that two of their three long-range aircraft, used primarily to interdict drug smugglers, were undergoing repairs, and the third was therefore in continuous use. The Coast Guard reported that the only plane capable of flying to Tbilisi was assigned to Homeland Security secretary Michael Chertoff and thus unavailable. The U.S. Marshals Service, which routinely flies inmates with a fleet nicknamed ConAir, said it would need weeks of advance notice to fly to Tbilisi. The Pentagon, which had helped HSI in the past, had recently created a new bureaucratic process for such assistance, a nonstarter because it offered more hassles than solutions. The HSI agents considered asking the CIA for help—the agency of course knew of the Ardebili case and had vast experience moving people around the globe, quickly and quietly—but in the end, with the unpredictable Georgian courts, Malandra and Ronayne decided it would be best if they just chartered their own damned plane. The week-long rental was budgeted at $250,000.

. . .

Hall and the agents waited through an anxious December and into mid-January as Ardebili fought extradition at various levels of the Georgian court system. In the third week of January, the Philadelphia agents received word that the Georgian Supreme Court would hear Ardebili's final appeal on extradition as soon as January 23 and issue a ruling within hours of the proceedings. The agents scrambled. On January 21, Hall and Malandra arrived at Dulles International Airport with their extradition team and boarded a leased Gulfstream IV jet. They planned to fly to Frankfurt and wait there until they were certain the Georgian ruling was imminent. The flight from Frankfurt to Tbilisi was just three hours. If they timed it right, the Americans hoped to land in Tbilisi within hours of the court decision, meet the Georgian police at the airport, and spirit Ardebili away before the Iranians realized what had happened.

But as the agents settled into the plush Gulfstream seats at Dulles that morning, someone from the charter company approached Malandra. With apologies, he explained that the Germans had rejected the pilot's flight plan, saying they hadn't received a required preauthorization from the U.S. government. The Germans were sticklers for procedure. Malandra tried to keep his cool. So close and yet another bureaucratic snafu.

Malandra asked the pilot where he could fly without preauthorization. Amsterdam, the pilot replied, the Dutch were easy that way, though the change would cost $50,000 more, given the distances and other logistics involved. Someone from the U.S. government would have to authorize it before they could depart Dulles.

Malandra needed to find someone in HSI International Affairs to approve the change, and fast. By a stroke of luck, following the sting Lechleitner had transferred to International Affairs in Washington. The evening before, Lechleitner had joined Malandra and the other guys for beers near the airport. Malandra reached Lechleitner on his cell phone.

"P.J.," Malandra said, "we're on board, getting ready to close the doors here and take off." Malandra laid out the problem. He didn't have to explain that this opportunity might represent their only chance to grab Ardebili.

Lechleitner called headquarters. It was Martin Luther King Day, and fill-in managers on holiday duty balked. Lechleitner phoned Malandra to apologize. The restless Malandra glanced down the cabin, his squad ready to go. The former street cop knew what to do. He began shouting into the phone at his friend, "What's that, pal?" Malandra said. "I can't you hear you. Sorry, you're breaking up. You're breaking up . . ."

Malandra snapped the phone shut and shrugged. "I guess we're okay," he said, motioning for the pilot to take off.

Lechleitner understood. He might lose his job for this, but his guys were operational. He called HQ back. "The flight change is authorized," Lechleitner said.

"Who's authorizing it?" the duty officer demanded.

"Put my name on it."

CHAPTER 21

Extraction

TBILISI, GEORGIA

Five days later—on January 26, 2008—the Gulfstream touched down in Tbilisi. It was shortly before dusk and the seven Americans filed out into the frigid January air, tense, tired, expectant. After departing Dulles, they had flown first to Amsterdam and then farther east to Vienna, where they had waited for the Georgian court to rule—a wait that stretched to three days. That morning, they'd been told the Georgian Supreme Court had finally convened to hear Ardebili's case, and was expected to issue a ruling that afternoon. The agents had been relieved to leave Austria. While waiting, they'd been tailed in Vienna by a series of Middle Eastern–looking men, maybe Austrians or Russians, but more likely Iranians. The shadows weren't subtle. One had clumsily followed Malandra into a bar bathroom and another had engaged Ronayne in a staring contest in a hotel lobby. The Americans figured they were meant to send a blunt signal: *We know you're here and we're watching you.*

Now, as darkness fell at the Tbilisi airport, the U.S. agents wondered whether the Iranians would attempt to stop them from leaving Georgia with their prize. After about an hour, a line of police lights appeared on the horizon, streaming along the airport highway, George W. Bush Street. The procession raced directly onto the airport tarmac and a white police van pulled beside the plane. An officer slid a side door open. Ardebili emerged, handcuffed, looking disoriented and gaunt. He had a beard and his hair was greasy and matted, as if he hadn't showered for weeks. Someone put a camera in his face and flashed a picture. The Georgians pushed a document in front of him and instructed him to sign. He did so, and an HSI agent guided him toward the short stairway that led into the plane. Malandra told him they were taking him back to the United States to face smuggling charges. Ardebili protested. They had the wrong guy, he insisted. He offered to help Malandra locate the real criminals, his American and Russian suppliers. "Those are the guys you really want—Darius and Patrick," he said.

The Gulfstream roared to takeoff speed, the pilot performing an emergency egress designed to avoid potential gunfire or surface-to-air weapons. The plane jerked up at a 60-degree angle, the maneuver pinning passengers to their seats, and sending anything that wasn't tied down—documents, magazines, soda cans, napkins—tumbling through the cabin. When the plane leveled, the agents uncuffed Ardebili and a steward brought the prisoner a bowl of chocolates, a Coke, and two sandwich halves, the crusts neatly carved off. Agent Mike Ronayne nudged the tray closer. Ardebili stuffed half a sandwich into his mouth. As the G-IV sped west across Georgia, over the Black Sea toward Amsterdam for a fuel stop, Ronayne laid out the situation. "If you confess now and plead guilty, you can go home a lot sooner. If you don't confess and go to trial, things will get complicated. You could face twenty years in prison."

Agent Mike Rodgers handed Ardebili a standard HSI "Statement of Rights" form, written in English. As the agent read each sentence out loud—"You have the right to remain silent. Anything you say can be used against you . . ."—Ardebili listened intently, unwrapping chocolates, popping them into his mouth. After a few minutes, he picked up a pen and signed the waiver.

Ronayne began the interview with basic biographical questions, designed to acclimate Ardebili to easy conservation. When were you born? Who are your parents? Where did you go to school? To test his veracity, the agents added questions to which they already knew the answers—things they had already gleaned from his laptop or facts captured on the Tbilisi sting video. Then they turned to the specifics of his crimes, and what he knew about the Iranian procurement network. For the next two hours and thirty-six minutes, Ronayne quizzed Ardebili as Rodgers scribbled detailed notes.

Was the American-made radar destined for Iran?
"Of course."

Did you know it was illegal?
"Illegal in the United States, yes. Not Iran."

Who did you buy the radar for?
"Friends at IEI. As a favor to them."

To whom did IEI intend to give the radar?
"The Iranian government."

Did you know it is illegal to wire money from Iran to the United States?
"Of course."

How did you do it?
"The money is sent from a third country."

How did you manage to buy the $1 million sonar package?
"I don't think it ever happened," he said.

For now the agents let lies like the last one pass unchallenged. They told Ardebili to get some sleep, and he nodded off in minutes. An agent flipped on the movie already loaded in the plane's queue, and it turned out to be *Lord of War*, a Nicholas Cage thriller about a fictitious arms dealer. Someone on the flight crew carried a warped sense of humor.

Ronayne looked out the window. He turned to the sleeping Ardebili, and then caught Rodgers's eye. It was a pinch-yourself moment, he thought. Ronayne couldn't believe where he was—on a chartered plane, racing through the dark European sky, interrogating a prized Iranian agent. It sure beat working at Planet Hollywood.

.   .   .

In a western Philadelphia suburb, Andrew McLees, the second-ranking HSI official in the region, slipped on a suit, bid his wife good night, and stepped into his government-issued SUV. It was approximately eleven o'clock on a Saturday night. On the drive to the tiny airport near Wilmington, Delaware, he picked up his boss, Special Agent in Charge John Kelleghan.

McLees had arranged for discreet security at the airport. He instructed the U.S. marshals to bring just enough men to ensure Ardebili's safety but not enough to draw attention from the media. For example, he nixed plans for a helicopter to patrol the skies and to shadow the prisoner's motorcade from the airport to the courthouse and prison. McLees also called a cousin agency, U.S. Customs and Border Protection, to request that agents be on hand to process and stamp the passports once the plane landed. The CBP agents were told only that HSI agents were escorting "a high-value detainee." The agents were instructed not to enter *any* travel information about the landing into the massive Homeland Security database. Although the database was accessible only to law enforcement, McLees didn't want Ardebili's name popping up anywhere accidentally. This would be a ghost landing.

. . .

Aboard the aircraft, the agents woke Ardebili as the jet neared the American coastline. As the plane descended toward the obscure Delaware airport, Ardebili began to recant. He'd only told the Americans what he thought they wanted to hear, he said, because he feared they were taking him to Guantánamo. Malandra cut in and gave Ardebili the advice he gave almost everyone he'd ever arrested: Confess and cooperate and we'll work with you. Lie and go to jail for a long time. "It's your choice, pal." Malandra added, "The facts are the facts. You take the route you want to go."

At 1:15 a.m., the G-IV touched down in Delaware. Under the watchful eye of sharpshooters, agents hustled Ardebili down the stairs and into a waiting SUV. There were handshakes all around and the exhausted agents joined a caravan that took off for the Wilmington courthouse, where a magistrate waited, ready to convene a 2 a.m. closed-door hearing. On the ride to court, Malandra's bosses, Andrew McLees and John Kelleghan, tapped out BlackBerry alerts to Washington: "The package has arrived." The reply came back in seconds: "Don't have to tell you. This is huge!"

Bail proceedings and the charges remained sealed from the public and the press. The agents also took the extraordinary step of keeping the case secret even from the jailers at the federal prison in Philadelphia, where Ardebili was held in solitary confinement, pending trial. They deposited him at the prison under a fake name, Hussein Shiraz, and a fake birth date. A judge arranged for Ardebili to be represented by one of Delaware's most prominent defense attorneys, Edmund D. "Dan" Lyons, a tall man in his mid-fifties with wise eyes and tousled brown hair. A few days after Ardebili arrived, Lyons visited him in prison. Ardebili, figuring this was just another trick, told Lyons that he didn't know what the case was about. "The U.S. government sure thinks you've done something," Lyons replied. "They've gone to a lot of trouble to bring you here." Ardebili told him he was just a simple man. Lyons grimaced and said, "Oh, cut the bullshit, will you?" The attorney's directness seemed to shake Ardebili, and he began to confide in his lawyer. Lyons left the initial meeting, wondering the same central question as Ardebili: Can the U.S. agents really do this? Can they charge a foreigner for violating U.S. law, even though he's never set foot inside the United States? Can they lure him to a foreign nation, run a sting operation, then extradite him to the United States, hold him under a false name and sealed charges? Lyons dove into the legal research.

By the time the Iranians learned of Ardebili's transfer to the United States—by way of a formal diplomatic note from Georgia—he was already in the Philadelphia prison. Tehran was furious, and repeated its threat against Georgian troops in Iraq and diplomats in Iran. Georgia took the warning seriously enough that it recalled its Tehran embassy staff to Tbilisi. The Georgians also queried the United States about going public with the case. In a message from Tbilisi, a U.S. diplomat warned the Homeland Security agents: "Iran is expected to make a public announcement, and likely a political one, about the case. We need to SERIOUSLY consider unsealing the case. Georgia needs the ability to prepare for the fallout and be in a position to mount a political defense." Malandra pushed back, arguing that the great pressure being exerted by the Iranians signified the importance of the case: "We didn't go through all of the effort, expense, difficulty and hardship to unseal charges that will essentially kill all of our future efforts to close the valve on U.S. military goods going to Iran. I do not take this position lightly and again, understand the Georgian position, but the Iranian response seems indicative of Ardebili's value." The Georgians acquiesced but within weeks someone—presumably a Georgian—leaked much of the Ardebili caper to an Israeli newspaper. Surprisingly, no other media picked up the Israeli news account. Feeling lucky, the U.S. agents returned their focus to the evidence inside the laptop.

Meantime, Ardebili's lawyer, having researched the law and studied the evidence, concluded that American courts had affirmed cases similar to this one. Lyons was surprised to find the case law so conclusive: fair or not, the United States could indeed charge a foreigner for acts outside the United States, lure him to a third country for a sting, and covertly extradite him here. The lawyer returned to see Ardebili and explained the grim options. If he proceeded to trial and lost—and he probably would, given the damning Tbilisi sting video evidence—the judge might sentence him to ten or fifteen years in prison. If he pleaded guilty, the judge would be more inclined to give him three to six years, maybe less. There was no sense fighting the fairness of the smuggling law, the lawyer added. The American courts had repeatedly recognized the right of prosecutors to charge foreigners with violations of U.S. law, even if the crimes were committed overseas and in countries where the acts weren't crimes. Reluctantly, Ardebili conceded, and in a sealed courtroom in Wilmington in May 2008, he pleaded guilty. Under the terms of his deal, Ardebili would be sentenced in public, but not until the agents' investigation had run its course. That was still expected to take months, if not longer.

Six months after his guilty plea, the American agents arranged a surprise visit for Ardebili. With the help of a friendly intelligence agency, and a bit of misdirection involving guile and a disguise, they smuggled Ardebili's wife, Negin, from Shiraz to Philadelphia. The newlyweds enjoyed two hour-long and closely supervised visits. She urged him to cooperate with the Americans—"tell them what they want to know"—so that he could serve his sentence as swiftly as possible and return home. Like most inmates, he tried to appear as brave as possible in front of his wife, stoically suggesting that everything would turn out well. After the visits, the U.S. agents obtained for Negin Ardebili a special visa that allowed her to live with an uncle in Beverly Hills while the case played out. Among other things, the agents figured, Ardebili might be more inclined to remain in the United States after he served his sentence if his wife was already living a comfortable life in Southern California. Indeed, she settled nicely into the large Iranian American community there, keeping the true nature of her open-ended visit secret from everyone but her uncle.

Over the next eighteen months, as Ardebili stewed in a solitary confinement cell and his wife enjoyed Beverly Hills, the HSI agents huddled in a Philadelphia safe house and continued to exploit the data from Ardebili's laptop and cell phone, as well as other sources. Posing as Ardebili, the U.S. agents picked up where he had left off before his arrest, resuming negotiations with approximately 150 U.S. companies, some of whom knew the Iranian only by his business name, Alex Dave. Ronayne and his colleagues used Ardebili's email accounts and mimicked his negotiating style, even his broken-English patois. The tech agents made the emails appear to originate from inside Iran. Malandra and Ronayne passed dozens of the suspicious replies they received from American companies to HSI colleagues across the country and kept a dozen for themselves. Homeland Security agents began stings against twenty American companies, firms targeted for agreeing to sell Ardebili military or restricted technology. The companies were based in Arizona, Texas, New York, California, Dubai, and Europe, and sold a range of military-grade equipment, from stealth technology to avionics needed to pilot a Predator drone. HSI agents raided businesses in Arizona and New York, though criminal charges were not brought against a majority of the companies investigated. In most situations, the agents were unable to prove that the U.S. companies understood the law and expressly intended to break it—and so instead of filing formal charges, the agents paid quiet visits to senior executives to issue stern warnings. In other cases, HSI leveraged what it had learned to help expand a network of American-citizen informants. Ultimately, the Philadelphia agents would bring charges against eleven more people or companies, primarily Americans, but remarkably, no agents in any other field office managed to make a case with the Ardebili laptop tips.

. . .

In July 2009, Malandra and Ronayne were handed an unexpected and fleeting opportunity to learn more about Ardebili's former partner, Sina Tavokoli, who was still believed to be operating out of Shiraz. From a source, the agents learned that the Shiraz woman who had worked as administrative officer for Ardebili and Tavokoli planned to take a vacation to Thailand. Malandra, Hall, and Ronayne believed the administrator might have access to Tavokoli's files or foreign travel plans. She might also be privy to the Iranian government's reaction to the Ardebili arrest. If she could be convinced to cooperate, she might be able to provide meaningful intelligence, perhaps help lure Tavokoli from Iran to a sting in another country. Malandra, Hall, and Ronayne hustled to get themselves to Bangkok. They brought along a handsome undercover Homeland Security agent who spoke Farsi.

In Bangkok, the Americans shadowed the woman during the first few days of her vacation and eventually arranged for the undercover HSI agent to bump into her in a hotel lobby. But the woman was reluctant to engage this strange man, and when it became clear that their undercover venture had flopped, Malandra told the agent to drop his cover and approach her directly. The agent managed to convince the woman to meet the prosecutor and American agents for drinks at a nearby Marriott. Hall, Malandra, and Ronayne laid out their pitch, implying that if she helped them learn more about Tavokoli and view his business records, Ardebili might be released sooner. She listened but did not commit. The agents gave her detailed instructions—which records to look for, how to copy and send them, and they discussed scenarios for luring Tavokoli out of Iran. The woman nodded often, but kept steering the conversation back to Ardebili's condition and potential release. Her deep affection for him—was it romantic?—surprised the Americans. After about an hour, they led her to a computer and demonstrated how to clandestinely communicate with them. The Americans parted ways with the woman on what they believed were good terms. But shortly upon her return to Iran, the woman broke off contact and they never heard from her again. The mission to Thailand—high-risk, expensive, time-consuming—was a bust.

In the fall of 2009, Ardebili's last name began appearing in Middle Eastern newspapers, cited by Iranian officials as one of eleven citizens illegally held by the United States. One story portrayed Ardebili as a "kidnapped nuclear scientist." The U.S. agents didn't know why the Iranians had suddenly started dropping Ardebili's name in regional news reports. Maybe it came in reaction to the Bangkok lure. Perhaps it was part of a coordinated Iranian effort to justify the recent arrest of three American hikers detained along the murky Iraq-Iran border. It didn't matter. With the Iranians openly talking about Ardebili, and their investigations having run their course, there was no longer any reason to keep the case secret.

On December 2, 2009, twenty-six months after Ardebili's arrest in Georgia, U.S. officials convened a press conference in Wilmington to announce the charges. Fox News covered the event live. John Morton, the director of Immigration and Customs Enforcement, the parent agency of HSI, told the reporters that the effort to catch men like Ardebili was a giant cat-and-mouse game. "There's no question there's an orchestrated effort by the government of Iran to acquire weapons," Morton said. "Unfortunately, there's a whole network of these guys out there trying to get weapons and sophisticated technology." To drive home the Iranian threat, Morton released four minutes of video excerpts from the Tbilisi sting. To the press, the most popular segment instantly became the one in which Ardebili explained to undercover agents why Iran was so eager to obtain U.S. weaponry: "They think the war is coming." The sound bite made news around the world, from *The Washington Post* to CNN to *L'Indépendant* in France. A few days later, the Iranian foreign minister Manouchehr Mottaki addressed the charges at his weekly press conference in Tehran. "They laid a trap in front of Iranian nationals and deceived them, an act which runs counter to the legal and judicial code of conduct," he said. "We urgently call on the U.S. administration to put an end to such illogical behaviors and immediately and unconditionally release Ardebili."

On the morning of December 14, Ardebili was brought to the U.S. courthouse in Wilmington for sentencing. The Wilmington police department and the U.S. Marshals Service ringed the building with squad cars. They closed two streets and positioned a command center on the courthouse plaza beneath a bright-blue tent. They sent up a helicopter and deployed an armored police car. It was the largest display of force in downtown Wilmington in nearly a decade. The security was necessary, the U.S. Marshal for Delaware told reporters, because "there's been information that the defendant's life is in danger."

The judge convened the hearing precisely at 10 a.m. Journalists and the public were barred from the opening proceeding, and what transpired during the first hour remains sealed by the court. When the doors finally swung open around eleven, it marked the first public hearing since Ardebili's arrest in October 2007. As it began, Ardebili's lawyer argued that the case against his client was overblown and that he ought to be sentenced to time served. "He was a little cog in the wheel," the lawyer said, adding that Ardebili could face retribution if he was sent home: "It's not clear to me that if he were returned to Iran, after the service of whatever sentence Your Honor imposes, that he could do so safely. . . . There is just a lot about this case where we don't know where it's going."

When it was his turn to speak, Ardebili shuffled in prison slippers to the well of the courtroom. He unfolded wrinkled, handwritten remarks. He opened his mouth but no words came. He slumped, gripped the lectern, and began to sob. The judge gave him a few minutes to compose himself and then Ardebili tried again. "I don't want to minimize the wrong thing which I done. I accept responsibility," Ardebili said at the outset, using buzzwords virtually all defendants use and judges expect to hear. He complained about the twenty-six months he spent in solitary confinement and then tried to downplay his crimes. "There is enough information in my laptop to understand a lot about me," he said. "There is nothing to indicate or suggest I am inclined to violence, religious extremes or any political activities or being an international arms dealer. I was just a businessman, but not for ammunition or gun."

Hall's rebuttal was biting. The prosecutor described Ardebili as a sophisticated procurement agent for his government, someone who understood that the products he sought from the undercover U.S.

agents would be used to help the Iranian military upgrade its F-4 jets, target American planes in the sky, and steer Iranian missiles. "He might not be a blood-and-guts type defendant—he is about invoices and spreadsheets. But what he is doing is very serious. He might not be the one with the gun in his hand, but he's the one who put the gun in somebody else's hand."

The judge, Gregory M. Sleet, was well suited to hear the case. A former public defender and a former prosecutor, Sleet had once worked for a large chemical and munitions company. He said that while he found Ardebili's remorse and tears genuine, his crimes had also damaged U.S. national security. "Additionally," the judge added cryptically, "additional information has been brought to my attention"—a reference to the sealed proceedings—"that will inform in part my view of an appropriate sentence." Without elaboration, the judge sentenced Ardebili to five years in prison, a slightly lengthier term compared to others charged with similar crimes. Ardebili's lawyer could point to more serious cases in which defendants got shorter sentences; the prosecutor could cite less serious cases in which the sentences were longer.

The Bureau of Prisons assigned Ardebili to its facility in Rochester, Minnesota, where he was moved from solitary confinement to a cell with bunkmates. He was given a job and afforded the same prison privileges as any other inmate who behaves. A few months after he arrived in Rochester, Malandra and Ronayne visited. The agents offered to relocate Ardebili and his wife in the United States once he completed his sentence, but he declined. In the months that followed, Ardebili typed angry letters to the Georgian government. "No force on earth can change the consequences of the actions taken and sanctioned by your government in conjunction with the United States who orchestrated the elaborate hoax and plot." In an interview, Ardebili insisted his case was politically inspired. "I'm nobody, but these U.S. people didn't understand or they didn't want to understand. It's propaganda."

During his first year in Rochester, a stream of news stories emerged suggesting that Ardebili might be swapped for the three young American hikers held by Iran—Shane Bauer, Sarah Shourd, and Josh Fattal. The Iranians certainly appeared to be linking their fate to Ardebili's. Indeed, on the same day the Americans sentenced Ardebili, the Iranians announced plans to charge the hikers with espionage. Some weeks later, Ahmadinejad proclaimed that negotiations were under way to trade the hikers for Ardebili and others. "There are some talks under way to have an exchange," the Iranian president said. "They [the U.S.] have sent messages. We have answered. . . . We are hopeful that all prisoners will be released." A few months later, MSNBC.com published a story headlined "Iran Arms Dealer May Be Key to Freeing U.S. Hikers." The story asserted that "the two cases are intertwined" and quoted an unnamed American official who said of Ardebili, "He's the prize." The U.S. agents and prosecutor Hall followed the public reports closely, knowing that if a trade materialized, it would be brokered by diplomats and politicians— the agents and prosecutor would likely be among the last to learn of it. Still, the reports intrigued them. If the Iranian president was invoking Ardebili by name, did it mean that he was more valuable than they realized, or merely a pawn in a cold war? The answer, Hall figured, probably lay somewhere in between. Hall kept returning to Ardebili's explanation to the undercover agents in Tbilisi: "They think the war is coming."

.   .   .

Ardebili's sentence expired on February 8, 2012, and he was transferred to a county jail in suburban Minneapolis to await deportation. The deportation process usually takes many months as paperwork slogs through the bureaucracy. But Ardebili's case moved with unusual speed. On an afternoon in mid-March, two ICE agents from Enforcement and Removal Operations arrived at the county jail to collect him. They brought gifts from the Iranian government—a new Iranian passport, a wristwatch, $2,300 in cash, and a new set of clothes, including a white T-shirt, a pair of Perry Ellis pants, a collared shirt, boxers, dress shoes, and a winter coat. The agents allowed Ardebili to change into the new outfit, handcuffed him, and prepared to drive him to the Minneapolis–St. Paul International Airport. He seemed nervous, and excited.

"You know what's going on?" one of the agents asked.

"Yeah, I'm going home."

At the airport, the agents guided Ardebili through security and the three of them boarded a KLM flight to Amsterdam before any other passengers. They settled into seats in Row 39 and from his pocket Ardebili withdrew a prison-issue Koran. Ardebili was chatty during the first hour of the overnight flight. He talked about his wife—she had returned to Iran and now worked at a university in Shiraz—and about his case and time in prison, especially the two years spent in solitary confinement. He insisted the charges against him were false. "I was just trying to buy electronics parts and they kept pushing me to buy other parts," he told the agents. "The United States kidnapped me." After about an hour, Ardebili put headphones over his ears, flipped on the in-flight entertainment console, and watched three movies in a row. As dinner and breakfast were served, he cautiously waited for the agents to pick an entrée or a drink, then ordered the same.

When the plane landed in Amsterdam early the next morning, the agents escorted Ardebili to a cell at the airport for the long layover. In the late afternoon, Dutch officers put Ardebili and the U.S. agents into a van and drove them across the tarmac to a KLM jetliner destined for Tehran. Once aboard, the agents shook hands with Ardebili and set him free. "Good-bye," he said, "and good luck."

. . .

Amir Ardebili was not the world's most fearsome arms dealer. He was no A. Q. Khan or Viktor Bout—he did not sell nuclear secrets or supply rifles and grenades to despots and rebels. But by smuggling American-made military technology that can be turned against U.S. troops—radar, sonar, missile guidance, and jet fighter components— Ardebili posed a similar, perhaps even more immediate threat. There are hundreds of state-sponsored brokers like Ardebili out there working for the Iranians, Chinese, Russians, and Pakistanis, trying to obtain the very weapon systems that give the United States its superiority on the battlefield. Bit by bit, deal by deal, black market middlemen like Ardebili are quietly, systematically stealing the technological advantages that sustain America's status as military and economic superpower. Is the United States doing enough to prevent this?

Although Operation Shakespeare was designed and executed by agents and prosecutors in the field, it happened to coincide with a coordinated counter-proliferation initiative in Washington. In the years that followed, the number of HSI counter-proliferation investigations and indictments nearly doubled, but it is difficult to determine if this statistical increase is an honest measure of success. The way The G compiles stats, the Ardebili case, with a single defendant, counts as one indictment; a minor case against a husband and wife and their mom-and-pop company can count as three; and an indictment in which sixteen Iranian citizens and companies are indicted (though only one person is actually arrested and the rest remain fugitives in Iran) can count as sixteen. Thus, the number of indictments provides a false measure of efficacy. Regrettably, only a handful of overseas stings materialized after Ardebili's extradition in 2008, and none involved procurement agents, at least as revealed by the public record. "That's a shocking fact," Hall said. "It's why the government fails at so many things—the war on drugs, violent crime. It's just a basic lack of will on the part of the government. Cases like this aren't encouraged. If you just wait for some knucklehead to get caught at the border, that's the equivalent of waiting to arrest the kid with a rock of crack in his pocket. You need to be going after the networks, the cartels, the distributors. But that's hard and you don't get results for years. It's not acceptable that this is the only time that a case has been done like this against an Iranian. How can that be? Iran has been under embargo since the Carter Administration."

Cases like Operation Shakespeare are hard, expensive, time-consuming, complex, and riddled with possibilities for failure, risks that don't mesh well with The G's stat-driven culture. What's more, the government does not release what may be the most relevant metric of all: the success with which the Iranians and Chinese have acquired or reverse engineered American-made military technology. Much of that information, if known, is classified.

No single case defines a law enforcement agency. Yet Operation Shakespeare proved to be something of a watershed for HSI. Inside the U.S. government, Operation Shakespeare demonstrated that HSI and ICE—best known as an immigration agency—could leverage its legacy Customs expertise to pull off a major international criminal case and provide the intelligence community with valuable information. "It gave HSI a seat at the crowded national security table," said a senior Homeland Security official. Operation Shakespeare became part of the counter-proliferation syllabus at the national law enforcement training center, and Malandra, Hall, and Ronayne gave lectures on the case across the country. In both settings, agents were encouraged to be proactive instead of reactive; to work closely with the intelligence community; to attack large foreign procurement networks, instead of focusing on arresting minor players; and to think creatively and operate overseas. In other words, HSI tried to formalize the kind of informal relationships and methods Malandra, Lechleitner, Hall, Darius, and others employed during Operation Shakespeare.

In late 2010, as if to certify HSI's expertise in counter-proliferation, President Obama selected the agency to lead a new, government-wide counter-proliferation program, the Export Enforcement Coordination Center, or E2C2, and HSI selected a Malandra protégé, Craig

Healy, to lead it. Unfortunately, this grand idea—taking a whole-government approach to tackle counter-proliferation—quickly fell victim to the kind of childish bureaucratic turf battles so pervasive in Washington. The coordination center's opening was delayed by nine months as the FBI, Commerce Department, and others bickered with HSI over a memorandum of cooperation. And yet by 2013, despite private grumbling among the agencies, the E2C2's potential began to emerge. As the E2C2 forced different law enforcement agencies to formally compare notes on counter-proliferation cases, they were surprised by what they discovered. In nearly two of every three cases, another agency had useful information about a target or was already investigating the same person or network.

Politicians talk tough on counter-proliferation. They proclaim it a matter of great and grave national security. Then little happens. A recent Justice Department plea to the U.S. Sentencing Commission to increase penalties for arms smugglers received no traction. Though President Obama made some technical changes to export rules and created the E2C2, the heart of his 2010 call for reform, which requires legislative action, is simply not a priority on Capitol Hill. When the U.S. House Committee on Foreign Affairs convened a hearing on export control in spring 2013, it marked its first on the matter in nearly two years. Most committee members took a pro-business position: they focused on the restrictive nature of U.S. export laws—how they make it harder for American businesses to compete with foreign companies that manufacture similar products. The law enforcement component of the export reform equation—preventing enemies from acquiring weapons that could be used against U.S. troops—rated only a passing mention at the hearing. "No one is interested in studying this," a congressional aide confided. "The landscape has shifted and now it's all about loosening controls." As if to accentuate its business perspective, the committee invited testimony only from officials who license legal exports—and no one from law enforcement.

As agents and prosecutors in the field, Malandra, Hall, and Ronayne were far removed from such policy debates. Besides, by the time Operation Shakespeare concluded, they were already well into another overseas sting, pivoting to the east and the next looming threat.

Epilogue

SAIPAN, NORTHERN MARIANA ISLANDS

In the predawn hours of June 7, 2011, approximately eighteen months after Amir Ardebili was sentenced, a small crowd gathered inside the airport on Saipan, an island in the middle of the Pacific Ocean. Most of those gathered awaited the overnight flight from China, which was expected to arrive within fifteen minutes. Saipan, like Georgia, is positioned between two great continents and offers an obscure crossroads for smugglers. The tropical airport is relatively modest, with just a few gates, and the pagoda-style terminal is considerably smaller and less modern than the one in Tbilisi.

On this morning, Dave Hall and Mike Ronayne stood surveillance beside the airport's small carryout café, cradling hot cups of coffee. Their target—the man they hoped would become the next Ardebili—was expected on the China flight. A half dozen other HSI agents milled about the nearly empty terminal, waiting, trying to look inconspicuous. After a few minutes, one of them stepped toward Hall and slipped him a manifest for the incoming flight. The prosecutor scanned the document until he saw the name he was hoping for—not a complete confirmation, but a damn good sign. Hall glanced at Ronayne and said, tongue-in-cheek, "This remind you of anything?"

The new sting, which they hoped would culminate that afternoon, did not involve Ardebili or Iran in any way. Yet Hall and the agents deployed the same successful Operation Shakespeare template. This time, the agents posed as U.S. buyers, rather than sellers, but they changed little else. The agents made contact with a

251

foreign broker through an undercover business near Philadelphia; they purchased stolen, American-made products from the broker; proposed a meeting to enter into an illicit, long-term, lucrative relationship; and lured him from the safety of his overseas perch to a place where U.S. agents could operate freely. At a nearby hotel, undercover cameras were set up, ready to roll. All the guy had to do was show.

The target, a man named Xiang Li from the Chinese city of Chengdu, was suspected of selling hacked and pirated industrial-strength American technology on a massive scale. According to evidence the agents had already collected, Xiang Li had resold password-protected U.S. software worth an estimated $100 million on the retail market, including national-security-sensitive satellite technology. The case against Xiang Li was not an arms export or espionage case per se, but some of the pirated software was restricted from U.S. export—which meant his enterprise might be providing China and other nations with sensitive technology that offered military applications. At a minimum, Hall believed, the case presented an excellent example of the way in which the wholesale theft of U.S. intellectual property by the Chinese was slowly stripping America of its great economic and military advantages. Some of the software at risk contained the kind of secret designs and engineering that helped make U.S. applications among the fastest, most accurate, and most efficient in the world.

Though the agents followed the general Shakespeare outline, Hall and the agents had added a wrinkle, one designed to expedite everything. They'd convinced the Chinese target to meet them in Saipan. Xiang Li was apparently unaware that in 1978 Saipan had become part of an obscure U.S. territory, the Northern Mariana Islands. Legally speaking, Saipan was as much a part of the United States as Puerto Rico or Philadelphia. No extradition was necessary. Upon his arrest, the agents could immediately bring Xiang Li before a magistrate judge at the U.S. courthouse on Saipan, then whisk him east aboard a chartered jet. Given the success in the Ardebili case, Ronayne had had little trouble requisitioning a G-IV this time.

.　.　.

Saipan also held personal significance for Hall, and the day before he'd shared the story with the HSI agents. Seeking to give them a sense of the kind of young soldiers their counter-proliferation program was designed to protect, Hall had gathered the agents at Green Beach on Saipan's southwest coast. In his hands he held a fat, dog-eared history book with a bright red cover, the official Pentagon account of the Battle of Saipan.

The prosecutor stepped out onto the serene, largely vacant beach. He looked out across the sapphire water, not far from the luxury hotel where the Americans expected to meet their Chinese target. The scene on June 15, 1944, looked quite different, Hall said as he began to tell the story. That morning, his father, Captain R. E. Hall, had stormed Green Beach with the Second and Fourth Marine Divisions, lunging from an amphibious assault craft into the sand and brutal Japanese crossfire. The Marines fought all day to establish a beachhead and they pushed, yard by yard, hour by hour, for ten days against relentless fire from Japanese soldiers holding the highest point on Saipan, Mount Tapochau. Hall drove the agents up to the summit and explained that the battle had not ended when the Americans reached the top. The fight continued for another two weeks in the face of suicidal Japanese banzai attacks. Three thousand American soldiers were killed during the Battle of Saipan. Hall's father survived. Later, Saipan and its sister island, Tinian, would become major staging areas for the coming assault against the Japanese mainland, and in particular, a new weapon, an American technological advancement that would forever change the face of war and geopolitics. The planes that carried atomic bombs to Hiroshima and Nagasaki departed from an airfield about ten miles from the spot where Hall began his walking tour. More than 100,000 Japanese were killed during the bombings, but the new technology ended the war within days. If U.S. troops, including Hall's father, had been forced to invade Japan, surely hundreds of thousands of them would have died.

.   .   .

In the Saipan airport lobby now, waiting for the target with Ronayne, Hall reprised the tension he'd felt in Tbilisi. He scanned for Chinese counter-surveillance. His mind swirled. Would the target show? Would he come alone? Would he bring his laptop, and if so, what would it reveal about China's efforts to steal American technology? Would the sting work or would they go home empty-handed?

An announcement came over the loudspeaker and the first passengers from China began exiting Customs, moving in bunches, mostly Asian tourists, weary from the long flight and the early hour. Hall and Ronayne took a position just outside the airport exit, studying the passengers, one by one, as they passed into the dark morning. Hall sneaked one more glance at their target's photograph. A few moments into the procession, Hall caught a glimpse of someone who looked like the man in the picture. He wore a white T-shirt, shorts, and flip-flops. The man looked relaxed, expectant.

Under his breath, Hall said, "Got him."

Afterward

Patrick Lechleitner continues to receive promotions. A few years after arriving at ICE headquarters in Washington, he became chief of staff to the ICE deputy director. He is now an assistant special agent in charge, supervising HSI activities in Colorado.

David Hall retired as assistant U.S. attorney in Delaware in 2013 and now works in private practice, specializing in export compliance. He also retired as a captain in the U.S. Navy Reserve.

John Malandra retired in 2012 from his post as HSI group supervisor for counter-proliferation, ending a three-decade run in law enforcement. He is now a security consultant to the U.S. government.

Michael Ronayne was promoted to group supervisor for counter-proliferation in Philadelphia. He continues to work on undercover cases that have reached into Asia, Europe, and the Middle East.

Andrew McLees, who supervised Malandra and his agents during Operation Shakespeare, became chief of staff to the acting director of ICE in Washington. He is now HSI special agent in charge for New Jersey.

John Kelleghan remains HSI special agent in charge for Pennsylvania, Delaware, and West Virginia.

Darius retired from HSI and returned to the United States, where he has embarked on private ventures in the international business community.

Clyde Pensworth still lives in London but says he has retired from the global arms market. American authorities aren't so sure.

Amir Ardebili was deported to Iran in 2012. His current whereabouts could not be determined.

Lieutenant Seth J. Dvorin is buried in Marlboro Memorial Cemetery in central New Jersey. His widow, **Kelly,** completed her doctorate in clinical psychology and works in the field. Lieutenant Dvorin's father, Richard Dvorin, counseled veterans in New Jersey until his death in 2013; his mother, Sue Niederer, is a peace activist. Friends have created a growing charity in Lieutenant Dvorin's honor, the G.I. Go Fund, which helps Iraq and Afghanistan war veterans transition to civilian life. For more information, visit gigofund.org.

Acknowledgments

Operation Shakespeare was made public in late 2009, while I was a reporter for *The Philadelphia Inquirer*, and I'm grateful that the editors agreed to allow me to write a 2010 series about it called *Shadow War*. I'd like to thank the dozens of people who met with me in the years after the newspaper series was published and provided the interviews, confidential documents, and videos that form the basis of this book. Special thanks to those who sat for repeated interviews from 2011 to 2013—David Hall, John Malandra, Michael Ronayne, P.J. Lechleitner, Andrew McLees, Darius, and others who asked not to be named. Thanks also to dozens of ICE/HSI senior officials and agents, including: John Kelleghan, John Morton, Brian Hale, Craig Healy, Clark Settles, Kumar Kibble, Harry Ubele, Michael Rodgers, Ron Grimes, William Argue, Brendan Cullen, Barbara Gonzalez, Chris Matarelli, Ross Feinstein, and Brandon Montgomery-Alvarez. Thanks also to Defense Criminal Investigative Service agent Robert Lerario and his boss, Ed Bradley; U.S. Department of Energy officials Joshua McConaha, Erik Deschler, and Sandro Volski for their guidance in Tbilisi; J. J. Klaver, Jerri Williams, Christopher Allen, and others at the FBI; and Lieutenant Colonel April Cunningham at the Pentagon. Many officials at the Justice Department were helpful—among them, Dean Boyd, Steve Pelak, Colm Connolly, David Weiss, Charles Oberly, Nancy Winter, David Webb, Patty Hartman, and Kim Reeves, and others.

Thanks to Amir Ardebili; his wife, Negin; his mother, Zahra Ahkami; and brother, Afshin, for the interviews and correspondence, and to Ardebili's defense lawyers: Temur Gogsadze in Tbilisi, Edmund "Dan" Lyons in Wilmington, and Ross Reghabi in Beverly Hills. In Georgia, thanks to my expert guide Eka Chitanava and Ministry of Internal Affairs officials Giorgi Gorelishvili, Archil Pavlenishvili, Akaki Akhaladze, and David Macharadze.

Thanks also to Mike Amitay, Jeff Goldstein, Zoe Reyners, Doug Frantz, Mike Sherman, Robert Sherborne, Dave Kinney, Chuck Ash, Patrick Gorman, Lucy Shiffman, Abigail Gorman, Ambassador Temur Yakobashvili, Rob Johnson, Maribel Yamat, Jake Cheney, Poe Piper Jack, Dave Anderson, Caitlin Lukacs, and the BCC Brewers.

In Iraq, the members of Outkast Platoon rotated in and out, but the heart of the group under Lieutenant Seth Dvorin's command included Sergeant First Class Dan Dusablon and sixteen young men from across the United States: Robert Finley, Steve Cates, Gregory A. Jones, Jr., Craig Stuart, Herm Howard, Ricky Martinez, Marco Barajas, Jeffery Williams, Cerron Hutchins, Brian Domitrovits, Larry Bowman, Richard Rosas, James Lambert, Chris Zarcovitch, Aaron Fultz, and Jeffery Shannon. At least seven of them were wounded and earned Purple Hearts. Dvorin, Rosas, and Lambert were killed by remote control IEDs. I'm also grateful to Lieutenant James McCormick, Lieutenant Dvorin's parents, Rich and Sue, and, most of all, his widow, Kelly, for spending time with me to talk about Seth.

At the *Inquirer*, thanks to: Tom McNamara, Avery Rome, Bill Marimow, Vernon Loeb, Stan Wischnowski, Mike Leary, Amanda Bennett, Ann Gordon, Frank Wiese, John Brumfield, Steve Glynn, David M. Warren, Joe Tanfani, Craig McCoy, Nancy Phillips, Mark Fazlollah, John Sullivan, George Anastasia, Michael Schaffer, Dotty Brown, Emilie Lounsberry, Dan Biddle, Troy Graham, Monica Yant Kinney, Peter Tobia, Conrad Grove, Julie Busby, Chris Hepp, Dylan Purcell, Ken Dilanian, Joe Slobodzian, Wendy Ruderman, Kaitlin Gurney, Edward Colimore, John Martin, and Rita Giordano.

At Reuters, thanks to Blake Morrison, Michael Williams, Alix Freedman, Brian Grow, Anna Driver, Mark Hosenball, Warren Strobel, Marilyn Thompson, Megan Twohey, Joan Biskupic, Jack Shafer, and, especially, to my counter-proliferation reporting partner, Duff Wilson.

Thanks to the retired founder of the FBI Art Crime Team, Robert K. Wittman, who taught me about stings and with whom I coauthored *Priceless: How I Went Undercover to Rescue the World's Stolen Treasures*; to Donna Wittman; to the authors of the books, articles, and court pleadings cited in the notes below; to fact-checkers Perry Stein and Nick Shiffman; and to friends who read manuscript drafts: Kevin Charles, Peter Eisler, Mimi Hall, Chuck Caspari, Alex Maduros, and, most of all, Peter Franceschina. Thanks also to literary agent Larry Weissman for his vision and tenacity, and to Jofie Ferrari-Adler at Simon & Schuster for his patience and wise edits, and his colleagues Sarah Nalle, Fred Chase, Elisa Rivlin, Ed Winstead, Anne Tate Pearce, and Jonathan Karp.

I'm eternally grateful to my sons, Nick and Sam, for their love, spirit, and sarcasm. Thanks also to my father, Paul; sister, Belle; and brother, Will, for support and inspiration, and for keeping my mother Sevah's memory alive. And to Cathy—for everything.

Sources

Interviews and research were conducted in Washington, Philadelphia, Wilmington, London, Boston, Beverly Hills, Dubai, and Tbilisi. Most people spoke on the record but a few spoke on a not-for-attribution basis, either because they were not authorized to speak publicly or because they feared retribution. In certain cases, the individuals listed below agreed to discuss certain matters, but not others—and in those rare situations, the anecdotes were verified by witnesses or documents. No one interviewed provided classified information, but I used dozens of State Department cables made public by Wikileaks to provide context and, in certain cases, information about specific incidents. General content from the following authors was also helpful: William R. Polk, *Understanding Iran* (New York: Palgrave Macmillan, 2009); Amir and Khalil, *Zahra's Paradise* (New York: First Second, 2011); Ronen Bergman, *The Secret War with Iran* (New York: Free Press, 2008); Catherine Collins and Douglas Franz, *Fallout* (New York: Free Press, 2011); and George Crile, *Charlie Wilson's War* (New York: Atlantic Monthly Press, 2003). Georgian court documents were translated by Tbilisi lawyer Nino Mtvarelishvili. The various divisions within Immigration and Customs Enforcement have changed names several times in the past decade. For the reader's sake, the units described here are cited by the names used as of early 2014.

PRELUDE

Interviews with Homeland Security Investigations agents Darius, John Malandra, Michael Ronayne, Harry Ubele, and P.J. Lechleitner; Defense Criminal Investigative Service agent Robert Lerario; prosecutor David Hall and U.S. attorneys David Weiss and Colm Connolly; Tbilisi International Airport police chief Giorgi Gorelishvili, Georgian Ministry of Internal Affairs special operations supervisor Archil Pavlenishvili, and other Georgian officials; business records from Amir Ardebili's laptop; White House transcript of President George W. Bush's Address to the 89th

Annual National Convention of the American Legion, August 28, 2007, Las Vegas, Nevada. Troop death figures are from *The Washington Post*, http://apps.washingtonpost.com/national/fallen/causes-of-death/ied/.

Interviews with Lieutenant Seth Dvorin's wife, Kelly; his father, Richard Dvorin; his mother, Sue Niederer; Lieutenant James McCormick; Sergeant First Class Dan Dusablon; Private First Class Jeffery Williams; Adam Dvorin; Kate Monteforte; Jack Fanous; Rev. Michael and Pam O'Brien; Lieutenant Dvorin's records from Rutgers and the U.S. Army; a scrapbook of memories Lieutenant Dvorin kept with Kelly.

CHAPTER 1: THE STOREFRONT

Interviews with Lechleitner, Ronayne, and other HSI agents; HSI counter-proliferation supervisors Malandra, Craig Healy, and Clark Settles; HSI special agents in charge Andrew McLees, John Kelleghan, and others; Cross International records; prosecutor Hall; a senior Department of Justice counter-proliferation official; Justice Department spokesman Dean Boyd; two senior Pentagon officials involved in arms procurement; court records for *United States v. Yasmin Ahmed*, District of Connecticut, 2002-CR-247; May 2013 interview for Reuters with former defense secretary Robert Gates; transcript of Gates's April 2010 speech, www.defense.gov/speeches/speech.aspx?speechid=1453; Jeff Gerth, "Two U.S. Aerospace Companies Agree to Fines over Helping China," *The New York Times*, March 5, 2003; order from U.S. State Department's Bureau of Political-Military Affairs, "In the Matter of Hughes Electronics Corp. and Boeing Satellite Systems Inc., March 2003"; Shirley A. Kan, "China: Possible Missile Technology Transfers from U.S. Satellite Export Policy—Actions and Chronology," Congressional Research Service, March 27, 2003; Joby Warrick and Carrie Johnson, "Chinese Spy Slept in U.S. for Two Decades," *The Washington Post*. April 3, 2008; James A. Hursch, director, Defense Technology Security Administration, "Report on Chinese Technology Acquisition for Modernization, Regarding U.S. v. Zhen Zhou, Chitron Electronics," the Pentagon, January 20, 2011; Max Boot, *War Made New: Technology, Warfare, and the Course of History, 1500 to Today* (New York: Gotham, 2006); Richard T. Cupitt, *Reluctant Champions* (New York: Routledge, 2000); James Romm, "Iran Arms Race in Ancient Times Echoes Today," *The Daily Beast*, April 12, 2012; Charles Higham. *Trading with the Enemy: The Nazi-American Money Plot 1933–1949* (New York: Delacorte,

1983); *Targeting U.S. Technologies: A Trend Analysis of Reporting from Defense Industry*, Defense Security Service, 2012; various HSI-generated materials for Operation Shield America outreach programs; various U.S. government records.

CHAPTER 2: THE CAPITALIST

Interviews with Amir Ardebili, his wife, Negin Ardebili, and his mother, Zahra Ahkami; financial, business, and email records from Amir Ardebili's laptop; Jessica Silver-Greenberg and Edward Wyatt, "In Laundering Case, a Lax Banking Law Obscured," *The New York Times*, August 8, 2012; court records and Justice Department statements in U.S. settlements with the banks Lloyds TSB, Standard Chartered, ING Bank NV, ABN Amro Bank NV, Barclays Bank PLC, and Credit Suisse; John Limbert, *Shiraz in the Age of Hafez* (Seattle: University of Washington Press, 2004).

CHAPTER 3: THE CAPTAIN

Interviews with Hall, Malandra, Darius, Weiss, McLees, Lechleitner; a person close to former attorney general Janet Reno; Chuck Ash; Dave Kinney; *U.S. v. Jasin*, 00-4185 U.S. Third Circuit Court of Appeal; former FBI art crime team founder Robert K. Wittman; former assistant U.S. attorney Robert Goldman; other federal agents and former prosecutors; Thomas Erdbrink, "Iran's Aging Airliner Fleet Seen as Faltering Under U.S. Sanctions," *The New York Times*, July 13, 2012; John Shiffman, "Corruption Case Ends in Deal," *The Philadelphia Inquirer*, June 7, 2007; U.S. Justice Department's *Summary of Major U.S. Export Enforcement, Economic Espionage, Trade Secret and Embargo-Related Criminal Cases*, updated February 14, 2013; *U.S. v. Zhou, Wei & Chitron Electronics*, District of Massachusetts, 08-CR-10386; Annual Reports, 2005–2012, Commerce Department's Bureau of Industry and Security; a review with Reuters's Duff Wilson of ITAR and IEEPA arms smuggling cases from 2003 to 2013; "Northrop Fined $15 Million for Exporting Air Force One Data," *Washington Trade & Tariff Letter*, April 7, 2008; *U.S. v. ITT*, Western District of Virginia, 07-CR-22, Appendix A: Statement of Facts, www.justice.gov/nsd/pdf/itt_statement_of_facts.pdf; ITT's corporate website, under its new name, ITT Exelis, www.exelisinc.com; *U.S. v. United Technologies Corp.*, District of Connecticut 3:12-cr-146; and Hall biographical material compiled by the author for *Priceless* (New York: Crown, 2010).

CHAPTER 4: THE PRODUCER

Interviews with Malandra, McLees, Kelleghan, Lechleitner, Ronayne, Ubele, Darius, and other HSI agents; interview with Hall; U.S. government records; John H. Anderson, *Through One Orphan's Eyes* (*The Girard Story*) (Pocono Publishers, 1997); court file documents, trial transcripts, and appeals court records from *U.S. v. John Reece Roth*, District of East Tennessee, 08-CR-69; Daniel Golden, "Why the Professor Went to Prison," Bloomberg BusinessWeek, November 1, 2012; http://www.plasmas.org/basics.htm; http://www.jameswgregory.com/plasma.html;

CHAPTER 5: THE INFORMANT

Four sources in the United States and Europe with direct knowledge of the informant's activities; related public records; Dubai Airshow website; U.S. government records.

CHAPTER 6: THE BAZAAR

Four sources with direct knowledge of the meetings; contemporaneous records; ICE/HSI agents interviewed in Dubai; records from Amir Ardebili's laptop; www.epa.gov/radiation/radionuclides/tritium.html#peopleshealth; U.S. diplomatic cables from Dubai posted by Wikileaks—for example, http://wikileaks.org/cable/2005/09/05ABUDHABI4102.html and http://wikileaks.org/cable/2005/09/05ABUDHABI4049.html.

CHAPTER 7: LOVE AND PROFIT

Interviews with Amir Ardebili; his wife, Negin; his mother, Zahra Ahkami; and a person close to the family; Limbert, *Shiraz in the Age of Hafez*; email and other records on Amir Ardebili's laptop; interview with an export specialist at the National Security Council; General Accountability Office report, *Analysis of Data for Exports Regulated by the Department of Commerce*, November 17, 2006; data from export.gov and the website of the Commerce Department and its Bureau of Industry and Security; www.rell.com/products//Triggered-Spark-Gap.html; declaration of Gary Milhollin, *U.S. v. Asher Karni.*, U.S. District Court for the District of Columbia, CR-04-396; defense and government sentencing memos, *U.S. v. Asher Karni*; Josh Meyer, "Man Gets Three Years for Sales Link to Nuclear Arms, *Los Angeles Times*, August 5, 2005.

CHAPTER 8: A WARNING

Interviews with Hall, Malandra, McLees, Lechleitner, Kelleghan, and other sources within ICE, DCIS, the Treasury Department, and the Commerce Department's Bureau of Industry and Security; other U.S. government documents.

CHAPTER 9: PROPOSITIONS

Records from Amir Ardebili's laptop; U.S. government records; recordings of phone calls between Darius and Amir Ardebili.

CHAPTER 10: THE MAGICIAN

Interviews with Darius, Hall, Malandra, McLees, Lechleitner, Ronayne, Lerario, Grimes, and Amir Ardebili; court records; data from Amir Ardebili's laptop; recordings of phone calls between Darius and Amir Ardebili.

CHAPTER 11: "A HERO WITH THE MINISTRY OF DEFENSE"

Interviews with Hall, Lechleitner, Ronayne, Darius, and Amir Ardebili; Amir Ardebili court records; emails and other records on Amir Ardebili's laptop; trial transcript, *U.S. v. Gowadia*, District of Hawaii, 05-CR-486.

CHAPTER 12: SHAKESPEARE

Interviews with Malandra, Lechleitner, Hall, Kelleghan, McLees, Darius, Ronayne; U.S. government documents; Amir Ardebili court records; Associated Press, "Ahmadinejad: U.S. Power 'Collapsing' in Iraq," August 28, 2007; White House transcript of President George W. Bush's address to the 89th Annual National Convention of the American Legion, August 28, 2007, Las Vegas, Nevada; Islamic Republic News Agency, August 30, 2007; Seymour M. Hersh, "Shifting Targets: The Administration's Plan for Iran, *The New Yorker,* October 8, 2007, posted online September 30, 2007; *Ahmadinejad: Soldier of God,* CNN: Special Investigations Unit, September 30, 2007; Hall, memo to Department of Justice headquarters.

CHAPTER 13: CONTAGIOUS ENTHUSIASM

Interviews with Darius, Amir Ardebili, Malandra, and Ronayne; email and other records on Amir Ardebili's laptop.

CHAPTER 14: MOTHER GEORGIA

Interviews with Georgian officials Archil Pavlenishvili, Giorgi Gorelishvili, Temur Yakobashvili, Akaki Akhaladze, David Macharadze, and Zoe Reyners; journalist/translator Eka Chitanava; Jeff Goldstein of the Open Society Institute; employees of the Old Tbilisi Hotel; World Bank report, *Fighting Corruption in Public Services: Chronicling Georgia's Reforms*, January 2012; interviews with Malandra, Hall, Ronayne, Lechleitner, Darius, Grimes, Lerario, and other U.S. officials working in Tbilisi.

CHAPTER 15: ARRIVAL

Interviews with Amir Ardebili, his mother, Zahra Ahkami; Lechleitner, Lerario, Ronayne, Grimes, Darius, Hall, Malandra; video from the camera hidden inside the car.

CHAPTER 16: THE MAGIC SHOW

Interviews with Amir Ardebili, Lechleitner, Lerario, Ronayne, McLees, Grimes, Darius, Hall, and Malandra; video from the camera hidden inside the painting and video from the camera hidden inside the wastebasket.

CHAPTER 17: "THEY THINK THE WAR IS COMING"

Interviews with Darius, Lechleitner, Amir Ardebili, Hall, Malandra, Ronayne, and Georgian officials; video from the camera hidden inside the painting and video from the camera hidden inside the wastebasket; audio recorded from the device carried by Darius.

CHAPTER 18: "VERY RICH MEN"

Interviews with Darius, Lechleitner, Amir Ardebili, Hall, Grimes, McLees, and Ronayne; video from the camera hidden in the restaurant and audio recorded from the device carried by Darius.

CHAPTER 19: TAKEDOWN

Interviews with Darius, Lechleitner, Amir Ardebili, Hall, Grimes, Malandra, Ronayne, and Harry Ubele; video from the camera hidden inside the painting and video from the camera hidden inside the wastebasket.

CHAPTER 20: COUPS AND COMPLICATIONS

Interviews with Lechleitner, Hall, Malandra, Ronayne, McLees, Kelleghan, Ubele, and other HSI officials; interview with Amir Ardebili and his Tbilisi defense lawyer, Temur Gogsadze; interview with U.S. Justice Department and Georgia court officials; Georgia court records; Human Rights Watch report, *Georgia: Prison Abuses Rife Despite Promises of Reform*, September 2006; U.S. government records; business and financial records from Amir Ardebili's laptop.

CHAPTER 21: EXTRACTION

Interviews with Lechleitner, Hall, Malandra, Ronayne, McLees, Grimes, Kelleghan, Ubele, and other HSI officials; interview with Amir Ardebili; U.S. government records; interviews with Amir Ardebili's lawyers in the United States, Dan Lyons and Ross Reghabi; interviews with Amir Ardebili's wife, Negin, and mother; press conference and sentencing hearing attended by the author; Islamic Republic News Service, "Mottaki Urges U.S. to Immediately Release Iranian National," December 7, 2009; letters to Georgian and U.S. officials provided to the author by Amir Ardebili; Associated Press, "Ahmadinejad Suggests Exchange for Jailed U.S. Hikers," February 2, 2010; Robert Windrem, "Iran Arms Dealer May Be Key to Freeing U.S. Hikers," NBC News, posted online May 17, 2010; interviews with ICE agents Ken Olson and Darin Gergen, who escorted Ardebili from Minneapolis to Amsterdam.

EPILOGUE

Interviews with Hall, Ronayne, and HSI agent Brendan Cullen; *U.S. v. Xiang Li*, District of Delaware, 10-CR-112.